'There is a lot of bad theology out there, and bad theology is toxic. In *Just Living*, Ruth Valerio answers bad theology with good theology. But this book isn't just about how we look at Scripture. It is just as much about how we look at the world. For too long Christians have used faith as a ticket into heaven and a license to ignore the world around us. So Ruth's book helps us discover a Christianity that is fully engaged. *Just Living* is not just about how we think. It is just about how we live. So often our problem has not been right thinking but right living, and thanks to Ruth Valerio we have a new resource to help us live more better, more just, more beautiful lives'

Shane Claiborne, author and activist

'*Just Living* makes an important contribution to the debate on how Christians (and others) can live a wise ecology in the world today, neither losing sight of the need for radical change, nor being so radical in approach that they need to live in a world of their own. Its drawing on Christian tradition, particularly that of monasticism and of Aquinas, provides an important foundation for the practical decisions that we need to make in working for a just and sustainable society'

Br Samuel SSF, Hilfield

'*Just Living* is a lively, compelling guide to a generous and faithful way of being alive, a way that can be shared between human and non-human life amid the realities of the contemporary context. It seamlessly combines personal reflection, insightful cultural analysis, rich theological meditations and sage advice'

Luke Bretherton, Professor of Theological Ethics, Duke University

'A book about justice that comes from the heart of a writer who has worked hard to live it out. Ruth's integrity and humility on top of careful scholarship and passionate activism makes this a must-read for anyone concerned with putting God's word into practice in today's world. Informing, empowering and liberating'

Dr Krish Kandiah, President of the London School of Theology and founder of Home for Good

JUST LIVING

Faith and Community in an Age of Consumerism

Ruth Valerio

HODDER

First published in Great Britain in 2016 by Hodder & Stoughton
An Hachette UK company

This paperback edition first published in 2017

3

ISBN 978 1 473 61335 5
eBook ISBN 978 1 473 61334 8

Typeset in Ehrhardt by Hewer Text UK Ltd, Edinburgh
Printed and bound in the UK by Clays Ltd, Elcograf S.p.A

Hodder & Stoughton policy is to use papers that are natural, renewable
and recyclable products and made from wood grown in sustainable
forests. The logging and manufacturing processes are expected to
conform to the environmental regulations of the country of origin.

Hodder & Stoughton Ltd
Carmelite House
50 Victoria Embankment
London EC4Y 0DZ

www.hodderfaith.com

Contents

Introduction   1

Part One: The Air We Breathe – the Context   25

1. The Elephant and the Blind Men:
   Just what is globalisation?   27

2. Skinny Jeans and a Broken Nose:
   The challenge of consumerism   57

3. Of Monks and Men
   The church context   84

Part Two: Breathing In, Breathing Out – the Theology   121

4. Get Thee to a Nunnery?
   Unhelpful retreat versus unhealthy narcissism   128

5. In Plenty or in Want:
   How to think about wealth   149

v

6. **Temperance, Justice and Human Flourishing:**
   A deeper look with Thomas Aquinas   180

Part Three: **A Life Well Lived – Putting It All Together** 211

   A Global Social Concern   218
   An Ecological Concern   225
   A Christian Approach to Money and Material Goods 232
   Ethical Consumerism   239
   Local Community   250
   Activism   259
   Time   265

   Final Words   274
   Acknowledgements   279
   Notes   281
   Bibliography   311

Introduction

I am sitting on a rock looking out over the sea. The bright sun bathes me in its heat, filling me with its radiance, warming my face and body. Across the smooth shimmering waters I can just make out the Wicklow Mountains of Ireland, hazy in the distance, while at my feet the water gently laps its calming rhythm, pulling my breathing into line with its own. As I look into its clarity I watch the undulating seaweed and the anemone fronds moving back and forth, dancing in unison.

The occasional seabird wheels overhead, looking for the mackerel that swim beneath the waters, and a bark makes me look ahead and smile at the seal, bobbing up and down, watching me with intense curiosity through its big black eyes. Back behind me, past the rocks over which I've clambered, sheep graze on the green slopes, their soothing bleats mingling in with the other sounds to produce a gentle choir.

I sit for a good hour or more. I do nothing. Say nothing. Pray nothing. Simply watch, listen, feel, and let the beauty of my surroundings take my thoughts and do with them what they will, working their alchemy on my being.

Peace.

I am on Bardsey Island, a place that has become a favourite holiday destination for my family and me. It is an amazing place. Just one and a half miles long by half a mile wide, it sits two miles off the Llyn Peninsula of north-west Wales. A monastic site from the sixth century (it still holds the ruins of an Augustinian monastery from the thirteenth century), it was known as 'the island of twenty thousand saints' as it became the burial ground of choice in medieval times. Three pilgrimages to Bardsey were said to equal one pilgrimage to Rome.

A number of farmhouses are dotted around the island, reflecting the period in the mid-1800s when it became a farming and fishing community (most of them are still without electricity). Now it is farmed by just one family who live here throughout the year, and the other houses are available for holiday rent.

It is outstandingly beautiful, with views across to Ireland from the one side and back to Wales and Snowdonia from the other. With a large colony of seals to swim with, a myriad of moths and birds to admire, a stunning night sky to marvel at, and the adventure of the Manx shearwater to experience, it truly is a place like no other.

This place has been formational to me as I have been thinking through what it means to follow Jesus in today's culture, which places so many demands on us in terms of our time, our finances and our relationships. This thinking culminated in me focusing my doctoral research on that subject, looking at how the concept and practice of simple living might provide some answers to the question of how we live well as Christians in our consumer society. I remember well spending my afternoons on Bardsey one summer week, perched at the kitchen table of our little farmhouse, with my cup of tea and favourite chocolate to hand, reading Aristotle and Aquinas, looking out over the fields to the sea. But most of the learning I have done on Bardsey has not come from the books I have read, but from the basic experience of being there and letting its rhythms and ways of life – so different from what most of us experience day to day – be my teacher.

Coming from a society that is built on the expectation of continuous growth, it is, quite frankly, a shock to spend time in a place where there are limits. For one, there is the food. Once on the island, other than honey, eggs and vegetables from the farm, or mackerel if you fish, you are entirely dependent on the food you bring with you. As the person responsible for this, I find that quite a worrying prospect. What if I haven't made enough cakes? What if my alcoholic provisions prove insufficient? What if the weather leaves us stranded here for a few more days? Have I brought enough extra food to see us through? As you can imagine, the phrase 'that's enough, this has got to last us all week' is one that the rest of the family get somewhat accustomed to hearing.

Second, there is the water. The island is entirely self-sufficient in water, and this is supplied from the mountain stream. Each house has one tap in the kitchen that comes from the stream (it kind of dribbles out) and a massive water butt outside. The water from the butt has to be used for everything (cooking, cleaning, washing, etc.) except drinking. If it has been a dry period, then the tap water might be rationed. The regular trips along the side of the house to the water butt to fill a bowl with water make me realise just how hugely precious this resource really is.

And then there's the energy. It is funny how instinctive it is, when it gets dark, to walk into a room and feel for the light switch. I caught myself doing that a couple of times when we first arrived and it took me a while to get used to there being no electricity and to get into the habit of getting particular things done (like taking out my contact lenses) while it was still light. Although there are lamps and candles supplied, there is a limit to what you can do with the light that they give out. Certainly I can't read, which is a definite drawback (and don't even think of bringing a hair dryer with you!).

So in many ways island life is inconvenient (and I haven't even mentioned the outside toilet and having to take all your rubbish home with you . . .), and there is no doubt that I am a fair-weather island dweller. I couldn't live here permanently. But it teaches me about limits and reminds me that I live on one huge island floating in the sea of the universe. The limits of Bardsey function for me as a metaphor for the limits of this earth that I inhabit and remind me that I shouldn't take the earth's resources for granted and use them as if they are unlimited. This is a theme to which we will return through the course of this book.

The island also changes my perception of time: something that so many of us struggle with in our fast-paced society.

'Just what do you do all week?' is the question I'm often asked whenever I tell people excitedly where we're going for our summer holidays. And it is an understandable question: what on earth do you do all week on a small island that has no electricity? Surely you have explored it by the first afternoon and then what else is there to do, with no televisions or computers?

The odd thing is that time has a funny habit of changing when you step off the boat onto the little beach that marks the start of your stay on the island. And that is just as well, because I have as bad a relationship with time as have most people, often struggling under the feeling of simply having too much to do.

It is amazing how much there is to do on an island where there's nothing to do. One year I didn't even make it to the tip of the island at the far end from our house – somehow there just wasn't the time!

To begin with there are the daily things of life. It takes time to boil the kettle for my morning wash. There is bread to bake and cooked breakfasts to fry. Then there is the daily swim with the seals and the walk to the farmhouse to say hello to Jo, the farmwife, and see if she has any eggs for me. There is the mountain to climb (well, a very big hill, really) and the cliff paths to walk along. Carol, the resident summer artist, holds craft workshops and Christine, whose husband was born and bred on Bardsey, holds a history talk and poetry reading in the old school building one evening a week. Sometimes there is help needed on the farm and we join in moving the sheep from field to field, or rounding up the cows when a careless day visitor has forgotten to close a gate.

We might join in with the Bird Observatory's activities, ringing Manx shearwater chicks one afternoon on the mountain and storm petrels on the beach at midnight. The children on the island get together regularly to play football and organise 'Five O'Clock Games' when they play Seekers (whatever that is . . .) in the fields.

At low tide you can sit out and watch the seals as they bask on the rocks, listening to their grumpy noises and watching their funny antics, and at midnight you can sit in the darkness in the valley where the Manx shearwaters return to the chicks in their burrows. The ghostly white shapes floating overhead and their eerie call is an experience like no other. Stargazing on Bardsey is incredible, with no light pollution for miles around. One year we found ourselves in the middle of a meteor shower and we lay on our backs at midnight and watched shooting stars whizzing through the heavenlies above us, and saw satellites and the International Space Station tracking their courses through the night sky. And of course there is time to spend with friends who sometimes come with us, drinking wine, eating together and talking life.

Foundational to it all is the regular rhythm of prayer that has been a part of the island for centuries. There are morning and evening offices held at 9 a.m. and 5 p.m. in the little Victorian chapel next to our house each day, and at the end of the day a number of us meet for compline, the children and teenagers taking it in turns to say the lines. The most memorable of these was held on our penultimate evening one year, after island football, on the sandy beach as the rain clouds gathered, with twenty or so seals bobbing in the water watching us as we huddled together around a candle.

So you see, there really isn't that much to do on Bardsey Island.

Undergirding it all is the impact of living so closely to the natural world and experiencing a deeper connection with nature. It is well documented how our lives today are increasingly separated from the wider natural world. Less than a quarter of children nowadays regularly use their local 'patch of nature', compared with half of all adults when they were children,[1] and a National Trust report said that children are unfamiliar with some of our most common wild creatures because they spend so little time outdoors. While many had trouble identifying a magpie and spotting the difference between a bee and a wasp, nine out of ten could recognise a Dalek![2]

The impact of this lack of connection with the outdoors has been memorably summed up by Richard Louv in his phrase 'nature-deficit disorder'.[3] We are the poorer where we are separated from the natural world, and it impacts us on all levels: psychologically, emotionally, physically and spiritually.[4] As a report from the University of Essex puts it in a wonderful understatement, 'This study confirms that the environment provides an important health service.'[5]

I live a fairly nature-connected life already, albeit quite a domesticated one, with a house and garden full of animals (chickens, guinea-pigs, free-roaming house rabbit, stick insects, python and chameleon), regular time spent in the allotment, and pigs to feed, scratch and chat to through my place in a pig co-operative, but one thing I have learned especially on Bardsey is the impact that nature connection can have on emotional pain.

Some years ago I was struck deeply by Steven Bouma-Prediger's writing in *For the Beauty of the Earth*. He comments on God's words to Job in chapters 38–39, saying, 'God's whirl-wind speeches forcibly remind Job not only of God's power but also of the expanse and mystery of the created world – a world not of human making.' He goes on to say, 'Such a world, beyond human control or knowledge, is able somehow to absorb the weight of human sorrow. In times of grief and pain there is great solace in fierce landscapes. When God is at the centre, and the human thereby displaced, there is a world wide and wild enough to absorb the pain of human suffering.'[6]

I am sure that I am not alone in resonating with what Bouma-Prediger writes here and, on Bardsey Island, whether out on the rocks, walking along the craggy coastline or sitting on the mountain with the choughs above and below me, I have begun to experience that for myself. Many of us reading this will also, no doubt, have known something of the beautiful ability of nature to take on our heart's longings and pains, not to make them disappear, but at least to apply a soothing balm to them, allowing us to experience respite.

Time, ecological limits and nature connection are among the different themes that we will be thinking about in this book. As I write this, however, I am not on Bardsey Island, but sitting at the kitchen table of our terraced house on a social housing estate in Chichester. We have just had dinner and our nearly-and-teenage children are out at a youth group. I'll need to go out soon in the car and pick them and their friends up.

A week or two on Bardsey Island may teach me some important things, but the challenge is how I live out what I learn in my everyday life. The reality, of course, is that most of us reading this live in fairly ordinary places and we are trying to live our lives as best we can in those places: trying to do our best at work; keep our mortgages/rents and other bills paid while putting aside something for the future; raise children (if we have them) as well as we can; keep our relationships steady, and not get too tired and worn out in the process. While we do that we face a cultural expectation that we should be regularly upgrading and buying new things, moving gradually upwards in our lifestyle, and making sure that we – particularly women – look as beautiful as possible in the process.

At the same time, for those of us reading this who are Christians (I am assuming a predominantly Christian readership, but please feel welcome to continue if that label does not apply to you, and I hope you enjoy what you read here), we know that we want Christ to be at the centre of all that we do and that this should make a difference to how we live and to what we view as our life priorities. My youngest daughter Jemba said to me just yesterday, 'Mum, if you were arrested for being a Christian, do you think there would be enough evidence to convict you?' It is a good question, and one I was not entirely sure I wanted to answer.

Added to all this, we know only too well that we live in a world with incredibly complex problems: inequality, injustice, climate change, rising sea levels, energy crises, hunger and lack of access to clean water, species extinction, crashing fish stocks and so on and so on. Most of us have a deep sense that these and other issues cannot be ignored, and a deep desire to try to do something about them. The least we can do, we feel, is give some of our money to charities (and we are often pretty good at that), but we know it is not enough.

We have a vague feeling that there is a connection between how we live our lives, the culture in which we live, our Christian faith and the broader issues of this world, but sometimes it is all too much and, honestly, it is all we can do to make it through to the end of the day and collapse in front of the television with a glass of wine.

I want to suggest that this connection *can* be made and that it need not always be onerous and burdensome, and it need not always lead to a life of deprivation. What I have discovered is that joining the dots can be a lot of fun and can take you on an adventure you never imagined you would have. Yes, it may lead to a life where you learn to say 'no' to some things you have previously enjoyed, but it also leads to a life where you say 'yes' to a whole lot more.

Joining the dots between lifestyle, our cultural context, faith and the issues of our world is essentially the focus of this book, and it is something that I have been trying to do for the majority of my adult life. It all began with three things.

First, while I was at university I read a book, written by a friend in my church, called *Whose Earth?*[7] This was the first time I had properly come across a biblical account of environmental care and I can only describe it as being like a second conversion. The penny dropped, and so began my journey of gradually reappraising my theological understanding (I was reading Theology at university at the time) to incorporate the wider creation, taking off my exclusively human glasses and reading the Bible instead through glasses that noticed where and how the whole of the created order fitted into the story of salvation that the Bible tells.

Second, after university, while studying for an MA part time, I also became research assistant to the then director-general of the Evangelical Alliance, a chap called Clive Calver. He was doing a huge amount of media work and public speaking and needed help with the accompanying background research.

One thing he did was a series of debates for the BBC World Service on ethical issues and, alongside the obvious ones of abortion, euthanasia, marriage, and so on, one of the debates was on the arms trade. Neither he nor I knew anything about this, so I set to work, reading all sorts of material around how our arms trade works. Some of this I did while in Addis Ababa, Ethiopia, on a trip with my husband Greg, working out in the slums. The combination of being in one of the poorest countries of the world and reading about the horrors of this multi-billion-dollar industry, and the way we are potentially all implicated through our bank accounts and pension schemes, blew my mind and showed me the links between our lives here and the lives and places of other people all around the world in a way that I could not ignore.

The third thing that catalysed my thinking over the last twenty years or so was a 'lifestyle audit' we did in our church, put together by the same friend who wrote *Whose Earth?* It was like a *Cosmopolitan*, 'how good is your sex life' quiz, where you added up your score at the end to find out how 'good a green Christian' you were. By this stage, I had become quite evangelistic about my new-found environmental theology and was talking about it a lot and telling people they needed to see the error of their theological ways. But doing this quiz made me realise that I was a hypocrite: I was talking about it but not living it out in any way. I knew that had to change, and so began the adventure of trying to find ways of living that did as little damage as possible to this world and its inhabitants, and maybe might even enhance it in some way.

I discovered something quite early on, though: this was not easy! Why? Because everything around me seemed to be set up to encourage me not to make the kind of choices I was wanting to make. The culture I was in did not want me to ask questions and think about where a product had come from; it wanted me to consume blind. It did not want me to be satisfied with what I already had; it wanted me to buy more. It did not want me to live differently and have my own alternative opinions on things; it wanted me to go along with what everyone else was doing and not worry about it.

It was also not easy, honestly, because very few people I knew really understood the deep change that had occurred in how I understood my faith and the world and, consequently, did not understand how important the changes I was trying to make were to me. Most of my family, friends and church simply thought I was a bit weird and weren't always backwards in telling me so! Aldo Leopold, one of the founders of the wilderness movement in America, once said, 'One of the penalties of an ecological education is that one lives alone in a world of wounds', and when I first read that I burst into tears because it was exactly how I felt.

I am glad to say (thanks particularly to getting to know the folk from A Rocha, the Christian conservation charity with which I now work) that this is not how I feel nowadays. But it is a reminder that the sorts of things we are looking at in this book are not considered 'normal' in our society and hence can take considerable energy and commitment to pursue. In one of the interviews I did for my doctoral studies (in the course of which I interviewed Christians who were trying to live more simply), one person said, 'I'm different in two ways: I'm different from secular environmental . . . groups by being Christian, and different from a lot of Christians in that I focus on simple living and environmental awareness.'

Things have changed hugely since my early adult life. There is now much greater environmental and social awareness both within and without the Church, and many of the things I do are not considered quite as weird as they used to be. Nonetheless, if you are reading *Just Living* then I know it will be because you are aware that our consumer society and globalised world are doing untold damage – to ourselves and to others – but that it can also be hard to live in a way that begins to address that damage. While I will make no attempt to provide all the answers, my hope is that what you read here will help you think through more deeply what it means to try to live differently: the challenges that presents, the tensions we have to hold together, and the practical ways by which we might actually do that.

But first, a word about where this book has come from. Some years ago I was asked to co-write a course coming out of the Alpha movement, entitled *Simplicity, Love and Justice*.[8] It was the first time I had properly met the word 'simplicity', but as I encountered others who were also travelling in this direction – whether virtually, in books or in person – I realised that this was the word they used to describe the way of life they were trying to lead, and I realised that it described what Greg and I were trying to do as well. Simplicity (or simple living) thus became something I began talking and writing about as I travelled the country and abroad on speaking engagements, and I discovered that it rang a loud and clear bell for many people.

However, I was aware that it is rather a vague notion with no accepted definition, and also that it is a bit of a misnomer since, as I often say, trying to live this sort of life is anything but simple – it is much simpler just to do what everyone else does! So, when I had the opportunity to do some doctoral studies, I decided to focus them on examining this notion of simplicity;

to determine whether it could be defined more closely; to see what were its key characteristics; and, particularly important to me in the context of my Christian faith, to ask from what theological basis simple living arises, bearing in mind that simplicity is not an exclusively Christian concept and can be found throughout the religions and faiths of this world.

As I began to explore how to do this, two things became apparent. First, as I read the more popular writings on simplicity and ran, spoke at and attended conferences, it became clear that contemporary understandings of simplicity are forged within, and are a response to, the context of consumer culture. Simple living cannot be considered by itself: it has to be understood within the context within which it is being outworked. Thus, trying to understand our contemporary culture became an important part of the task.

Second, as I read the more academic literature, I became increasingly uncomfortable with the way so much of what I read seemed to float up in the ether somewhere with little reference to what was actually going on in people's lives, on the ground, so to speak. I wanted my conceptual thinking to be more rooted, and so I decided to begin the doctoral thesis with a piece of empirical research on a group of people trying to live more simply, and to let what I discovered there direct and inform the rest of my thinking.[9]

This book is based on my doctoral thesis and on what I learned from it. It is not simply a cut-and-paste job, though: I have rewritten significant sections, added others, and made it more autobiographical and practical than the thesis inevitably was. I have also not included the actual empirical research, as fascinating as that was, although I will mention some of its findings at various points. Nonetheless, the substance of my thinking over the course of my doctorate is what forms the foundation of the following pages.

The book itself is divided into three main sections, so a word about each to help you navigate them successfully.

Part One is about *context*: what is the context within which we are living? We will be thinking about globalisation (chapter 1) and consumerism (chapter 2), trying to gain a greater understanding of what they are, how we experience them, and what their positive and negative impacts are, on us and more broadly. We will then consider the church context (chapter 3) that many of us inhabit. I think there are a number of different paths that are coming together in church life at the moment which are leading to this particular emphasis on lifestyle and global issues. Things like a rediscovery of the ancient paths of monasticism and the tradition of radical dissent within Christianity are all part of what we will be exploring here.

Part Two is about *theology*: what are the key theological issues behind Christian attempts to live more simply in response to the context seen in Part One? What becomes apparent is that trying to live well as a Christian today leads to some significant tensions that we must try to negotiate. There is a *via media*, as Aristotle would say – a middle path to be walked carefully, with extremes on either side to be avoided. It is these tensions that we will consider in this part of the book, and I hope this will be a useful discussion as I believe that identifying and understanding these tensions is the first step towards negotiating them successfully.

Chapter 4 will look at two particular dangers that can face us. One is the danger of a Christianity that retreats too far from society and leads to us creating an oppositional enclave rather than engaging with what we see around us. The second is the danger of a Christianity that is unhelpfully 'me' focused and narcissistic, a trap into which, ironically, some attempts to live more simply can fall. Chapter 5 will then focus on the critical question of how we develop a Christian approach to money and material goods and will consider the danger of embracing the opposite of a therapeutic form of Christianity: a world-denying attitude towards material goods. The early Church, St Benedict and St Francis will be our companions here as we think through this issue, and we will spend some time considering what the Bible has to say about money and possessions.

With chapter 6 we get to the real meat of the book as we consider Aristotle and Thomas Aquinas and the concept of *eudaimonia* – well-being or flourishing – and Aquinas's understanding of the relationship between the virtues of temperance and justice. Here I get to the heart of what my doctoral thesis focused on and it may be too heavy for some readers. If that is the case then you are very welcome to skip this chapter and move on!

Part Three is about *practice*. Bearing in mind all that we have seen so far, what then might a Christian life, well lived, in today's globalised, consumer society, look like? What might be some of its key features? In this final part of the book we will explore seven features of such a life: a concern for global, social issues; an ecological concern; a right use of money and material goods; ethical consumerism; an active engagement in local community; a faith that is engaged across the whole of our lives, particularly in advocacy; and a healthy balance in our use of time.

*   *   *

Before we turn to chapter 1, though, I want to take some time to tell you about what gets me out of bed in the morning, doing the things that I do. It all comes down to the way I read the Bible and how I understand the story of God that it contains. So let us go back to the very beginning . . .

In that beginning, as the opening words of the Bible tell us, God created the heavens and the earth. This is not the start of a debate about evolution, simply the statement that, whatever views you hold on how the universe came into being, God was the cause.[10] And the world God created was *very good* (Gen. 1:31). This little statement is dynamite because it blows up all the unbiblical dualism that the Church has adopted through the centuries of its existence: a dualism that has taught that what is earthy, physical, material is somehow inferior to what is ethereal, non-physical, immaterial. In contrast to the dominant Babylonian creation myth (called *Enuma Elish*) that was circulating around the same time as Genesis was likely being put down on papyrus – which portrayed the world as evil, having been fashioned out of the defeated god in a cosmic battle – the Genesis narrative makes the fundamental point that the created world is wholly good (because, of course, it comes out of a wholly good God).

This world is soon teeming with life: in the seas, on the earth and in the skies, and the final species God creates is an earthy one, an earth creature (more commonly known as Adam).[11] The similarities between this earth creature and the other living things are many. All are blessed to multiply and fill the earth. All have the breath of God in them (Gen. 1:20: it is not correct to see God breathing into Adam's nostrils as God giving humanity a soul or spirituality, in contrast to other living beings). But there is one difference: only *'adam* is made 'in the image of God', and it is in this description that we learn what makes us uniquely human.

This phrase, 'the image of God', reflects the Babylonian context within which the Genesis texts are thought to have found their final form. Archaeological discoveries have found royal tombs with the inscription describing that particular king as being 'in the image of' whichever god it was they worshipped. To be made in the image of a particular god meant that the king represented that god to his people, ensuring social harmony and fertility of crops and livestock.

We have been made in the image of the Creator God, to represent him to the wider creation and carry out God's kingly rule. The Old Testament scholar Chris Wright has written persuasively (so persuasively that the most recent NIV translation has changed in line with what he says) that the most faithful translation of Genesis 1:26 should read, 'Let us make *'adam* in our image, in our likeness, *so that* they may rule over the fish of the sea, etc.'[12] In other words, we have been made in God's image *so that* we may look after the rest of what God has made (remembering that the idea of 'ruling' in the Old Testament is not about oppression and domination but about servant care – see, for example, Prov. 31:1–9).

If we are to represent God – if God's image is an essential part of who we are – then we represent God's fundamental nature, and that nature is relational, as expressed in the Trinity. To be human is to be in relationship: 'beings in communion', as the theologian John Zizioulas has expressed it.[13] Although ultimately these things cannot be separated, I find it helpful to see those relationships as threefold: our relationship with God, our relationship with other people, and our relationship with the wider creation.

We have seen already that we have been created to be in a healthy relationship with the wider, natural order. The earth creature, *'adam*, was placed in a garden, to tend it and look after it (Gen. 2:15), and was given the responsibility of naming all the other animals. But alongside that we have also been created to be in relationship with the God who gave us life – to walk with him in the garden (Gen. 3:8) – and with each other. *'Adam* alone with the animals was not enough: a partner was desired, and so Eve was created and human community was born.

When Adam and Eve ate the forbidden fruit, whether we take this story literally or metaphorically, those relationships were broken. Suddenly the human couple were afraid of God and hid from him. Their relationship with each other is fractured as the blame-game starts and God tells them that their relationship will be disordered (Gen. 3:16). And communion with the wider creation breaks down too: the snake will now be hated by human beings (I know, we have one, and seeing people's seemingly instinctual aversion to it is fascinating) and the ground will be hard to work and dominated by thorns and thistles (again, I can testify to that on my allotment!). The earth (the *'adamah*) is now cursed because of the *'adam*.

The story of the Old Testament is the story of those fragmented relationships.

Many of us will be familiar with reading the Old Testament as the story of Israel's relationship with God and of the ups and downs involved with that as they alternate between walking in God's ways and following him, and deserting him and following other gods. The command against idolatry, primary in the Ten Commandments of Exodus 20, is fundamental to that and is, actually, an issue of trust and security. Who will they trust to keep them safe from attacking neighbours and ensure their harvests are abundant? The laws and the sacrificial system is given to them as a means of repentance and restoration for when they sin and walk away from God.

But the Hebrew Scriptures also document the tragic outcomes of the human relational breakdown that occurs in Genesis 3, and makes for some pretty horrendous reading. There is fratricide (Gen. 4). There is rape (Judg. 21). There is jealousy (1 Sam. 18), adultery and murder (2 Sam. 11). There is oppression, dishonest trading and greed (1 Kgs 9:20–21; Amos 8:6). You name it: whatever you can think of, it will be there in the stories of the Old Testament. The laws and the sacrificial system aim both to legislate against these things happening and to provide the means for reparation once they do.

Woven into the relationships between God and humanity is that of humanity's relationship with the wider natural world. The laws of the Israelite people are clear that it matters how the land and all its inhabitants are treated. For example, the laws of the Sabbath apply more widely than to humans alone (Lev. 25) and a mother bird sitting on her nest is not to be taken (Deut. 22:6). Interestingly, meat eating is only allowed after the story of Noah. Is this, perhaps, the ultimate indication that something is wrong between human beings and the wider creation?

The state of the land acts as a spiritual barometer for the health of the Israelites' relationships with God and each other.

Amos 8 is a good illustration of this: because the people have turned away from God and are not practising social justice, the land responds accordingly and there is environmental upheaval (see also Deut. 30:15–16; Jer. 5:23–5). In contrast, when the people turn from their 'wicked ways' and listen to God, then the trees, the mountains and the hills will rejoice (Isa. 55). This is not simply pretty poetic language: there is something in this about the positive impact on the land when there is peace between people, God and each other, and therefore the non-human inhabitants of that land celebrate when that happens.[14]

The Old Testament finishes on an ambiguous note. The people of Israel are back in their land, the temple is rebuilt. And yet . . . And yet it cannot be said that they are living in the fulfilment of the words of the prophets spoken around the time of the exile in Babylon. For emerging out of the wreckage of the people's desertion of Yahweh, and the subsequent destruction of Jerusalem and taking of their key people into exile, are amazing words of comfort and hope: of a time coming when

> the Spirit is poured on us from on high,
>   and the desert becomes a fertile field,
>   and the fertile field seems like a forest.
> The LORD's justice will dwell in the desert,
>   his righteousness live in the fertile field.
> The fruit of that righteousness will be peace;
>   its effect will be quietness and confidence for ever.
> (Isaiah 32:15–17)

The Hebrew prophets begin to look forward to a time of peace, of *shalom*, when the harmonious relationships originally established would be put back to rights again. And crucially, they begin to envisage that this time would be brought about by one particular person, specially chosen and anointed by God (Isa. 9:6–7; 11:1–9).

About four hundred years later, one night, when a large company of angels bursts into song in front of some very surprised shepherds, they proclaim, 'There is glory for God in highest heaven, and on earth there is peace among the people whom God has favoured.'[15] Their words about peace are not just a nice way of saying 'hello', they are like a great big flashing neon sign, telling the shepherds and the world that the hopes of the Old Testament prophets are being fulfilled, in a very particular newborn baby.

The good news is that through Jesus there is peace: his life, death, resurrection and ascension together have brought about reconciliation (see Peter's words in Acts 10:36). And that reconciliation happens in the three areas we have already been considering.

We know, of course, that Jesus came to restore our relationship with God. That is the basis on which our life with him rests. John 3:16; Romans 5:1, 8–11; 2 Corinthians 5:18–21 and Philippians 4:7 all speak manifestly into that area. But Jesus also came to restore our relationship with one another. Romans 12:18; 1 Corinthians 7:15; Galatians 5:22; Ephesians 2:14–17; 1 Thessalonians 5:13; Hebrews 12:14 and James 3:18 again are loud and clear about that.

And he came to restore the broken relationship between ourselves and the wider creation. That is the meaning of Romans 8:19–21: creation has been 'subjected to frustration' as a result of humanity's fall, and so when we know what it truly means to be the children of God again we will be set free to fulfil our original calling, and so the whole creation will also be set free. As the theologian Colin Gunton said, 'We human creatures are the centre of the world's problems, and only by our redirection will the whole creation be set free.'[16] As Colossians 1:19–20 makes clear, then, Jesus' blood was shed on the cross not only for the sake of human beings alone, but for the sake of the whole created order.

Peace with God, peace with others and peace with the wider creation. That is what Jesus came to bring about, and the amazing news is that as we work towards these things in our own lives, we experience peace within ourselves too (Rom. 15:13; Phil. 4:7; 2 Thess. 3:16).

For me, it is this three-dimensional understanding of relationships – with the fourth dimension of peace with self running alongside – that defines who I am and what I do. Putting it simply, I want to live my life in such a way that my relationships with God, with others and with the wider natural world are being developed rather than stunted. That leads me to give time and attention to my interior life with God; to how I treat other people (both those I know – my family, friends, neighbours, work colleagues – and those I do not – living somewhere in my local community or many miles away, growing my tea or making my clothes); and to how I live in this world. Because I am a naturally enthusiastic and evangelistic person, I then want to help others do the same, hence why I spend so much of my time speaking, writing and communicating in general.

I hope it is obvious that this framework provides us with a full understanding of what it means to be a follower of Jesus:

worship, evangelism, the spiritual disciplines, social justice, campaigning, ethical consumerism, spending time outside, practically helping those financially poorer than myself, and so on . . . all these things, and more, are natural outworkings of this relational scheme. And the wonderful thing is that I do not see any of them as having priority over the others – any one thing as being more important to do than anything else: they all blend together into a harmonious whole, and that whole is weakened if any one of those things is missing in our lives.

This is not about pitting evangelism against community engagement, or poverty relief against environmental care, or a life of prayer against a life of action. A life sold out to the gospel of Jesus Christ does all those things and more, not out of duty, but naturally, out of love for our trinitarian Creator God.

So as we delve into this book and turn our attention to the contemporary context within which we are all trying our best to be followers of Jesus, it is this biblical framework of relationships that lays the foundation for the rest of our discussions.

PART ONE

The Air We Breathe – the Context

Chapter 1

The Elephant and the Blind Men
Just what is globalisation?

Take a few moments before reading any further to think about what countries you have been in contact with so far today. Have a look at the labels on your clothes: where are they from? Maybe you are wearing jeans from Morocco, or a top from Pakistan. How about the food you have eaten so far today? Maybe you have had some coffee from Nicaragua or tea from India, cornflakes from US corn, tomatoes from Spain, potatoes from Egypt and beans from Kenya (although possibly not all in the same dish). Take a look around you: your carpet might be from Australia and your furniture from Scandinavia. And then what have you (hopefully) washed yourself with? Your soap might come from Germany, your facial cleanser from France and your deodorant from Ireland.

Now think about actual people with whom you have had contact. If you have been on social media today, then chances are you have seen posts or tweets from people all over the world. Greg sometimes has days when he feels like he has spent the whole day in his office, following the sun on Skype, talking with different people around the world as it becomes their daytime.

Once you begin to think like this, you realise that in the course of a day we might each have had some sort of a connection with ten . . . twenty . . . thirty countries. Of course, trade between countries has always taken place, but the speed at which this now happens and the sheer number of countries with which we all have connections every day is unprecedented and in stark contrast to life in the sixteenth and seventeenth centuries, when many people rarely travelled more than twenty miles away from their homes.[1]

It feels like our world is getting smaller. When the Jesuit missionaries of the sixteenth and seventeenth centuries set off from southern Europe, they knew it would take them two years before they reached Goa in India. For those who were headed for China, it would take them another year from there, or possibly two if the winds were not in their favour, thus making a possible journey time of four years from Italy and Spain to China (it is also sobering to think that around half of all passengers on such journeys died en route). By the time my great-great-grandfather went to India to be a missionary in 1846, his sailing boat could get him there in four months: what a revolution in speed! When my parents went to Singapore in the 1960s and my grandfather (who himself had been a missionary in China) heard that they could travel there by boat in three weeks, he exclaimed, 'How amazing to get there so quickly!' Now, of course, we can fly out there in around fourteen hours.

What we are talking about here is _globalisation_, a word that 'encapsulates our latest contemporary story'.[2] Globalisation might sound like a big word that has little to do with the life we are living, but actually it is the framework within which we are each living out our lives, and it is of particular relevance for those of us who want to think through how we serve Jesus well in a world of inequality and environmental suffering.

Globalisation is a much debated term, but at its simplest it describes – as illustrated above – the way our world is increasingly interconnected. It is a process that has been accelerating since the onset of the Industrial Revolution in the mid-1700s and it has moved us from a world that is exclusively national and transnational, in which the primary world actors are those that exist within national boundaries (i.e. national governments), to one that is global, in which nation-bound actors jostle on the stage alongside those that operate across – and whose concerns are not restricted by – national boundaries, such as business corporations, global NGOs (non-governmental organisations) and institutions like the IMF (International Monetary Fund) and World Bank.

It needs to be recognised that there is constant debate over globalisation. For some (what we could call the hyper-globalisers), the whole world is being globalised and homogenised, with the national completely superseded by the global, and economies coming together into a global system. Others question whether it really exists and point to the increasing rise of fundamentalism and a concern for national identities. The Slow Food movement, for example, was a classic backlash against what was seen as the 'McDonaldisation' of food around the world, with a desire to reaffirm the importance of local, regional food. People wondered whether the events of the 9/11 terrorist attacks and the 2008 banking crisis and recession would bring globalisation to an end. While the terrorist attacks highlighted the lack of homogeneity in the world and the clash of cultures that existed, the banking crisis revealed the vulnerability of a globalised economic system and potentially encouraged nations to withdraw and turn in on themselves. Even the former head of the IMF, Dominique Strauss-Kahn, acknowledged this possibility and said that the events since 2008 have 'devastated the intellectual foundations of the global economic order of the last twenty-five years'.[3]

However, when we count up the countries we touch in just one day (or even just one meal), it seems that, although events such as 9/11 and the recession brought in new dynamics, globalisation is alive and well, albeit undeniably fluid and shifting.

David Held and Anthony McGrew are two leading commentators on globalisation and they identify three particular reasons why globalisation has continued apace, despite the potential of international crises to derail it. First, it is socially embedded. Globalisation is now so much a part of both our social narrative and our experience that it is hard to conceive of going 'back' to anything else. Second, it is institutionally entrenched. In other words, the global institutions of our day are ideologically embedded to the economic philosophy of free trade that underpins globalisation and they show no signs of moving away from that (we will explore this a bit more shortly). Third, crucially, there is currently no politically mainstream alternative to the open world economy of globalisation.[4]

In its current form, globalisation is a phenomenon that has a whole range of different approaches to it and is understood in a number of different ways, reflecting many different networks of relationships. It is evolving constantly and is very complex to define.

A well-known Indian story tells the tale of six blind men trying to describe an elephant. One man touches the leg and describes the elephant as being like a pillar; one touches the tail and says it is like a rope. Another man touches the trunk and says it is like the thick trunk of a tree, while another touches the tummy and says the elephant is like a huge wall. The fifth man touches the ear and believes the elephant to be like a big hand-held fan, and the final man touches the tusk and describes the elephant as being like a solid pipe. They all begin to argue, each one convinced that they are right. After all, they know what they have felt! And it takes a wise man to come to their rescue and explain to them that each one is right because they are describing the part of the elephant that they have experienced, but that each one is also wrong because none of them have experienced the elephant in full.

This is a helpful way of understanding why there are so many different opinions on what globalisation is and why it is so hard to define: each commentator's definition comes from their own experience of globalisation, which varies depending on their geographical and social location. Like in the story above, no one person has overall sight. Indeed, one could go further and suggest that there is actually no one elephant called 'globalisation': what it is differs according to which part of our global scene we are looking at.

Despite all these many debates around globalisation, however, there is a general level of agreement that globalisation has four main aspects to it – what I call the four faces of

4 faces of it

globalisation – and I want to look at these (the economic, political, technological and cultural[5]) and consider what relevance they have to the overall subject matter of this book.

Economic globalisation

When the 9/11 terrorist attacks focused on the twin towers of the World Trade Center, they were going right to the heart of the dominant economic system of the world. Trade is what our world is built on, but not just any form of trade: a very specific form of trade called 'free trade'.

Free trade is all about removing the barriers to trading between countries that nations can impose. These barriers are often in the form of tariffs, where a government places a tax on a product that is being exported out of the country. On the one hand, such a tariff can help provide revenue for that country, but it can also have the effect of discouraging others from wanting to buy from them, hence creating a barrier to trade. Because of this, supporters of free trade generally want to limit the degree to which states can intervene in the trading processes (this is called deregulation) and allow market forces to find their own equilibrium.

When Bill Clinton, as President of the United States, said, 'The United States has 4.5 per cent of the world's population but 22 per cent of its income. We cannot sustain our standard of living unless we sell some things to other people', what he was pushing for was an American economy that did not close in on itself protectively but opened up its borders and traded more openly with other countries.[6]

This way of running the economy – both nationally and therefore globally – is based on what is called the Washington Consensus. This was a set of ten principles, laid down in 1989 by economist John Williamson and agreed by the American financial institutions, that brought together the main tenets of free market economics and acted as a guide for economic growth. While thinking has developed and we are now into the 'Post-Washington Consensus', these initial principles together formed a distinct ideology on which economic globalisation has been built – an ideology labelled 'neo-liberalism'.

Underpinning these principles was – and is – the belief that the economy must grow continually. It may not be quite true that in the aftermath of 9/11 President Bush urged Americans to 'go shopping', but it is easy to see how that urban myth arose when, in his address to the nation on 20 September of that year (at which he announced his 'war on terror'), he stated that it was imperative for them to continue their 'participation and confidence in the American economy'.[7] Participation in the American economy (i.e. shopping) has to continue because, without it, the American economy would not keep growing, which would bring collapse and disaster.

Economic globalisation in the form of free market economics is highly contested and it attracts intense criticism from those who are concerned about the numbers of people still living in poverty.[8] The criticism comes from different voices, speaking from diverse perspectives. Some speak from a position of power and essentially agree that free trade is the way to bring people and countries out of poverty. However, they also acknowledge that the so-called 'invisible hand' of the market has not done the job it was expected to do: it has not brought a natural state of balance between supply and demand to the global economy, and it has not led to all societies being better off, and so it cannot be left entirely to its own devices. Therefore, some measure of state control is needed to encourage the market forward but without its negative side effects.[9] Others fundamentally reject globalisation as little more than a selfish ideology advanced by rich elites.[10]

In between these two ends is a variety of views. One of the most interesting global developments from this perspective in recent years has been the rise of the anti-globalisation movement (possibly better named 'alter-globalisation' by Geoffrey Pleyers[11]). This has been made visible at large-scale gatherings such as the protests at the Genoa Group of Eight meeting at Genoa in 2001 and at the WTO (World Trade Organisation) meeting in Seattle in 1999, the regular World Social Forums and the Occupy Wall Street/London movements. These gatherings attract a mass of different groups and individuals, representing a wide range of views, but all agreeing that globalisation as it currently exists is intensely problematic.

Many of these groups are large but often generally invisible because they represent the powerless: groups such as Via Campesina and the Landless Workers Movement in Brazil. Of increasing importance, additionally, are the internet-based pressure groups that are able to mobilise sometimes hundreds of thousands of citizens around the world within hours.[12]

What makes the debates around globalisation confusing is that, for many, there is no doubt that it has brought enormous benefits. One of the amazing success stories of recent years has been the fall in poverty rates in Asia. In East Asia, the proportion of people living in poverty fell from 60 per cent in 1990 to 16 per cent in 2005. Most spectacular has been the transformation in China where Deng Xiaoping's policies of export-led growth resulted in China's economy growing eight-fold in the 1980s and 1990s and, between 1990 and 1998, the number of Chinese living on less than a dollar a day fell by 150 million. This is the fastest fall in poverty the world has ever seen.

Good news indeed. The problem, though, is that it is now well acknowledged that those benefits have come at a threefold price. First, they have been extremely unevenly distributed. So, while it is true that East Asia has experienced dramatic falls in poverty levels, this has not been the case in other areas. Indeed, the UNDP (United Nations Development Programme) states that if China is taken out of the equation, the number of people living on less than a dollar a day actually increased by 36 million between 1990 and 2005.[13]

Second, one of the undoubted consequences of the focus on economic growth is that it has come at the expense of the environment, which has been stripped and changed almost beyond recognition in order to provide the resources upon which the growth has been built.[14] That has had, and will have, profound impacts on both human life[15] and on other creatures[16] – changes that are ultimately likely to undo much of the positive economic growth and social development.[17]

The third price that has been paid for the incredible economic rise of East Asian countries is that the 'rising tide lifts all boats' narrative has not turned out to be the case, as growth for some has resulted in increasing inequality for others. Despite arguments to the contrary, it has become apparent that this inequality seems to be endemic to the neo-liberal approaches to economic globalisation. Globalisation, as we currently have it, while certainly having lifted many out of poverty, operates a win/lose scenario in that the very success some experience causes the increasing poverty of others.[18]

As I indicated in the Introduction, the deeply persistent poverty and environmental destruction that accompany this economic face of globalisation are of immense concern to many, if not all, of us. The economic debates over globalisation are thus stimulated precisely by those who desire to see an end to such desperate poverty and inequality and who believe that the status quo, built as it is on a continual-growth model, needs to be challenged.

One of the interesting things for our purposes, bearing in mind the biblical overview we looked at previously, is that the debates around economic globalisation involve deep issues of what it is to be human, what sort of development is therefore required, and hence how to achieve it. The problem with the dominant economic ideology that we have been considering (a neo-liberal approach that is focused on growth through free trade) is that its definition of development is too narrow and restricted. The 'rising tide lifts all boats' scenario, held to by those who advocate for free trade, holds to the belief that a growing global economy will inevitably result in everybody catching the wave and being lifted out of poverty. However, this view focuses on economic growth without considering other implications such as environmental concerns and issues around social cohesion.

Ian Christie is from the University of Surrey and co-ordinates the Sustainable Lifestyles Research Group. He writes that 'the growth model of development focuses on individuals and their consumption [but] it neglects the social and environmental relationships in which people are embedded'.[19] In other words, while reaching a certain level of material prosperity is absolutely to be desired and worked for, there is more to human development than simply getting financially richer. Such an understanding diminishes what it means to be human and forgets that we flourish and find who we are through the relationships of which we are a part. Material gain can be a positive (and for many in our world it is an imperative), but it must never come at the expense of other human beings and the wider world. When it comes to development, we need to foster a model that recognises the importance of economic growth, but places it in a subservient role, necessary to serve the more important goals of human well-being and peacefulness with the wider natural world.[20]

Political globalisation

On a shelf in Greg's office is a chunk of concrete, about the size of my hand. It is pretty rough, but one side of it is smooth with colourful markings on it. Some of you might recognise that description instantly: it is a piece of the infamous Berlin Wall that was used to separate capitalist West Germany from communist East Germany for twenty-eight years. On 9 November 1989, people all around the world watched as thousands of jubilant Germans dismantled it and brought it crashing to the ground. It is almost unbelievable now to think that Germany used once to be separated in such a way.

The fall of the Berlin Wall is one of the most significant moments in recent history and it triggered the collapse of communism in Eastern Europe. Like a pack of cards, once the Berlin Wall had gone all the other communist countries followed. Hungary, Czechoslovakia, Poland, Romania, Bulgaria: all saw their communist leaders toppled by the end of 1990 and replaced by democratically elected governments, and the process was completed when, at the end of 1991, the USSR (Union of Soviet Socialist Republics) was dissolved. The Cold War was over: capitalism had won.

The collapse of communism under the triumphant march of capitalism shifted the political scene vastly and changed the world balance of forces. Crucially, it enabled the development of today's global financial system as there was now no longer any significant group of countries that was not a part of this system.

As we saw earlier, this has meant that we have moved from a world that is international to one that is global. Christian ethicist Roy McCloughry explains the difference between the two very helpfully: 'A world which is international conducts its business between nations. It is inter-national. But in a global world the state has become one player among others, all of whom have power and influence.' Thus 'we now live in a world in which the influence of states, multinationals and international non-governmental organisations all have an impact on global governance'.[21]

One consequence of the economic face of globalisation then is that the relationship between states and the economy has been reversed. Whereas the economy used to be subservient to the nation, the nation now works to serve the global economy.

The most important thing driving state policy is increasing competitiveness in the world market. What becomes clear, therefore, is that the economic face of globalisation does not exist in a vacuum: it is enabled to happen through specific political decisions taken at both a national level, through state governments, and at a global level, through institutions such as the IMF and the World Bank, as well as at a regional level, through blocs such as the EU (European Union).

If the economic face provides the *ideology* of globalisation, through free trade market capitalism, then the political face is the *engine* of globalisation. What we witness is the conflicted nature of this political face as nation states push for other countries to lower their trade barriers, while trying to maintain control and protection over their own. What is patently clear is that the level of ability with which a state government is able to do this reflects their status and position of power within the world scene, thus in fact making a mockery of the free trade mantra.

And so the playing field is far from level. One only has to look at the number of delegates sent to global negotiations by different countries to see how this is the case. For example, at the United Nations COP (Conference of the Parties) meeting on climate change in Warsaw in 2013, China was able to send 112 delegates, the Maldives just 4. No one from Tanzania was there; 5 went from Honduras and 6 from Lesotho. Brazil sent 142 delegates.[22]

A friend of mine from the relief and development agency Tearfund told me of one COP meeting he went to where he got chatting to the sole delegate from a francophone country in West Africa, who said that it was hard to take part because he was on his own and his English wasn't very good. All the sessions were in English and, although the plenary sessions were translated, the crucial working groups were not. Similarly, someone else told me that his experience of discussing with representatives from Least Developed Countries revealed that they had much less 'voice' in discussions, as often the same person was trying to cover a number of different negotiation tracks and so on occasions barely had time to read new text before negotiating sessions. Often in group meetings, too, China and other large developing countries dominated the discussion on which position was to be agreed by the group (if, my friend said, they were able to agree a position at all!).

As nation states have lost some of the power they have historically enjoyed, they have handed it over to the business world, whose position on the global chess board has become hugely advantageous as they have gained immense political power. Nokia provides an example of how one company can impact the policies of a whole nation. Based in Finland, the 'communications and information technology multinational corporation' at its height represented two-thirds of the Finnish nation's stock market value and a fifth of the nation's total export value. Its $25 billion in annual sales almost matched the entire national budget. This, of course, benefited Finland hugely on an economic level, but it also gave Nokia political power to pressure the government to move away from its strong welfare system in favour of lower corporate taxes.[23]

The situation in the UK is somewhat different, but it is apparent that, as Monbiot asserts, our 'leading politicians, like those of Australia and Canada, appear to be little more than channels for corporate power'.[24] Take, for example, the attempts by the coalition government that was elected in 2010 to reform the NHS (National Health Service) by way of increasing privatisation. An investigation by the trade union Unite discovered that twenty-four of the Conservative MPs and Lords who voted for the 2012 Health and Social Care Act (which introduced one of the biggest reorganisations of the NHS in England) have links with companies that benefited from the changes that were made. These included Prime Minster David Cameron and Andrew Lansley, who was Secretary of State for Health and the person whose policies resulted in the proposals. Unite calculated that in two years after the Act was passed, £1.5 billion left the NHS and went into the fifteen companies linked to those twenty-four people.[25]

Technological globalisation

In 1920 the first commercially licensed regular radio broadcast was begun in the US. From this point, it took forty years for it to gain an audience of 50 million. When PCs were introduced, it took fifteen years before 50 million people were using them. It took just four years, after it was made available, for 50 million Americans to be regularly using the internet.[26] By 2015, the United Nations' agency for information and communication technology (ITU) calculated that 3.2 billion people globally had access to the internet and there were 7 billion mobile phone subscriptions.[27]

If the political is the *engine* of globalisation, then the techno-logical face is the *fuel*, since it is what makes the engine work.

Very little of either the economic or the political advancements that we have seen would have been possible were it not for the incredible pace with which technology has developed.

The economic sphere of globalisation relies on the computerised virtual world. Currency transactions, speculations, the daily workings of the stock exchange: all happen virtually; no 'real' money actually changes hands. And technology allows companies to split their assembly lines between countries on different sides of the world, sending designs and orders and shifting components from one country to another to minimise costs.

Politically, on a mundane level, it is a simple fact that technology enables global politics to function through facilitating travel and communication. But technology also plays a role in facilitating the political sphere in other ways.

It has been a fascinating feature of the seismic shifts in world politics that modern technology has stood behind so much of what has happened. The 1989 revolutions that we saw at the start of this section have been dubbed the 'TV revolutions' because one of the major reasons for the downfall of the communist regimes was the access the people had to Western ideas through the televised media. As McCloughry puts it, 'In the twenty-first century borders come down not so much because physical dividing walls are dismantled but because there is no effective restriction on the free flow of information across them. The information society has made it difficult for totalitarian regimes to isolate their societies since the Internet can be used to convey information around the world.'[28]

Technology is used not just to convey information, but also to connect people. The incredible events of 2010 and 2011 with the protests, riots, revolutions and civil wars of the so-called Arab Spring (so called because most of the events happened in the springtime and were in the Arab world) have also been labelled the 'Twitter revolutions' because one of their notable characteristics was the key role that Twitter played in helping activists to connect with each other and co-ordinate their activities.

In fact, Twitter is becoming an increasingly important feature of the political sphere in general as it is such a powerful means of communication, with campaign activists, politicians and businesses all using it to get their various messages across. One very successful campaign was by Greenpeace, calling on Legoland not to renew their sponsorship deal with Shell. They devised a brilliantly creative campaign, based around the 'Everything is Not Awesome' YouTube video depicting a Lego Arctic being covered in oil, and lots of still images of Lego characters protesting against Shell in various places. It caught the public's imagination and, for a few days in July 2014, the Twittersphere was full of what Greenpeace was doing, with the result that the video was watched by nearly 7 million people, and over 1 million people signed their 'Tell Lego to Dump Shell' petition. After initial resistance, in October 2014, Lego announced that it would not renew its contract with Shell once the initial one had come to an end.

Cultural globalisation

These three faces of globalisation – the economic, the political and the technological – have together had a profound effect on culture, which is the *manifestation* of globalisation. What does this all look like to the average person on the street? Well, the answer is that we are not on the street, we are in the shops.

As we have seen already, humanity is more interconnected and more mobile than ever before (although that is not always for the good, as we shall see shortly). Television and the internet have enabled a communications and social revolution that has not only impacted the economic and political spheres of globalisation: they impact *us* as well (and here we begin to see how closely related the different faces are). We now have news, information and values transmitted and disseminated to us more extensively than at any other time in history and, as my illustration at the start of this chapter demonstrated, we are connected with more people in more places than has ever been experienced before.

Television, of course, remains the ubiquitous symbol of globalisation, with some 98 per cent of homes in the USA and the UK owning at least one television. In fact, television has become so much a part of our lives that we hardly notice how much it has encroached on our time and space. This was brought home to me strongly when I went with a friend to see a house they were in the process of buying but which was currently vacant. She talked me through the various rooms and when we reached the sitting room the main point of the conversation was where the television would go and how to arrange the furniture around it.

I am nervous about coming across as a total snob here, but I find it sad that the room where people might sit together the most is dominated by something that sucks in our attention, takes our focus off the people we are with, and often limits

– if not entirely shuts down – our conversation. I know, for example, that when we decided not to replace the television in our bedroom when it broke, Greg and I discovered that we actually talked when we got into bed at night, rather than sitting next to each other staring at a screen in the corner! I think, too, of my daughter's friend who came round for dinner after school one day and commented on how nice it was to be all eating together, talking. She lives with her mum in a flat with no kitchen/dining table. Her mum would often cook something for dinner for her daughter, and she would eat it on her lap in her room watching the television. Then later, her mum would make something for herself and she would eat it on *her* own, on her lap, watching the television in the sitting room. I am not against the television *per se*, but we have let it intrude into our lives far too much and we turn it on far too quickly.

However, the TV might not always be the screen of choice. Look around you next time you are on the train and the majority of people will be on a screen of some sort, texting, playing a game, watching a film, working, reading a book . . . And now we have the phenomena of double (and sometimes triple) screening, where a person is engaged with more than one screen at the same time. I have to say that this particular skill is well practised in the Valerio household, including by myself!

Looking back at the last two paragraphs, it is perhaps obvious to say that globalisation, in all its facets, has hugely impacted the family. Sociologist Anthony Giddens highlighted this particularly in his fourth BBC Reith Lecture on globalisation, in which he stated, 'Among all the changes going on today, none are more important than those happening in our personal lives – in sexuality, emotional life, marriage and the family. There is a global revolution going on in how we think of ourselves and how we form ties and connections with others.'[29] The advent of sophisticated contraception, the feminist movement, social media and the intensification of consumer culture have all played their part in radically changing relationships and familial identity and practice, with complicated family arrangements and both parents out at work as the norm.[30]

We have already looked at some of the problems of poverty and inequality inherent within globalisation in our consideration of the economic face, but one of the strongest changes that has been seen culturally has been in contemporary understandings of social stratification (i.e. how people are ranked hierarchically in society), and this only serves to highlight globalisation's uneven character. New patterns of inclusion and exclusion have developed and these are based on how far an individual is able to participate in technology-driven, consumer society.

So we can categorise people into three main levels. First, there are those at the top. They are the ones who are integrated into the management levels, who make the decisions, carry out the research and maintain the system. Then there is the second level, which is the vast number of those who support the top category. This level consists of people with lesser skills, who exist where the work is offered and are often in precarious positions. Finally, at the third level, are those who are excluded from international production. They are the unemployed, the myriad of small, low-technology enterprises in the richer countries, and a large part of the marginalised population in poor countries.[31]

Another interesting characterisation of our modern world that categorises people is mobilisation. We have seen already that humanity is more mobile than ever before, but this observation operates on different levels. On the one hand, differentiation exists between those who are able to be mobile and those who are not. Zygmunt Bauman is a sociologist whose work we will consider more fully in the next chapter, but it is appropriate to bring him in at this point because much of his exploration of globalisation is built on this stratification. For Bauman, the 'top level' person is the one who is extra-territorial and who has most in common, and networks, with those at a similar level across the globe. Thus 'mobility climbs to the rank of the uppermost among the coveted values – and the freedom to move, perpetually a scarce and unequally distributed commodity, fast becomes the main stratifying factor of our . . . times'.[32] The mobile are able to pursue employment opportunities and escape more localised problems.

One of the significant implications of mobility is that it results in the loss of responsibility for any specific location: something that the German sociologist Ulrich Beck, whom we shall consider shortly, describes as 'organized irresponsibility'.[33] Kentucky farmer and celebrated author and poet Wendell Berry describes this brilliantly and is worth quoting in full to get a grasp of what he is saying:

My part of rural America is, in short, a colony, like every other part of rural America. Almost the whole landscape of this country – from the exhausted cotton fields of the plantation South to the eroding wheatlands of the Palouse, from the strip mines of Appalachia to the clear-cuts of the Pacific slope – is in the power of an absentee economy, once national and now increasingly international, that is without limit in its greed and without mercy in its exploitation of land and people. Between the prosperity of this vast centralizing economy and the prosperity of any local economy or locality, there is now a radical disconnection. The accounting that measures the wealth of corporations, great banks, and national treasuries takes no measure of the civic or economic or natural health of places like Port Royal, Kentucky; Harpster, Ohio; Indianola, Iowa; Matfield Green, Kansas; Wolf Hole, Arizona; or Nevada City, California – and it does not intend to do so.[34]

At the heart of this 'organized irresponsibility' is a lack of relationships, since one does not love what one does not know. As we saw in the Introduction, relationships are at the heart of the biblical framework for the themes of this book and we will see often that part of the move towards simpler living is the desire to solidify relationships. Relationships cannot be solidified by people who are constantly on the move, and so an essential part of relationship building is about staying and being rooted in one area.

So, having the freedom to move is one thing that characterises the different levels that exist in society. But, conversely, having the freedom to *stay* is also something that can define one's social place.

The Notre Dame Global Adaptation Index is an authoritative annual index that ranks the majority of the world's countries based on their vulnerability to climate change and their current ability to adapt to the impacts of droughts, extreme weather events and other natural disasters.[35] At the time of writing, Norway is the most prepared to respond to climate change, followed by New Zealand, Sweden, Finland, Denmark, Australia, the United Kingdom, United States, Germany and Iceland. At the bottom, however, are Chad, Eritrea, Burundi, the Democratic Republic of Congo, the Central African Republic, Sudan, Niger, Haiti, Afghanistan and Guinea-Bissau.

It is no surprise to note that it is the economically more developed countries that have the better rankings and whose citizens will not experience the worst of the predicted environmental and social problems. One of the biggest implications of that for the citizens of those countries, even if they are unaware of it, is that it leaves them (us) secure enough to settle down and not live with the constant fear of being forced to move. Contrast this with the Bangladeshi farmer, constantly moving his dwelling place, family and possessions back each year as the sea encroaches, and one realises that the freedom to stay will increasingly become a luxury afforded only to the privileged minority of the world.

We can see this happening closer to home as well, as younger generations are forced to leave the area in which they have grown up because of either a lack of jobs or unaffordable house prices, or both. This has a direct impact on social cohesion as extended families are spread further and further apart, with increasing pressure and expectation then placed on the nuclear family to provide all its needs. People cannot live near their elderly parents to help look after them; grandparents cannot live near to and help out with grandchildren, and so on.

There is thus a strong link between those who are able to move and those who are able to stay; both of them are about being able to choose, and they are both advantages that not everyone will be able to enjoy. At the bottom of society are those who are forced to move, and the global refugee problem continues to escalate. Although Bauman's main preoccupation is with the freedom to move, he does also write strongly about this, describing how 'hundreds of thousands, sometimes millions of people are chased away from their homes, murdered or forced to run for their lives outside the borders of their country'. In typical Baumanesque polemic, his judgement of the global situation is that 'perhaps the sole thriving industry in the lands of the latecomers (deviously and often deceitfully dubbed "developing countries") is the *mass production of refugees*'.[36]

The 'Risk Society'

This is the world in which we live, and it is incredibly complex. Our next chapter, on consumerism, will give us the opportunity to consider it – and our place within it – still further. But before we do that, I want to conclude our discussion of the global context by looking at the German sociologist Ulrich Beck and his thesis on the 'Risk Society'. His thinking is useful for us, particularly his notion of 'sub-politics', because it relates to the desire that many of us have to use the everyday decisions of our lives well, in ways that work towards building a world of *shalom* – peace – with each other and the wider creation.

'Citizens of the world, unite!' is the clarion call that Beck wants to sound out through his writing on what he has termed the Risk Society.[37] For Beck, it is this notion of risk that encapsulates the global world in which we live. Beck's notion of the Risk Society is that we live in a society today that experiences the concept of risk very differently to 'pre-industrial' and 'industrial' societies. In those societies, risk was predominantly localised, arising as it did from natural disasters. In Beck's evocative words, risks 'in those days assaulted the nose or the eyes, and were thus perceptible to the senses'.[38] Our contemporary risks, by contrast, are global, arising as after-effects of our own technological and scientific advances.

For Beck, these risks are both real and also socially constructed. From a realist perspective, these risks 'are': they exist in actuality, as seen in the Chernobyl disaster, 'when an "atomic cloud" terrified the whole of Europe and forced people to make changes even in their day-to-day private lives'.[39] Yet the presence of risk is also a perception, moulded by the narratives that a society tells of itself. Those risks relate to meta-disasters – risks such as climate change, crop failure and nuclear disaster (and we might want to add the spread of disease to that list, living as we do with the Ebola epidemic in our recent history) – but they also relate to more personal risks felt by people living in Western culture, risks concerning areas such as relationships, identity, employment and economic security. Reflecting what we have already seen in relation to the impact that globalisation has had on the family, even marriage becomes a component of the Risk Society: marriage 'is a much more open system with new forms of risk . . . The very decision to get married is constitutively different from before. There has never been a high-divorce, high-marriage society before. No one knows . . . what its consequences are for the future of the family or for the health of children.'[40]

Is this something you would relate to? In many ways we live in one of the most secure, prosperous and comfortable societies ever. And yet we are constantly frightened of what might happen to us: the economy might fail; immigrants might steal 'our jobs'; our partner might leave us for someone more attractive; our children might experience cyber-bullying; our parents might be abused in their care home; the little nick on our windscreen from a flying pebble might spread and cause the whole thing to shatter . . . and so on. 'Sunday night sleeplessness' is now a recognised problem for many people: it is the night when we sleep our worst because we are worrying about what the week might hold with unreasonable bosses and tight deadlines. This notion of living in a Risk Society is something that will emerge again in the next two chapters: we will see it in different form in chapter 2 when we consider Bauman and Liquid Modernity, and we will meet it again in chapter 3 when we look at the rediscovery of the way of monasticism and how its practices can help us counteract that sense of fear that arises from living in the Risk Society.

Beck's work has become a sociological classic – it has been discussed, debated, disputed and celebrated – and there is more to it than we have space to consider here. What is particularly relevant to our interests, though, is the acutely political nature of Beck's sociological analysis. Correlating to our earlier discussion of the political face of globalisation, Beck observes that what has emerged is a 'powerplay between territorially fixed political actors (governments, parliament, unions) and non-territorial economic actors (representatives of capital, finance, trade)'.[41] As that powerplay has ensued, the nation state has proved incapable of dealing effectively with the problems with which our industrialised liberal society is beset and the non-territorial actors have stepped into the vacuum.[42] This is problematic since, as we have already seen, non-territorial actors bear little territorial responsibility and are not automatically overly interested in democratic principles. Moreover, when nation states are involved in decision-making processes, the power weightings ascribed to different countries are disproportionate, reflecting those countries' economic and military strength: a problem exacerbated by the lack of some sort of parliamentary control at an international level.

The impact this has had on politics is interesting. For some, democracy has become a casualty of globalisation, leading to disillusionment among the voting population.[43] Sharply declining electoral turnouts in the UK would seem to confirm this.[44] On the other hand, for those with the motivation to do so, it has pushed them out to explore other channels of political involvement, beyond the realm of the traditional representative institutions of the state.[45] For Beck, globalisation has generated new kinds of democratic sub-politics as the political restructuring means that politics cannot any longer be fully equated with the political system: 'the truly political disappears in and from the political system and reappears, changed and generalized, in a form that remains to be comprehended and developed, as *sub(system) politics* in all the other fields of society'.[46] Politics is thus conducted at 'social "sites" that were previously considered unpolitical', sites such as 'the firm, the laboratory, at the gas station, or in the supermarket'.[47]

This is key for what we are thinking about in this book. *Just Living* is about joining the dots between how we live our lives, the culture in which we live, our Christian faith and the broader issues of this world, and Beck's notion of sub-politics relates directly to this. We will see at various points that, while we make those connections partly by retreating from the negative aspects of globalisation and consumerism, we also use our life actions positively to engage in global structures and bring about change. In many ways, what we are doing when we use our life actions in this way is precisely engaging in the sort of sub-politics that Beck describes.

What becomes apparent is that joining the dots, as Beck has demonstrated, is an inescapably political activity: it is not a purely privatised lifestyle initiative. Because we live in a world in which the global economy plays such a large part in the political system, everything we do that has a bearing on that economy becomes a political act. So, buying fairly traded goods, practising generosity, reducing the amount of energy we use, limiting the amount of time we spend watching the television, growing our own food and many more similar actions have political implications because we inhabit a world in which the political, economic and social are so closely intertwined. To use political scientist Michele Micheletti's memorable phrase, we are engaged in acts of 'thinking politically privately'.[48]

However, we need to be aware that there is an interesting discussion to be had here around the effectiveness or otherwise of such sub-politics. Australian sociologist Kim Humphery undertook an excellent analysis of the anti-consumerism movement, and he makes the salient criticism that an emphasis on individual lifestyle cannot carry the political weight that its proponents imagine it to do and that, on their own, these sorts of acts do not bring about the challenge to consumerist ideology that is hoped for.[49] The result is that 'the subject on which much Western anti-consumerist commentary becomes frustratingly timid is that of systemic economic and political change, beyond that of attending to the self'.[50]

Mary Grigsby is an American sociologist who wrote a detailed account of the voluntary simplicity movement in the US.[51] She has the same criticism to make as does Humphery and notes that the 'simple livers' she studied were silent on the structural issues of class, race and gender and seemed unaware of how those issues shaped the ability of individuals to partici-pate in consumer society.[52] As she says, 'I don't believe . . . that self-change in keeping with the prescriptions of voluntary simplicity will result in an evolutionary shift to an ecological era without major political and economic shifts that will need to be achieved through policies aimed at structural and cultural change as well.'[53]

There is thus a tension between macro- and micro-political involvement: between traditional political engagement and sub-politics, and also between the 'hard' resistance of the more visual manifestations of actions such as the Occupy movement or the Seattle demonstrations, and the 'softer' resistance of smaller, everyday actions. As we look later on at some of the practices involved in living well in this globalised, consumer culture, we will do well to bear this tension in mind and to remember the criticism of Humphery and Grigsby. Nonetheless, rather than seeing the sub-politics of our life actions as invalid or impotent, we should view each kind of political involvement as operating along a continuum and inhabiting different social locations as we search for a better world.

Globalisation is probably *the* determinative framework within which we attempt to live out the Christian faith. However, there is still much more to be said about our context, and the next chapter turns to a consideration of the consumer society within which we live, to help us come to a better understanding of the cultural air that we breathe.

Chapter 2

Skinny Jeans and a Broken Nose
The challenge of consumerism

Friday 28 November 2014 was a day that many of us living in the UK will remember, even if we are not aware of the precise date. If we were not out shopping ourselves, it was a day when our screens relayed to us pictures of mass hysteria as people swarmed into shops to get themselves a discounted TV or coffee-maker. As the events of that day unfolded, we watched incredulously as scenes were shown of shoppers around the country trampling over each other to get into the shops first. Checkout ladies cried; people fought each other to get the goods they wanted; one person ended up in hospital when a TV fell on their head; police were called to restore order; shops had to be closed down. Online, retailers' computer systems went into meltdown as they were unable to cope with the volume of orders being placed.

It was the day that Black Friday became a truly recognised day in the British calendar, having been imported from the US four years previously by Amazon. It was also, many agreed, a national disgrace.

Overall, however, the British economy was happy. For the John Lewis retail chain, it was its busiest shopping day ever, and topped off a week that saw it sell £179 million of goods. In total, it is thought that over £800 million was spent shopping on Black Friday 2014, an important figure for an economy that has become increasingly dependent on consumer activity.

I doubt many of us were in the front line back on Black Friday 2014, pushing our fellow consumers out of the way in a frenzied attempt to get the best deal. But maybe we might resonate more with my friend who came to see me once and became distinctly embarrassed when I unconsciously looked down at her shoes. She gave an instant reaction. 'Oh, don't look!' she exclaimed. 'I bought them over the weekend and I have so many pairs already. I knew I shouldn't, but once I'd seen them I couldn't put them out of my mind till I'd got them.' She went on to tell me that she just loved the feeling that came from buying things and that often she would buy some clothes because doing so gave her a buzz, and then when she got home she would feel bad and the next day would take the purchased goods back.

I remember another conversation with someone I bumped into one day. She was wearing a top I hadn't seen before, so I commented on it, said I liked it and asked if it was new. 'Oh yes,' she said laughingly. 'It's just one of those silly things. You know what it's like: you're a bit early meeting someone in town so you pop into the shops while you're waiting and pick up something silly.'

Or maybe, before I point the finger too much at other people, I should confess to the time I bought a pair of skinny-fit jeans. Before doing so, almost right up to the counter, I took part in a pained internal dialogue. Did I need them? No, I had other jeans at home that were in good condition. What was I doing?

Taking part in a blatant act of needless consumerism. Why did I want them? Simply because 'everyone else' had them and I thought I would look good in them. Why did I think I would look good in them? Because I'd seen images and pictures that showed me how I could look. How could I do this when I spent most of my time encouraging others to live more simply and trying to do so myself? Without too much difficulty, as it turned out: this time, anyway, my desires overtook my ethics. At least, I consoled myself as I licked my guilty conscience, I was buying them from H&M, one of the more ethical options out of the main high street stores.

These illustrations are all about clothes, but of course we consume far more than that and no doubt you can think of stories similar to the above relating to other sorts of consumer goods. The fact is that we live in a consumer society. That will hardly be news to us. It is the culture most of us will have grown up in and a culture with which we are very familiar. The majority of us reading this will be used to living in a culture whereby our primary activity and focus is on consuming things rather than producing them, and in which producing or making something has become more of a niche activity than an everyday experience or necessity (and where there is still production it tends to be of more nebulous things like 'services' rather than physical products).

But what actually *is* consumerism and is it really as negative as the opening to this chapter would seem to imply? Commentators, both within and without the Church, have been discussing consumerism for decades and there is a danger that it becomes a worn and weary subject. In fact, I worried about even having the word in the title of this book for fear it would put people off. However, the above illustrations demonstrate amply that this issue is still very much a live one. Consumerism continues apace and develops constantly. Trying to keep up with it can be quite hard, which is why writing on consumerism is proliferating rather than dying down and comes from all fields, including geography, marketing, history, economics, anthropology, psychology and sociology. If we want to think through how to live well as Christians in today's culture, then we simply *have* to get to grips with consumerism, and do so in a way that is not naïve or overly simplistic. So in this chapter we will attempt to do just that, and we will do it by looking at two foundational issues: (1) what dynamics are taking place when we consume? And (2) what are the main problems with our highly consumptive society?

As with the previous chapter on globalisation, the aim is not to come to a definitive understanding of what consumerism is as such, but to explore this subject in order to become more aware of the impact that it has on us – both positively and negatively; to help us see it from some new perspectives, and thereby to help us think through how we might formulate a response to living in this day and age. A discussion on globalisation leads us to consider concerns around issues of global poverty, inequality and environmental destruction. Much of what we are interested in with this book is about an outward-focused life that is lived in order to help other people and places. However, when we turn to think about consumerism we see that intertwined with that outward-focused approach is one that is interested also in the impact of our contemporary society on ourselves, as we consider the consequences on our own lives of living in a society that places a heavy emphasis on busyness and identity, and that pressurises us to buy and 'succeed'.

So let us begin by thinking through what is actually going on when we consume things. There are two basic sides involved in any act of consumption: the side of the producer and the side of the consumer. Standing in between these two sides – bringing them together – is the product that is being consumed (and remember that product might not be material; it might also be a 'service' or something that cannot be seen like electricity). The relationship between these three (producer, consumer, product) is complex and can be seen in different ways.

From the side of the producer

One way of understanding consumerism is by focusing on the producer side. I wonder, when you get into your car (if you have one), if you ever think that you have one person to thank for that? Over a hundred years ago Henry Ford made it his mission to make cars cheap enough that anybody in middle-class America could afford one. In order to do that he developed (he did not invent) the production line approach to manufacturing. Mass production was born, and so was the revolutionary economic system known as 'Fordism'. I remember one holiday job when I stood for hours on end in a production line and screwed one single screw into whatever it was that was being made. This was the impact of Fordism: it moved production away from one person making a product, to a product being broken down into its component parts and individuals focusing on one of those particular parts. At the same time, it paid the workers a decent wage that meant they could afford the goods they were producing.

Although these things are never clear-cut (many would now say we are living in a post-Fordist era), modern consumerism is associated with Fordism and the impact that it had on American culture as first cars and then other goods began rolling off the production lines. By the 1920s, a whole new array of consumer goods was being produced and there was a large population eager to be educated about what they could buy.

When we focus on the producer side, two things emerge. The first is an awareness of the danger that, as consumers, we can simply become *passive participants in* the act of consumption: we are duped and exploited into cultural conformity and stripped of any sense of acting independently or making our own free choices. Through advertising and marketing we are told what we want: our desires are stimulated for things we had not realised we either wanted or needed (think back to me buying that pair of skinny jeans).

I was struck by this danger some years ago when celebrity chefs Hugh Fearnley-Whittingstall and Jamie Oliver were running their campaign to improve the welfare of supermarket chickens, and in particular to ban the sale of whole chickens at '2 for £5'. Some of the supermarkets responded positively, but Tesco insisted that they keep their budget line of chicken. Why? Because, they said, their priority was consumer choice: it was what their customers both wanted and expected. The problem with this argument is that it could be said their customers want and expect chicken to be sold at a very cheap price exactly *because* Tesco have introduced it and have educated their clientele to think along those lines.

In this way (and we will meet this concept further on too), through the producer, consumerism influences and controls the consumer. The key word for this is that consumerism is *hegemonic*: in other words, it dictates to us how we are to live and what we are to buy.

The second idea that emerges when we focus on the producer side of the equation is that of *detachment*. As Western society has changed from being a society of producers to one of consumers, and as globalisation has taken hold, and advertising has encouraged goods to be purchased from all over the world, we have lost touch with the origins of those products. The place of production has become far removed from the place of consumption – with long and complex supply chains – and the advertising industry has attached meanings to objects far from their original use-value (a Jaguar isn't just a car, it has a meaning to it).

In theologian Vincent Miller's excellent book on consumerism and religion he locates this detachment within broader societal moves that have led to the development of the single-family home and the need for those homes to rely on a whole range of electrical appliances that replace the work that would traditionally have been done by the extended family, thus resulting in mass de-skilling.[1] The consequence is that 'our countless acts of consumption and evaluation of commodities large and small train us daily to value things *out of their contexts*'.[2]

The impact of this has never been brought home to me more strongly than in the conversation that ensued after a talk I gave once when a young woman said to me, 'You know, I'm only just beginning to realise that meat comes from animals.'

We can thus see three particular ways in which consumer-ism detaches people as consumers.[3] First, we have become detached from material production because we do not actually make things any more. Second, we have become detached from the producers because we do not know who has made the things that we buy or consume (and, again, remember this may not be physical goods: how many of us reading this could say which power stations our gas comes from or what it is like to work there?). Consequently, third, we have become detached from the actual products themselves: because of the first two detachments we treat the things we consume with less respect and so we discard, move on to the new, very quickly. I know, for example, that since installing PV (photo-voltaic) solar panels I am much more aware of our electricity and keen to use it well, and I know that I will often treat vege-tables I have grown myself with more care than ones I have bought in the supermarket.

The Christian ethicist Stanley Hauerwas sums this up nicely when he says that 'capitalism has no memory'.[4] Amnesia becomes an important feature of consumerism as we forget how to make things, who has made them and what we bought them for in the first place. And we forget the time that has gone into so much of what we consume: the years the tree has grown before it is cut down for paper and wood; the slow passing of millions of years that have produced the (literally) fossil fuels that are burned with such speed. Thinking back to one of the illustrations at the start of this chapter, such amnesia results in us being able to view an item of clothing as 'something silly' because we have no understanding of where that item has come from, who made it, how many back-breaking hours they put into it, what environmental costs were paid for the production of the material, and so on.

If we want to learn how to live and consume well in our current culture, then understanding this key characteristic of detachment, and setting ourselves on a plan of action to tackle it, is crucial. We will pick this theme up again in Part Three as we look at practices to help us re-engage with how and what we consume.

From the side of the consumer

So one way of looking at consumerism focuses on the producer side and makes us aware of issues of passivity and detachment. However, this only gives us a partial picture of the relationship between producer, consumer and product and, when we focus on the consumer side, we see that there are other dynamics taking place as well. In particular, there is more to the consumer than simply the passive.

When we consume, at its most basic, we do so in order to purchase something we think we need or want. We buy the product because it has an underlying use-value: I buy an oven dish because I want something I can put food into in order to cook it in the oven. Often that is as far as the act of consumption goes. I am merely buying something to do a job I need or want doing.

However, partly due to us having so much choice, an act of consumption can carry further meaning. When we consume something, we also often communicate something about ourselves. If, for example, you were to come round for dinner and see that I had cooked my food in the oven in a Le Creuset casserole dish, I might be communicating that I am a woman who appreciates the importance of using quality equipment to cook with; who therefore understands what good food is all about; and who has the money to buy such equipment. I don't have such a dish, by the way – if only because I wouldn't have the strength to lift the darned thing out of the oven – but I hope the point is clear: when I choose something to buy, I am implicitly (like it or not) communicating something about who I am.

How that works is, of course, very complex and those little pieces of communication can be hard to read. I may, for example, have the money to buy the whole Le Creuset range but not want to be stereotyped in that way and so decide to buy more generic cookware. Or I may have found such a dish in a charity shop.

Sometimes our acts are about making statements of 'conspicuous consumption' (a term coined at the end of the nineteenth century by the economist Thorstein Veblen in his study of how rich Americans were communicating their wealth in their new urban industrial environments, in which the old rural ways of communicating wealth were no longer viable[5]). A large house, expensive car and frequent holidays abroad are conspicuous ways of communicating very clearly a level of wealth not enjoyed by most people.

Sometimes our consumer acts are carried out in such a way as to create 'marks of distinction' (a term coined by the sociologist Pierre Bourdieu in his ground-breaking work on class classification, conducted through the 1960s[6]). Our consumer practices are often designed to position ourselves within a particular class or social grouping. Intertwined here are interesting discussions around 'taste' and what is considered to be tasteful. A person's understanding of taste is inevitably culturally determined (Bourdieu's empirical research demonstrated that taste was generally determined by education and parental profession[7]) and always works by setting itself up in distinction from that which is thought to be distasteful.

As consumers, then, we use goods to make statements about ourselves (and we are aware that others use those goods to make judgements about us back, whether we want them to or not). Alongside this, one of the drivers of consumerism is a pressure to conform to – and sometimes exceed – the consumerist habits of one's peers. This happens at different levels for different people. While for some, Veblen's 'conspicuous consumption' might be an appropriate term (a current radio advertisement for a competition to win a car finishes with the line that if you win the car you will generate 'the envy of all your neighbours'), others of us might resonate more with what Bauman describes as 'marks of belonging'.[8] I think of the clothes I wore as a teenager which were clearly designed to mark me out as belonging to a particular group of people who listened to a particular type of music.

It might be helpful to think of our acts of consumption as something akin to an arms race: many people are not really that interested in buying more things, but we do not want to be left behind socially and so, as our peers consume in particular ways, we gradually do as well.[9] I am reminded at this point of Adam Smith's statement that people wish simply to 'live a life without shame'.[10]

It is at this point that trying to understand the dynamics of consumerism can begin to feel like trying to pick up sand. It is not possible to formulate one defining macro-thesis as to what is taking place when people consume: people are trying to keep up, keep ahead or keep in, and of course more mundane factors such as age and personality type are also determinants of how one acts and responds within consumer culture.

So understanding consumerism from the side of the consumer is complex. As we look at it from this side we must not lose what we saw previously in terms of the power held by the producer. While we live in a society that extols the virtues of consumer choice and crowns the consumer as queen or king ('the customer is always right'), we must never forget that the parameters of our consumer choice are prescriptively set within the structures of the consumer society in which we live.[11]

Nonetheless, the last few paragraphs have shown that it is not enough simply to label consumers as passive dupes, dancing mindlessly to the tune of the Ad Man: the real picture is far more nuanced. The relationship between consumer, producer, the sphere of exchange and the material goods themselves is complex and it is most helpful to view consumerism as something that both constrains and enables both consumer and producer – positively and negatively – and to describe the consumer, in the words of Luke Bretherton, as 'neither an autonomous chooser nor a gulled fool, but an active and reflexive participant'.[12]

There is another way in which we use consumer goods, beyond using them as social markers: we use them relationally. The anthropologist Daniel Miller has undertaken several studies of everyday objects and their owners. In one particularly interesting piece of research, he studied the residents of a London street and looked at how they related to and used the objects in their homes.[13] He came to the conclusion that they do this in multifarious ways, some of which could be positive and conducive to building good relationships. So, for example, one woman had a huge array of photographs displayed and she used those as a way of building an inviting environment for her many foster children. One man had sold some of his record collection to raise money to help pay for his sister's wedding. One couple had filled their home with objects filled with family memories as a way of creating a welcoming atmosphere for returning children.

I am sure we can think of our own illustrations. I know, for example, that my parents have filled their sitting room with objects that they have been given on their many overseas travels. This helps connect them with the people they have met, the churches and Bible colleges they have spoken in, and the needs that have been related to them.

I use food in this connective way too, and know I am not alone in doing so. Food shopping is in one sense a functional thing: I have a list that I want to get through as quickly as possible and get home again. On another level, though, this is more than simply buying calories to fill up the people in my household: I am constantly thinking about what food I know will make particular members happy and/or benefit them in some way, and what ingredients I need to buy in order to do that, all of which will have the effect of strengthening the bond between me and my family.[14] For my last birthday, my eldest daughter cooked a three-course meal. She went out with her older cousin and they bought the ingredients together. This was consumerism through and through, and yet it enhanced our relationships, both for us as a nuclear family and then more broadly too as photos of the meal were shared around my wider family (and on Facebook and Twitter).

Looking at this relational side to our use of consumer goods (Miller goes so far as to say, 'the closer our relationships with objects, the closer our relationships with people'[15]) brings in a more positive understanding of consumerism than we have been considering so far. I want to spend the rest of the chapter looking more specifically at some of the challenges that consumerism poses to us, but before we do that, this positive side is important to highlight. On a purely material basis, as author James Twitchell asks, who among us *really* would want to go back to 1900?[16] I am constantly thankful for the high level of material comfort that I enjoy. But, more broadly than this, consumerism can provide intellectual stimulation and enjoyable entertainment; it fosters innovation and can provide meaningful work; it leads to a more interesting and aesthetically pleasing society; it can support social relationships, and it helps people express their identity.[17] There is a sense in which all of this should be not just acknowledged, but celebrated, without a knee-jerk anti-consumerist reaction.

Before we turn our attention to the negative side of consumerism, there is one other aspect that we must make note of because we will meet it again in our next chapter, and that is the rise of the concept of 'consumer' itself as an identifiable subject in its own right. We must not forget that this is a novel social development: through history people have been categorised as peasants, citizens, subjects, republicans and so on, but never before has there been a category of person known as 'consumer'. The sociologist Celia Lury suggests that it is this – the emergence of the consumer as a category – that distinguishes consumer culture from all other cultures and that differentiates us from all that has gone before.[18] All societies shape their inhabitants, and being a consumer entails being located within a society that shapes us in particular ways that relate to the values of consumerism. Roberta Sassatelli (and she is not alone) makes the significant point that 'the particular cultural politics of value which underpins the development of "consumer society" is thus not a natural one: it is one which requires a process of learning whereby social actors are practically trained to perform (and enjoy) their role as consumers'.[19] This is the culture that we inhabit and the question for us to wrestle with is this: how does one function well as – and indeed how far should one even be – a consumer when one's primary identity is as a follower of Jesus Christ?

Liquid modernity: into the shadows

As we have said, we must be wary of viewing consumerism through a wholly negative lens. It has brought many of us many benefits, and the consumer relationships that exist in society are multi-layered and complex. Nonetheless, there is no doubt that consumer culture should also not be seen as entirely benign, and part of learning how to negotiate it well is recognising its darker aspects. One of the most piercing and prolific critics of consumer society has been Polish sociologist Zygmunt Bauman, and we will look now at his idea of 'liquid modernity' as a way of uncovering consumerism's shadow side.

Part of Bauman's genius – and what has made his writings on consumerism so notable – has been his ability to use metaphors to capture his cultural analyses, and one of his most arresting is that of 'liquid modernity'. He sees the earlier stage of modernity as 'solid', as a time when overarching ideologies fixed people in place and power was securely tethered to national politics; a time of stability and permanence.[20] In contrast, the period in which we now live has turned those solidities into liquid:

> The solids whose turn has come to be thrown into the melting pot and which are in the process of being melted at the present time, and the time of fluid modernity, are the bonds which interlock individual choices in collective projects and actions – the patterns of communication and coordination between individually conducted life policies on the one hand and political actions of human collectivities on the other.[21]

There are obvious links here with our earlier discussions around globalisation and the impact that this has had on the economic and political faces as both faces have lost their rootedness: the economic melting away into the virtual realm, the political into a multitude of disparate and contested areas. (In fact it was Bauman's increasing desire to focus his attention on a moral critique of globalisation that led him to develop the concept of liquid modernity.[22])

'Liquid modernity' is thus Bauman's term for what he frequently also calls 'negative globalisation' and he sees this as having had a number of intense impacts on social life. One of the most pervasive of these impacts is the development of a society based around fear, reflecting Beck's concept of the Risk Society that we saw in the previous chapter. Fear is the result of living in a society that has lost its moorings; where the pace of change is 'mind-boggling', unpredictable and uncontrollable.[23] Fear becomes a controlling aspect of society and we spend our lives trying to secure ourselves against those fears, through retreating into our private spheres and erecting physical and emotional barriers.[24]

Insecurity then becomes the hallmark of 'liquid modernity' as uncertainties are experienced in all aspects of personal life: from our job security and personal finances to our identities; from our faith in politics and political leaders to the shape and strength of our personal relationships; from our perceptions of fear and crime in our communities to our – and our children's – future prospects.[25] The most worrying aspect of this for the individual is that 'the burden of pattern-weaving and the responsibility for failure [falls] primarily on the individual's shoulders'.[26]

Bauman calls this 'individualization' (a term that resonates with Beck and Giddens' use of the term[27]). This term moves beyond the commonly understood meaning of individualism to the very specific idea that the onus is put onto us, the individual, both to create our own identities and to sustain our 'saleability' in the marketplace. To do this well places intense pressure on us – and it is interesting to note that this process actually has the result of turning us, the consumer, into a commodity ourselves.[28] This involves both considerable skill and also an ability to negotiate and use the various 'authorities' on hand to offer advice (think about all the different online adverts offering advice: how to attract more followers on Twitter; how to burn off that tummy fat; how to succeed at your next interview, etc.).[29] But – reflecting the point made earlier about whether or not as consumers we really are the ones in control – it also comes with the awareness that, while shouldering all the responsibility, we often are not actually really free in the choices that we have set before us: 'all too often, however, one needs to exercise that responsibility under conditions that entirely elude one's own, intellectual as well as practical, grasp'.[30]

One of Bauman's most piercing critiques is around the worryingly detrimental effects on relationships that he perceives this to have, because the need to promote ourselves in the marketplace of life leads to a culture of competition rather than co-operation, and this can be on a personal level as well as at work. Bauman has an intensely negative view of the 'liquid modern' consumer as someone who 'only cares for themselves and does so by demeaning others'.[31] Relationships become those that are only kept 'until further notice'.[32] Society becomes a place where human bonds grow increasingly frail as long-term relational commitments decrease and 'where few if any people continue to believe that changing the life of others is of any relevance to their own life'.[33]

Relationships are damaged in liquid modernity because of issues concerning time. As the bonds that hold people in place dissolve, so also they face a life that is too busy and pressured to be able to cultivate friendships. As Bauman says, 'consumption takes time': 'the sellers of consumer goods . . . are interested in cutting down as far as possible, or eliminating altogether, those necessary activities that occupy much time but bring few marketing profits'.[34]

Technology, too, plays its role and acts as a signifier of what is taking place culturally. Although technology in its own right is not something that Bauman seems particularly concerned with, he does highlight the mobile phone – and in particular its texting function – as the embodiment of 'liquid modernity', with its ability to collect large numbers of social contacts without commitment; its ability then effortlessly to delete those contacts; and its pressure on owners to prevent themselves from being deleted by answering promptly.[35] This fear of being deleted reflects Bauman's understanding of the casualties of 'liquid modernity' as those who are *excluded* from the consumerism that is at its heart; an understanding that, in his later writings, he increasingly expresses as *human waste*.[36]

It is interesting to see that Bauman's understanding of *waste* extends beyond the human to the environmental implications of contemporary society. Reflecting what we have already seen about detachment, he maintains that we have developed a culture of waste that thrives on the need to buy ever-increasing amounts of goods to satisfy the 'ever rising volume and intensity of desires'. The consumerist economy, therefore, 'thrives on the turnover of commodities, and is seen as booming when more money changes hands; and whenever money changes hands, some consumer products are travelling to the dump'.[37] Our lack of attachment to things leads to a high-waste society.

A key feature for us, which Bauman explores, is the failure of consumer society to satisfy. He questions the correlation between economic growth and increasing happiness, stating that we were wrong to choose such economic growth as the road to satisfaction.[38] Of course, Bauman recognises that the 'point' of consumerism is not ultimately to bring happiness, but to stimulate the desire and search for happiness. After all, if happiness were reached, then the consumer would stop consuming; something that must never be allowed to happen![39]

I think Bauman's analysis of consumerism is helpful, and it highlights three particular areas that are important for us and the themes of this book. Before I specify those, however, it is worth noting that, although the narrative he has created around consumerism and 'liquid modernity' is eloquent and powerful and teaches us much about the negativities of contemporary society, I want to sound a note of caution as well.

Picking up earlier discussions, my one problem with Bauman is his unrelentingly critical assessment of 'liquid modernity'. By way of contrast, the feminist sociologist, Carol Smart, asserts that 'connectedness' is every bit as much a feature as 'individualization'. Her research leads her to move away from words such as fragmentation, differentiation, separation and autonomy, towards words such as connection, relationship, reciprocal emotion, entwinement, history and memory.[40] Certainly it was poignant that, as I was reading Bauman's analysis of the loss of social bonds, the residents of the most socially deprived road on the estate on which I live were collecting Tesco vouchers to give to a family whose husband was in hospital over Christmas.

Thinking back to our third 'face' of globalisation, technology, Bauman's brief analysis of the mobile phone is a helpful example of how his negativity blinds him to any appreciation of the positive role that such devices might play. As we saw above, he views mobile phones (or, more appropriately today, smartphones) as illustrative only of 'thin' acquaintance. However, in a world of mobility such as he describes, they can also function positively as part of the maintenance of 'thick' friendship. Technology thus can be used for good or for ill, as is well demonstrated by the contrast between the Egyptian protests for democracy and the riots in the UK in 2011, both of which used phones to organise and mobilise.

Smartphones are thus one example of how people use a variety of tools to make their lives work within 'liquid modern' society, and for the majority of us reading this, the way forward will not be to reject such technology outright, but to look at how to use these devices well, as tools to help us make our lives work as Christians – within the framework of recognising that we carry within ourselves the identity of consumer. The key is that we use these things well, rather than letting them use us. Having our priorities – what, as we shall see later on, Marva Dawn calls our 'focal concerns' – firmly in place enables us to do that.

These are things that we will return to throughout this book, but smartphones provide a good, initial example of how we do that. Thinking back to our biblical framework of relationships, our focal concerns will be around living in ways that enhance the development of each of those relationships: with God, each other, the wider creation, and ourselves. That will then give us cause to think through our approach to smartphones, a consumer product that might feel so ubiquitous nowadays as hardly to deserve a second thought. We will all want to be aware of the complex social and environmental problems that are embedded in our smartphone technology. Because of that, for example, some of us may decide not to own one at all, but to use simpler technology (ever heard of a mobile phone?) which therefore has a lesser environmental impact. Others of us may decide never to buy a new phone but always to seek out one that is second-hand and sitting superfluous in someone's drawer. Others of us might decide to get a FairPhone, which uses conflict-free minerals. The least we can all do is not go along with the upgrading culture that encourages us to discard our current phone and move 'up' to the latest version. And whatever phone we have, we can all make choices about how much we use it and what we use it for.

As we begin to move towards the end of this chapter, I hope it has become clear that consumerism is not a topic we can approach naïvely or simplistically and we must always remember that we are all enjoying the benefits that it has brought. Nonetheless, at the same time many of us are also deeply concerned with the negative impacts it is having.

I well remember one of my children coming back from her first party, walking through the door and promptly throwing up all over the hallway! She had eaten too much chocolate: something she hadn't been brought up to eat in such large quantities. That taught her that it is possible to have too much of a good thing, and she learned not to eat so much when she went to parties again. And so it is with consumerism. We simply have not known when to stop. We have gorged ourselves on it, regardless of the consequences, and instead of controlling it wisely, it now controls us.

There are three particular facets of consumerism that make it intensely troubling and that are pertinent to what we are thinking about in this book. The first – as we have seen already in Bauman's critique of consumerism, and previously with Beck's description of marriage in the Risk Society – is the impact that living in this society has on our relationships. I am not going to go into all the statistics around marriage, but we know the general trend: the incidence of marital breakdown is increasing, and, while more people are choosing to cohabit, those relationships also are breaking down. The most recent data at the time of writing states the expectation that 42 per cent of marriages will end in divorce.[41]

The factors involved in this are complex, of course, but the fact is that no matter how many advertisements we may see of happy families laughing and playing together, we do not live in a culture that facilitates long-term relationships. Consumerism produces a high-pressured society where both partners have to work in order to meet the costs of living, and it can be hard to find either the time or the energy to invest anything more than the bare minimum into the relationship. For all that we sing the praises of those who display acts of sacrifice and heroism, we also constantly imbibe messages that tell us to put ourselves first and prioritise our own needs. While this can be a crass comparison, I do not think it is going too far to say that the same values that lead us to upgrade to a newer version of technology seep through into how we view our personal relationships, so that if our partner does not meet our needs it is acceptable to put them back on the shelf and replace them with a better model. Add to this the enormous amount of emotional expectation that we place on marriage, and the simple fact that, because of our high levels of health and life expectancy, marriages now potentially can last longer than at any other point in history, it is not hard to understand why we struggle to keep them together.

And of course it is not just marriage relationships that are feeling the strain. Families and wider friendships are suffering as well, often for similar reasons, with the result that loneliness and mental health problems have become endemic features of our society.

The second troubling facet of consumerism is its environmental unsustainability. For me, this is where the rubber hits the road (or should I say, the rays hit the PV panels). We can have all manner of differing views over the positive and negative benefits of living in a consumer society; its psychological impact; whether the producer or the consumer is in control; what role the consumer products themselves play . . . and so on. The one thing that is unarguable, however, is that our current rates of consuming are unsustainable environmentally.

Did you know that August is the most important month in the year? Why? Because this is the month when, as a human species, we reach 'Earth Overshoot Day'. Calculated by the Global Footprint Network, this is the day when we reach the sustainable limit of the amount of natural resources we can use in a year, and of our capacity to absorb our waste (including carbon dioxide). In 2014 it was 19 August, but each year that date is creeping forward. In fact, back in 1961, humanity used about three-quarters of the earth's capacity, but this has been increasing so that now we have used everything up within less than eight months. That means that for the rest of the year we are running on an ecological deficit and building up a mounting ecological debt in the form of deforestation, fresh water scarcity, soil erosion, biodiversity loss and increasing climate change.[42]

Drawing similar conclusions of a worrying overreach of our ecological capacity is the Stockholm Institute's widely used work on planetary boundaries.[43] They have identified nine limits within which we must live and function if we are not to cause irreparable damage, both to ourselves and to wider ecosystems: climate change, biodiversity loss, ocean acidification, land use, fresh water use, chemical pollution, ozone depletion, atmospheric aerosol concentration, and nitrogen and phosphorous cycles. Their research indicates that we have crossed the threshold of at least four of those boundaries.

Population growth is, of course, a key factor in humanity's large global ecological footprint, and it is no longer the elephant in the room that it once was, with increasing debate now focused on how a population that reached 7 billion in 2011 and is on track for reaching 9 billion by 2050 will feed, clothe, shelter and water itself. But questions of population must go hand in hand with issues of consumerism and the knowledge that those of us living in the more economically developed nations simply consume more than our fair share of resources. Take food, for example. People in the USA consume on average around 3,265 kilocalories of food a day, whereas in the Democratic Republic of Congo that figure drops to 2,103.[44] But it is not just food, of course: everything we buy or consume comes from somewhere and has taken resources to produce it. And the fact is that we are seriously overusing those resources.

Is it possible to maintain today's consumer society without using too many natural resources? Personally, I do not think it is, and the challenge set before us all is will we change and, if so, how?

The final troubling facet of consumerism is the illusionary nature of the happiness that it promises. Consumerism encourages us to equate happiness with financial and material success and we forget that this is not what happiness is rooted in. According to the IMF, in 2015, Costa Rica was the seventy-seventh richest country in the world and yet, according to the

NEF (New Economics Foundation), it has the happiest citizens in the world. The NEF rates countries according to their Happy Planet Index, a measurement that uses global data on experienced well-being, life expectancy and ecological footprint to rate how well countries do in delivering 'long, happy and sustainable lives' for their people.[45]

In the previous chapter we noted criticisms of the growth model of development and it is no surprise that as we consider consumerism we find ourselves inevitably part of a discussion around the relationship between economic growth, ecological sustainability and life happiness. A really interesting piece of work has been done by Druckman, Hirsh, Perren and Beckhelling, looking at the concept of a green Minimum Income Standard (MIS).[46] Coming out of the Joseph Rowntree Foundation, the MIS is the financial figure reckoned to be the minimum income needed by individuals and families in order to have an acceptable standard of living in the UK.[47] It is based on society's expectations of what makes for a socially acceptable quality of life and is a fascinating concept to look into. At the time of writing (2015), a lone parent with one child is thought to need to earn a minimum of £27,100; a couple with two children need to earn more than £20,200 each, and single working-age people are thought to need to earn a minimum of £16,200.[48]

The research of Druckman et al. looks at the ecological footprint of a person who lives life at the level of the MIS and then considers what lifestyle changes are needed in order to reduce that footprint. The conclusion they reach is that when an individual reduces their ecological footprint, this leads to a reduction in the MIS. Hence economic growth becomes less of a necessity.

It is interesting to note more work from the NEF that produces evidence to suggest that individuals with the smallest ecological footprints (in a developed Western country) had similar levels of well-being to those with the largest. High levels of well-being did not correlate with high ecological footprints.[49] In other words, living a highly consumerist life will not lead to happiness.

We all know this in our heads, of course, and yet isn't it so hard actually to translate that into living differently? So many of us – myself included – suffer from what I call 'consumer creep'. We know, once a basic minimum of our needs is met, that our sense of happiness and well-being does not come from having increasing amounts of things, but from other areas of our lives: good friendships, a healthy spiritual life, meaningful work, contact with the natural world, and so on. And yet somehow we just buy this . . . and then we buy that . . . and before we know it our lives look no different from anyone else's; we have a house filled with things we do not really need, and we realise that consumerism has crept up on us nonetheless. I hope the final chapter in this first part of the book will begin to point the way forward to resisting that 'consumer creep'.

Chapter 3

Of Monks and Men
The church context

Barn dances, international evenings, meeting people from all round the world, walking through the woods gathering chestnuts, carpets of daffodils and bluebells, visiting my dad in his study with its Afghan rug on the floor . . . these are some of the strongest memories from my childhood at All Nations Christian College, a Bible college in the south-east of England.

All Nations was – and is – primarily a missionary training college. Over its fifty-plus years of existence it has sent thousands of people out around the world to do mission work in a variety of different forms. My parents were both lecturers there for thirty years and we lived half a mile from the bottom of its long drive, in the local village. It is fair to say that our whole lives revolved around All Nations and the people who came from all over the world to study there.

One of the most notable features of All Nations is its stunning old country house (Easneye Mansion), set in the midst of beautiful countryside. The house was built by and belonged to the Buxton family, themselves a godly family with overseas mission in their blood. The main hall is beautiful, with a huge fireplace, a large sweeping staircase leading up to the main bedrooms, and some lovely stained-glass windows.

In one of these windows, in pride of place on the Buxton coat of arms, between two stags, is something you might not expect to see quite so prominently celebrated by a Victorian Christian family: a barrel of beer! The Buxtons were a family who knew that Christianity was not a private religion but a vibrant faith that pushed a person out to get involved in bringing good to all sectors of society, both at home and abroad. Easneye was built by Thomas Fowell Buxton Jnr in 1868, and his father (Thomas Fowell Buxton Snr) was a leading Abolitionist and member of the Clapham Sect. It was actually Buxton Snr, in the end, who got the Emancipation of Slaves Bill through Parliament in 1832 when William Wilberforce retired due to ill health. In fact, in the stone coat of arms that sits over the fireplace, one of the stags has a medallion around its neck with a picture of a little African boy on it, representing the Buxton family's work to bring freedom to those caught in the slave trade.

But back to the barrel of beer. In those days, gin was what was mostly drunk by the working classes and it was causing massive health and social problems. It was also made with sugar from the slave-worked sugar plantations. Beer, on the other hand, was thought to be a healthier drink, being a much watered-down version of what we might drink today. It was also made with hops, which therefore supported a local British industry. The Buxtons were thus strong advocates of beer drinking and indeed ran a brewery business (and, it is only fair to note, made their fortune from it). In doing so they joined in with the Abolitionist creation of one of the earliest examples of consumers using their purchasing power to push for ethical trade, as thousands of people around the UK boycotted sugar that came from the slave plantations.

So next time you drink a bottle of beer, raise a toast to the transforming influence of the Christian faith, to consumer power, to fair trade, and to the amazing work of the Abolitionists!

In this first part of the book we are looking at some of the overriding features of our contemporary culture within which we live as followers of Jesus, exploring its complexities and nuances so that we might be able to think through more deeply how we can follow Jesus well within those contexts. For those of us reading this who would call ourselves Christians, it is important also to be aware that there is a church context within which we live too. As Buxton's barrel of beer shows, there have always been Christians concerned to think about the connections between their faith, their lifestyles and the issues of our world, but the last two chapters have shown us that we face social and environmental problems on a global scale that we have not encountered before. There is a high degree of awareness in the Church of these global, social and environmental issues and a growing awareness of the detrimental impact of living in a consumer-focused society. For those who are thinking through these issues, it is clear that both concerns are rooted in a strong understanding of faith and of what it means to be a Christian.

We stand at a particular juncture in church history: a juncture at which a number of theological discourses are converging that help us think through how we respond wisely and positively to the many challenges we face today. It is to five of these different strands that we turn in this chapter.

1. The place of simplicity in a concern for issues of global poverty and ecological breakdown

Let me be honest with you: when I think about the different issues that we have touched on so far – things such as poverty and starvation; species dying out and coral reefs being destroyed; increasing numbers of refugees and family breakdown; defor-estation and climate change – I often feel utterly helpless. Then I begin to think about the different things I could do to help and I end up feeling overwhelmed by the options.

When I first started thinking about these things, some twenty or so years ago, the most immediately obvious way to help was by using our money to help people and groups who were work-ing in these areas, and so Greg and I began doing that. It then became clear that this was supporting the proverbial people down the stream who were fishing drowning people out of the fast-flowing river (a crucially important job in itself, mind you), rather than doing something to stop them falling in in the first place, and so we began getting into campaigning. I joined the board of the World Development Movement, set aside regular evenings to write letters to companies and politicians (yes, I did live before email!), and did all I could to push for systemic change. We then felt too complicit in the system we were trying to change, and so considered moving to Addis Ababa to work in the slums there with a fantastic project we were supporting (the Integrated Holistic Approach to Urban Development Project – a snappy title if ever there was one). They told us in no uncertain terms that we could help them much more by staying in the UK and raising awareness and money than by coming to live with them.

These, and other options, are all things that fizzed around my head and continue to do so. Should I be giving more money than I currently do? Where should I be focusing my campaigning efforts? Should I be up a tree somewhere or chained to a newly proposed power station? Should I forget the big issues and just go live in a slum and concentrate on helping those around me? Should I stand as a local councillor (I have been asked to do so quite a few times) and work out these concerns in my local area, or retrain and get into international development politics or economics? So many different paths, and I often have to stop and remind myself to trust that where I am and what I am doing is what God has intended for me, and that I should rest secure in that rather than worrying about all the things that I could be doing but am not.

In the midst of all these options, though, one thing has become obvious to me: however we choose to respond to the problems around us, that response must make a difference in how we actually live our lives. I very soon realised that I couldn't give my money and push politicians and businesses to change their behaviours without changing my own as well. I am constantly called back to the prophet Micah's words in the Old Testament that what is required of us is that we act justly, love mercy and walk humbly with our God. A concern for both people and planet has to be outworked in one's own life, and trying to live more simply is a fundamental part of that.

There are three people, in particular, whose books have been most instrumental in encouraging the development of this understanding over recent decades.

Perhaps most influential of all has been Ron Sider and his classic *Rich Christians in an Age of Hunger*, first written in 1977, which has since gone through five editions and sold hundreds of thousands of copies. Its purpose is very straightforward: to open Christians' eyes to the realities of what is happening in our world; to demonstrate that responding to issues of poverty (and also to environmental degradation, although his main emphasis is on human poverty) is thoroughly biblical, and to call the Church to respond, giving various practical ideas along the way.

Sider makes a strong link between the massive injustices he reports and the need to respond by living more simply. So he asks questions like, 'Dare we care at all about current fashions if that means reducing our ability to help hungry neighbours? Dare we care more about obtaining a secure economic future for our family than for living an uncompromisingly Christian lifestyle?' His overall thesis is stated plainly when he says, 'We simply cannot continue these present economic patterns, *and* reduce global poverty, *and* preserve a liveable planet all at the same time. We could choose both justice for the poor and a liveable planet – but only if we give up rampant materialism and make hard choices to reverse environmental destruction.'[1]

Rich Christians in an Age of Hunger is, of course, an old book now, and many younger Christians have never even heard of it. Yet, for many others, reading *Rich Christians* signalled a defining moment in their lives. Amazingly, in my Bible-reading notes just this morning, the chap who writes them talked about *Rich Christians* and what an impact it had on his life when he first read it. Its uncompromising, hard-hitting style was, for many, a wake-up call to what was (and is) going on in the world and to the need for us to change the way we live as a result.

The second person, Richard Foster, is one of Christianity's most widely read modern authors, with *Celebration of Discipline* and *Money, Sex and Power*. Another well-appreciated book of his, though, is *Freedom of Simplicity*, which is one of the very few books on simple living written by an evangelical Christian. Foster approaches simplicity from a broader perspective than does *Rich Christians* and his aim is to show that living a simple life is not just something that Christians do out of concern for current issues, but is 'a call given to every Christian': a call rooted in the Bible and lived out by 'all the devotional masters'.[2] Nonetheless, Foster emphasises the relevance that simplicity offers to contemporary society and the many struggles that it faces (and for him, coming from an evangelical perspective, this includes world evangelisation), not least of which are global concerns. In his final chapter ('Corporate Simplicity: The World') he sends out the clear message that '*our undisciplined consumption must end*. If we continue to gobble up our resources without any regard to stewardship and to spew out deadly wastes over land, sea, and air, we may well be drawing down the final curtain upon ourselves.'[3]

Through all of this, simplicity is the key for Foster. He states unequivocally that 'it is the Discipline of simplicity that gives us the basis for developing a strategy of action that can address this and many other social inequalities. Individual, ecclesiastical, and corporate action can spring from the fertile soil of simplicity.'[4]

Sider's and Foster's books are inspirational, but, written originally in 1977 and 1981, it is fair to say that they are coming from an earlier and older generation (the generation that was also involved in convening the Lausanne International Consultation on Simple Lifestyle in England in 1980, which produced a Commitment that is well worth reading[5]). I remember, when I first started getting excited about the importance of simple living, my parents saying to me in some surprise, 'But we used to talk about this stuff years ago. Why are you feeling like this is something new? What happened?' What happened, I told them, was Thatcher and Reagan, who brought in a new era of individualism, which impacted the Church as much as it did the rest of society.

After Sider and Foster, then, things went quiet from the mid-1980s to mid-2000s and there was very little mention within the Church of the need to respond to global problems by changing the way we live – although there have been some lone voices, such as that of American evangelical Tony Campolo. So it has been heartening in recent years to see a new focus on lifestyle springing up and beginning to take root in the hearts of younger generations, with new voices coming through.

One of the clearest voices has come from Shane Claiborne and his book *The Irresistible Revolution*, which has become a contemporary classic amongst certain groups of Christians. Part of the New Monasticism movement (which we will look at more below), Claiborne is a Christian radical who uses examples from his own life (such as his peace visits to Iraq during the war, his time with Mother Teresa, and his efforts in galvanising a student movement that saved a group of homeless families from eviction), as well as from the lives of others, to pierce what he perceives to be the comfortable bubble of (US) evangelical Christianity and turn it upside down:

We can admire and worship Jesus without doing what he did.
We can applaud what he preached and stood for without caring

about the same things. We can adore the cross without taking up ours. I had come to see that the great tragedy in the church is not that rich Christians do not care about the poor but that rich Christians do not know the poor.[6]

A founding member of the faith community The Simple Way, Claiborne's life and words are an extended outworking of the call to simplicity that we have seen with the previous two authors. As he says, 'Simplicity is meaningful only inasmuch as it is grounded in love, authentic relationships, and interdependence. Redistribution then springs naturally out of our rebirth, from a vision of family that is larger than biology or nationalism. As we consider what it means to be "born again" . . . we must ask what it means to be born again into a family in which our sisters and brothers are starving to death.'[7]

Sider, Foster and Claiborne have been leading voices in calling us as Christians to respond to the problems of globalisation and consumerism with our own lifestyles; leading a more simple life that will consume less of the world's resources and free up our own financial resources to help others who are poorer than ourselves.

Of course, the links between our consumption and the poverty of other people are far from straightforward. I cannot say, for example, that by not buying a litre-bottle of water I will release a litre of clean water to someone living in the Sahel in Africa. I know that if I choose to eat less meat I won't thereby guarantee that an equivalent amount of food calories will reach a person who is hungry elsewhere, nor will using less electricity in my house automatically send more energy to someone else who needs it. There are systemic, structural issues that

need addressing alongside lifestyle changes (hence the importance of the discussion at the end of chapter 1 around the
tension between macro- and micro-political involvement:
between traditional political engagement and the sub-politics
of our smaller, everyday actions).

Nonetheless, when you consider the fact that Americans spent
$11.8 billion on bottled water in 2012 while it is estimated that it
would take only around $7 billion a year to provide the entire
world with clean water and basic sanitation,[8] it is clear that
although lifestyle change alone is not sufficient, that does not
mean we do nothing and just carry on living in a highly consumptive manner. We are part of a global system in which a rich
minority (i.e. us) consume far more than their fair share of
resources; a world in which the fossil fuel consumption of one
American is equivalent to that of around 4 Chinese, 20 Indians,
or 250 Ethiopians.[9] If everyone in the world lived as we do in the
UK, we would need around three planets to support us all, and
it hardly need be said that we do not have three planets. We only
have one and we must learn how to live within the constraints of
the resources provided by that one planet.

I often feel that the steps I have taken are small and insignificant. What difference does it really make to another, poorer
person if there is one woman in Chichester trying to live a little
more fairly? At the same time, I sometimes try to imagine how
the world might look if everybody made those same small and
insignificant steps, and I realise that it would look very different indeed. Far fewer things would be made, hence less of the
world's resources would be consumed. I do not make this statement easily or naïvely, but the whole economic order of our
world would change. People in the more developed countries

would work less hours and earn less, but that would be fine because they would consume less. Time would thus be freed up for voluntary and leisure activities. Fewer essential agricultural commodities would be grown for export: most would be grown for domestic consumption, and more people would earn their keep by growing food and working on the land. Green energy would be massively invested into and would provide employment opportunities all over the world. Landfill sites would shrink and there would be a thriving economy around innovative upcycling. More time and energy would be invested into local communities and travel abroad would become a luxury only undertaken every few years. The balance of power between nation states would change as oil would not be as crucial a commodity as it currently is.

Taking steps to live more simply, then, is a necessary response to the very simple reality that we are consuming too much and need to consume less. It is a spiritual discipline that reflects our worship of the God who denounces those whose rich lifestyles come at the expense of other people.

It needs to be said, however, that although the call to live more simply is being well made, the Church in the rich world (and remember that can include the more wealthy sections of poorer countries) is a long way from heeding that call in a major way.

I see this when I think of the legacy left by one of the most influential UK Christians of the last century – John Stott, who died in 2011. In his final book, *The Radical Disciple*, Stott looked at eight characteristics of Christian discipleship which he thought should be embraced by everyone who is serious about following Jesus.[10] One of those was Simplicity. However, although he was well known for his simple lifestyle, it is other aspects of his teaching that have been celebrated since his death. So I have heard much about his approach to the Bible and his classic formula of 'double listening', whereby we are called to listen both to the Word of God and to the world, in order to relate them together as faithful disciples – but his belief that 'Christian obedience demands a simple lifestyle' because 'the fact that 800 million people are destitute and that about 10,000 die of starvation every day makes any other lifestyle indefensible' has gone largely ignored.[11]

Why is this? The obvious answer is that it is incredibly difficult to live counterculturally. It can be done – and this book will hopefully take us some way towards helping us see how we might do that – but it is difficult. As we saw in our last chapter, we live in a society that moulds and shapes us to think and act in particular ways, and to go against those ways takes an awful lot of courage and persistence.

It was interesting in this regard to listen to the people I interviewed for my doctoral research, all of whom were trying to one degree or another to live more simply. There was a ready willingness to admit to the challenges of what they were trying to do, and the interviews demonstrated a high degree of wrestling with how, practically, to live out the principles of simple living within a consumer society. Very noticeable within this was an acute sense of failure. Nearly every person interviewed added a caveat, at some point, showing their awareness that they were not reaching their goals. Phrases such as 'I don't think I'm anywhere near succeeding', 'I try in a number of things, but I fail in more aspects than I succeed in', and 'I'm sounding like this is something that I'm completely sorted at and it's totally not at all', were just some of the comments. They felt they ought to be doing more but that life mitigated against them: 'I think probably time is a big factor . . . there's lots of things I could do that would be more sustainable, but they require time.'

Thus the challenge of living in a society systemically structured to channel people into a life of high materialism was acutely felt. This is not a theoretical issue, but something that plays out very practically in the everyday detail of life. In the interviews, people talked about difficulties with travel, both locally (not being able to live near work; living in a town where it is easier to drive than take public transport) and more widely (challenges over whether or not to fly, with family and/or friends living in other countries). Housing was also discussed, with the only feasible option being to live in a three-bedroomed house, which then mitigated against community and sharing; as was clothes, with struggles over ethical sourcing. Family pressures were mentioned, with one woman in particular wrestling with how to live out her values when her family saw things differently. Food was discussed, with someone commenting, 'It's just difficult because our whole system's . . . based on supermarkets and long transport lines and big farms.' One of the consequences of this, as I noted in the Introduction in relation to myself, is that people can feel isolated and at odds with those around them: 'It is against the grain of the culture of the way everyone else is living, so sometimes you feel that doing the things that you do is a little bit odd.'

Despite these challenges, however, if there was one thing that shone through all the interviews, it was that the attempt to live a more simple life – while seen by participants as a necessary response to society's national and global problems – was not viewed as a duty, but rather as a delight. Some of the main words that people used in the interviews were 'joyful', 'thoughtful', 'freedom/freeing', 'liberty', 'open', 'space/ spaciousness', 'light/ness', 'gratitude', 'authentic/ity', 'creativity', 'footloose', 'enjoyment', 'connected', 'blessed', 'abundant', 'rich', 'deep', 'transformative' and 'contentment'.

People talked about 'discovering the joy of giving'; of how 'simplicity has a beauty about it, that allows the unnoticed to be noticed, and the unexpected to be pleasurable'; of how simplicity 'is life giving', and that 'it's something that can release beauty and be releasing of joy and laughter'.

There was a keen sense that reducing the amount of 'stuff' one has brings a freedom not experienced by those enmeshed in consumer culture. One person said, 'I feel like I've been freed of having to be part of that buying frenzy', and another said, 'I think it's very freeing to choose what's important to you and then to be able to pursue those things.' Freedom from the need to consume was important to the interviewees, who often emphasised that a reduced focus on consumer goods led to less worry and more gratitude: 'I think the more you reflect on God's generosity and the more you move into a place of depending on him, and not on what you have already, the less anxiety there is in your life, because I think the more you have the more worries you have.'

It is wonderful to see that there are fresh moves within the Church to embrace lifestyle choices that help tackle injustice, materialism and a broken environment. A Rocha UK runs its own lifestyle programme called 'Living Lightly', which is full of ideas to motivate and help people make practical changes in all areas of their lives, and it is encouraging to see people engaging with it in a number of different ways, such as in churches, with our monthly EcoTip and in social media discussions.[12] Tearfund, too, launched their 'Ordinary Heroes' campaign in 2015, with a focus on inspiring a movement of people who will 'think differently, live more simply and speak up about creating a just and sustainable world'. In an unpublished pre-campaign survey, they found that significant numbers of those who responded had already adopted lifestyle-changing actions and were doing things such as buying fairtrade, choosing to consume less, trying to reduce their transport emissions and reducing their meat consumption.

So there is a growing understanding within the Church that as we look at the problems of our world, yes, we must give; yes, we must campaign; yes, there are all manner of things we can do to help; but foundationally we must challenge these things in our own lives and be prepared to live differently.

2. The recovery of an environmental theology

'I look upon this world as a wrecked vessel. God has given me a lifeboat and said, "Moody, save all you can."' So said D.L. Moody, the influential nineteenth-century American evangelist, providing us with a perfect illustration of the dualism that we saw at the beginning of our biblical overview in the Introduction, that Genesis 1:31 blows away.

Moody's words would have been very well accepted by his hearers and represents a view that is still around today: this world is doomed for destruction and our focus as Christians should be on saving souls. If there is anything good about the world it is that it is there for our use – our dominion – as Genesis 1:26–30 makes clear.

It is this theological view, of 'man's transcendance of, and rightful master over, nature', that was famously interrogated by the medieval historian Lynn White Jnr in his 1967 article entitled 'The Historical Roots of Our Ecologic Crisis'.[13] In this article he claimed that 'Christianity bears a huge burden of guilt' for our current environmental catastrophe.

White's thesis has been pulled apart many times and it is not my intention to add to that. In fact, we owe White a debt of thanks because his criticism (and it should not be overlooked that he was a churchman himself and finished his article by recommending St Francis be made the patron saint of ecology), coming at a time when the environmental crisis was beginning to take root in people's consciousness, caused the Church to sit up and look afresh at what theological resources it could offer. And so the last fifty years or so have seen a growing wave of books offering an ecological theology and understanding of the Bible.

Of course this discovery of an environmental theology is not an entirely new thing, and a broad sweep of church history shows that, while not a dominant theme, the Church has not always neglected the ecological implications of the Bible's words. Clement of Rome, Basil the Great, John of Damascus, John Scotus, Hildegard of Bingen, St Francis, Meister Eckhart, Martin Luther and John Woolman are just some of the more well-known Christians who have written and spoken about God's wider creation, seeing it – in John of Damascus's beautiful words – as 'a living icon of the face of God'.[14] Nonetheless, it is also true that the wider creation has been almost entirely absent from the thought and writings of recent church history and so seeing such thinking and writing emerging in such quantity in recent years is notable.

The Anglican Church – as the central denomination in the UK – provides a good illustration of the change that has occurred within mainline Christian thinking. Acknowledging that it has been slow to bring environmental concerns onto the main agenda, former Archbishop of Canterbury Rowan Williams has admitted that 'the church was inheritor of a school of thought which did not see the environment as a good and appropriate environmental behaviour as a virtue'.[15] In 1986 the General Synod held its first debate on environmental issues (there had been a brief mention in 1970), but it was not until 1998 that the Lambeth Conference adopted four principles on the environment, which included the principle that 'the covenant of God's love embraces not only human beings but all of creation'.[16]

The major pieces of work on the environment conducted by the Church of England have been the book *Sharing God's Planet: A Christian Vision for a Sustainable Future* and its 'Shrinking the Footprint' campaign, which focuses on the energy consumption of church buildings.[17] More recently there has been a move within the Church of England pushing for disinvestment from fossil fuel companies,[18] and an 'Eco-Bishops Conference' bringing together bishops from around the Anglican Communion in South Africa to discuss a united response to climate change and other environmental issues.

Perhaps most significant is simply the fact that 'to strive to safeguard the integrity of creation and sustain and renew the

life of the earth' is explicitly stated as the Fifth Mark of Mission.
These marks comprise the Anglican Church's statement on
mission (first formulated in 1984), and they seek to demonstrate that mission goes beyond personal evangelism to embrace
a more holistic – or integral – understanding. The original list
was made up of four, and then the fifth statement was added in
1990. The Anglican Church cannot ignore the call to wider
creation care.

The most significant ecclesial development in the recovery
of an environmental theology has been the papal encyclical
from Pope Francis, released after much anticipation in June
2015. The encyclical, entitled *Laudato si'* ('Praise be to you'),
was a call to all people around the world and was the first encyclical in the history of Roman Catholicism to address environmental issues specifically. Following the example of his name-
sake, Pope Francis referred to the earth as 'a sister with whom
we share our life and a beautiful mother who opens her arms to
embrace us'. The earth, as its subtitle stated, is our common
home. This sister, Francis said, was crying out to us because of
all we have done to her. Drawing on rigorous scientific and
theological foundations, Pope Francis laid out the moral, social
and ecological imperatives for urgent action to tackle climate
change and other related environmental issues. The encyclical
attracted immense global attention and, for the first time,
put the Church centre stage in discussions about the
environment.

As I write this book and think about its themes, I am aware
that I am doing so within a church context (in the UK anyway)
that, verbally at least, takes environmental issues seriously.
Even when I wrote the first edition of *L is for Lifestyle: Christian*

Living that Doesn't Cost the Earth back in the early 1990s, the context was quite different. The book goes through the alphabet, taking a key global issue for each letter and giving a brief explanation and then some clear action points. E is for Energy, possibly the most important topic in our world today, alongside food. When my manuscript was given to the theological editors, the feedback was that they wanted me to change that chapter to E being for Evangelism, and they wanted me to explore and explain where environmental care fitted into the biblical call to evangelism. They were nervous about a book with such an explicitly ecological focus and needed convincing of the biblical mandate for that. Needless to say, I refused to change the chapter.

Perhaps most shockingly, when I wrote the Bible study guide *Rivers of Justice: Responding to God's Call to Righteousness Today* in 2005, I included a session on 'caring for the earth'. The publishing company asked me to take it out, on the grounds that environmental issues were not really a Christian concern (obviously I refused again). Then just three years later they approached me to write a whole Bible study guide for them on the environment. At that point I realised just how much the church landscape had shifted. In this regard it is striking that, in research on evangelical Christians in the UK (traditionally the wing of the Church most resistant to seeing environmental care as part of Christian life), 94 per cent of the more than 17,000 people surveyed agreed that 'it is a Christian's duty to care for the environment'.[19]

This change in the ecclesiological landscape is vital if we are to have any hope in averting the ongoing and oncoming global crises affecting both people and planet. Why? Because it is well recognised that there is massive potential in the Christian Church (and other faith groups) to create a movement for change that significantly impacts our world, tackling overconsumption, lifting people out of poverty and seeing a balanced relationship between ourselves and the wider natural world.

Christiana Figueres, executive secretary of the UN Framework Convention on Climate Change, addressed faith leaders at St Paul's Cathedral in 2014, saying, 'It is time for faith groups and religious institutions to find their voice and set their moral compass on one of the great humanitarian issues of our time. Overcoming poverty, caring for the sick and the infirm, feeding the hungry and a whole range of other faith-based concerns will only get harder in a climate challenged world.'

It is also vital because we know that, ultimately, the root of our environmental crisis lies not in a lack of scientific understanding, but in human sin: in greed and selfishness. As Carmelite Father Eduardo Agosta Scarel (a climate scientist who teaches at the Pontifical Catholic University of Argentina in Buenos Aires) says, what is needed is 'a change of heart. What will save us is not technology or science. What will save us is the ethical transformation of our society.'[20]

The Church has been a sleeping giant on these issues, but it is beginning to wake up and I look forward to seeing what it can do.

3. The rediscovery of the 'ancient paths' of monasticism

In September 2015 church history was made when the Archbishop of Canterbury, Justin Welby, opened the doors of

Lambeth Palace and welcomed sixteen young people to come and live at the Palace for a year, undertaking a programme of prayer, study, practical service and community life. Accompanying them are around forty people who live in London and have remained in their workplaces but are joining them on a part-time basis. Under the direction of Prior Andes Litzell, the group is living in a way that, as Archbishop Justin described it, 'the ancient monastics would recognise: drawing closer to God through a daily rhythm of silence, study and prayer'.[21] But, at the same time, through those disciplines, they are engaging in the modern challenges of the global twenty-first-century Church. The inspiration for the name of this new community has come from St Anselm, a Benedictine monk who was Archbishop of Canterbury from 1093 to 1114.

This radical step by Archbishop Justin reflects a massive surge in interest in the monastic tradition and in what it is perceived to be able to offer contemporary Christian spirituality. The Modern Monk, Punk Monk, The Contemplative Network, Chasing Columba, Chasing Francis, The Contemporary Monk, Contemplative Activists, The New Monk Project, The Society of St Columba, Columba's Barns and many more such titles of books, blogsites and projects all illustrate that interest. I notice personally that almost any conversation with a Christian friend that goes to any depth will lead at some point to a discussion around how they have been discovering the value of silence and stillness and scriptural meditation. While of course these things are not entirely the preserve of monks and nuns, it is to that tradition that my friends are turning in order to find the encouragement and resources to help take these practices further.

In the earlier years of my adult life, my evangelical church context taught me to be somewhat derisive of monasticism. After all, it was something for old people and reflected a retreatist spirituality, and the offices and pattern of prayer represented dead religion! When someone in the church tried to bring in something of monastic spirituality, they were humoured but gently sidelined. Little did I know then that by this present stage of my life, some twenty years or so later, I would have my own twice-daily rhythm of prayer, which includes a period of silent meditation each morning, and that it would be this regular rhythm that has kept me in one piece emotionally when the storms of life have threatened to tip me over the edge.

We will look at this practice in more detail in the section on Time in Part Three, but suffice it to say here that, while in some ways this has been a continuation of the 'quiet time' practice with which I was brought up, it has differed from it too. My understanding of the 'quiet time' had been of something quite active: I read the Bible (making notes when in a particularly diligent phase) and then prayed, often with a list of things to pray about. My times now are much less active: I have a prayer book that I use, but much of the time is spent simply sitting in God's presence, opening myself up to him.

Coming from a North American context, the resurgence of interest has found expression in the emergence of 'New Monasticism' (NM), for which Shane Claiborne is a prominent spokesperson. NM has what it calls 'twelve marks' which characterise how it has developed.[22] These marks are written about in a fascinating book called *School(s) for Conversion: 12 Marks of a New Monasticism*, edited by the urban American

Christian community Rutba House. Each chapter focuses on one of the marks and is written by someone trying to live out that particular mark. What is notable is that a number of the marks relate specifically to the issues that we have seen raised so far through this book. There is a strong focus on relationships and community, such as in mark no. 9, 'geographical proximity to community members who share a common rule of life', and no. 3, 'hospitality to the stranger', and earth care is specified too in no. 10, 'care for the plot of God's earth given to us'. The NM attitude towards money (something we will be focusing on later in the book) is clearly evinced: 'sharing economic resources with fellow community members and the needy among us' (no. 2), and 'support for our local economies' (no. 10). Finally, relationship with God threads through the marks as there is a commitment to 'intentional formation in the way of Christ' (no. 6) and 'a disciplined contemplative life' (no. 12).

At the beginning of *School(s) for Conversion* the authors make the statement that 'the church's response to compromise and crisis has always been one of new monastic movements'.[23] That might be a bit of a sweeping statement but it is an interesting one that, I think, begins to point the way to why this renewed interest in monasticism has developed.

This monastic turn is perhaps not surprising given what we have already explored in our previous two main chapters on the experience by individuals of the challenges and disorientations of globalisation and consumerism. One of my favourite books ever is called *Living in Hope: A Rule of Life for Today*, and is the revised rule of life by the Society of St John the Evangelist, the oldest Anglican religious order for men. It is a wonderful book that can only have come out of deep reflection and prayer and I cannot recommend it highly enough. Get hold of a copy and take time to think, pray and discuss its different sections.

In the Introduction, Martin Smith SSJE (the then superior of the North American Congregation of the Society) says that 'change is overwhelming society and the Church at an unprecedented rate, and it is easy to become paralyzed by the sense that everything has become provisional'.[24] The parallel between this sense of things being 'provisional' and Bauman's 'liquid modernity' is patent. The Introduction goes on to explain that the Society has decided to publish its rule because it addresses 'deep issues of vocation, prayer, community and ministry that are common to Christians everywhere who are seeking to express the life of union with God in forms that are authentic for the beginning of the third millennium'.[25]

Mary Grigsby, whom we met towards the end of chapter 1, in her theory of the voluntary simplicity movement in the USA, sees simple living as one way by which people can challenge the hegemony of consumerism and globalisation. The attraction of monasticism occurs in this context. With its emphasis on 'spirituality', its concern for the earth, its daily rhythm of prayer, its rootedness in community and its countercultural attitude towards money and possessions, it appears to offer a thick, rooted antidote to the fissiparity of modern life. When confronted with a terrain in which the life challenges faced by men and women have been, as Brian McLaren describes it in his book on monastic practices, 'surreptitiously yet radically transformed, invalidating the extant life wisdom and calling for a more thorough revision and overhaul of life strategies', it is no surprise that individuals look backwards in search of those older life wisdoms in order to provide a more secure anchor.[26] This sentiment is nicely expressed by McLaren, who says that the alternative path to what is offered by society 'needs to derive strength from the old religious traditions; it needs to face new-age challenges with age-old wisdom. The challenge of the future will require, we realise, rediscovery and adaptive reuse of resources from the ancient past.'[27]

We will be looking further in the following chapters at where monastic ideals can help us as we seek to navigate some of the tensions of trying to live Christianly in contemporary society. For now, though, it is sufficient to note that the revival of interest in monastic forms of living has provided important tools for many of us as we make that attempt, and is a key strand of the ecclesiological context in which we find ourselves today.

4. The tradition of Christian simplicity and radical dissent

Tortured . . . burned alive . . . accused of incest and cannibalism . . . I do not think that is how I would describe any of the people sitting in church with me on a Sunday morning! And yet this is an apt description of the circumstances and fate of many of the earliest Christians. Living – as many of us reading this book do – in a society in which Christianity is accepted and tolerated, albeit somewhat begrudgingly, and in which open hostility is not a regular feature of our everyday lives, we can find it hard to remember that the Christian faith started its days as a subversive, minority group who refused to acknowledge anyone as Lord except Jesus Christ, and suffered the consequences for so doing (and of course we must always remember that many Christians around the world still suffer those consequences through imprisonment, torture and death).

While monastic practices and thinking play an important role in the ecclesiological framework within which the desire to live more simply sits, there are other movements that play a key role too, and this desire stands within a long tradition of Christians living within culture yet in a manner that runs counter to the cultural norms, particularly regarding wealth and status. This tradition includes some forms of monasticism (so, for example, it is notable that NM does not involve living away from society, but is concerned with living right in the midst of it: a feature we will explore in the following chapters) but extends more broadly to encompass a whole range of movements that have occurred down through church history. In this short section I am not going to provide anything like a comprehensive overview of the many different forms that this countercultural living has taken, but I want to highlight two that I think are interesting for us as we think about simple living today.

The first is the Quakers: a remarkable group who refused to pay attention to the divisions of status and wealth. Quakerism today is associated with its silent meetings and pacifist views, but its roots in the seventeenth century are fascinating to uncover. Many people know that the movement started as a protest against the established Church during the English Civil War in the mid-seventeenth century, with a desire to practise a form of Christianity that allowed a direct encounter with the divine, rather than relying on the mediation of priests, but this does not tell the whole story. The movement also arose as a protest against the socio-economic conditions of the day and several of the first converts in the 1640s had been in conflict with landlords over excessive rents and services.

And so, as the Quaker scholar Reay says, 'from the start, the Quaker movement was a movement of political and social as well as religious protest'.[28] They became known, among other things, for their refusal to remove their hats in the presence of nobility; their insistence on addressing all people as 'thee' and 'thou' when convention stipulated that a different mode of address pertained to the elite; and their preference for plainness in clothes, possessions and speech. The important thing, as their leader George Fox said, was to 'let your lives preach'.

The Quaker movement was linked sociologically with the upheavals of the Civil War and when Charles II was restored to the throne in 1660 Quakerism went into a period of adjustment and institutionalisation.[29] Quakerism post-1660 is a complicated phenomenon and we do not need to worry about the details here. What is significant is that early Quakerism laid the foundations for a movement that has played a significant role in the pursuit of social justice and it has had a massive influence on society.

Elizabeth Fry, for example, is one of the most well-known Quakers. She did amazing work to bring about reform to the notorious English penal institutions of the 1800s. Barclays Bank, too, was established by the amalgamation of twenty Quaker private banking firms. Some of the family members became partners and were able to use their wealth and influence for the benefit of the Abolitionist movement. One such, David Barclay, became the owner of a Jamaican sugar plantation due to the repayment of a loan and took the bold decision to free all the slaves and transport them to Philadelphia at considerable cost.

Cadburys is also steeped in Quaker roots, set up as a small grocery store by John Cadbury who, being against alcohol, focused on tea, coffee, chocolate and drinking chocolate instead. As business grew and they needed to find larger premises (they had by this time become a manufacturer of chocolate and cocoa), they bought some land outside Birmingham and established 'Bournville'. By this point, the Industrial Revolution was in full tilt and working conditions for many were horrendous. One of Cadbury's aims was to produce a clean, pleasant and healthy working environment for his employees, and this remained one of the heartbeats of the company for many years, in stark contrast to so many others.

Many of the issues that Quakerism touches on are right at the heart of concerns we have already met in this book – issues both local and global, concerning wealth and poverty, status and relationships, and the transformation of society.

Moving away from Quakerism to something completely different, there are interesting resonances with Latin American liberation theology.

Liberation theology was birthed out of the ground-breaking teachings of Vatican II, the second Vatican Council, which took place between 1962 and 1965. Vatican II focused on renewing the Church through fresh understandings of (among other things) its relationship to the world, the role of Scripture in the life of the Church, and the relationship of the Catholic Church to the ecumenical movement. There was new emphasis on the Church as being about all God's people and so the priests were now encouraged to celebrate mass facing the congregation rather than facing away, thus facilitating a greater sense of participation, and new vigour was breathed into the development of Catholic social teaching, which brought themes of social justice into the heart of Catholic life.

Liberation theology came from the attempts by the Latin American Catholic Church to apply these teachings to their own situation, which was one of mass suffering among the populations of Latin America. This was due to the failure of the economic development measures of the 1950s and the enforcement of national state security.[30] How would the modernisation and renewal of the Catholic Church inspired by Vatican II translate into the favelas of Latin America? The Second General Conference of the Latin America Bishops in Medellin in 1968 sought to answer this question in depth, and it was at this conference – with the pivotal theologian Gustavo Gutiérrez a central figure – that the programmatic statement for liberation theology was laid down. Here the principle was provided that the Church 'must become not only a church *for* the poor, and not only a church *with* the poor: it must become a church *of* the poor'.[31] In particular, they developed the concept of 'base ecclesial communities' as being the foundation of the Church. These were expressions of church in small neighbourhood groups that retained their Catholic practices and beliefs, but existed in poor communities (such as the favelas in Brazil) and were mostly run by lay women and men.

Liberation theology proved controversial, with some accusing it of Marxism and others accusing it of a less-than-Christocentric approach, with its emphasis on the exodus as a paradigm. John Paul II, and the then Cardinal Joseph Ratzinger (who became Pope Benedict XVI) were famously opposed to it. But liberation theologians such as Gutiérrez were insistent that this was not about using the gospel as a platform to serve the interests of a social justice agenda, but was rather about developing a holistic understanding of the gospel that rooted the concerns of the poor into the Christian faith.

Gutiérrez' discussion about the meaning of poverty is particularly pertinent for some of the discussions concerning money and possessions we will pick up in subsequent chapters. He differentiates between *material* poverty (which is 'a scandalous condition') and *spiritual* poverty (which is 'an attitude of openness to God and spiritual childhood') and then brings them together into *voluntary* poverty. Voluntary poverty – which he bases on the *kenosis* of Christ in Philippians 2:6–11 – is about solidarity with the poor which 'must manifest itself in specific action, a style of life, a break with one's social class'. In doing that, 'one can also help the poor and exploitated [sic] to become aware of their exploitation and seek liberation from it'.[32] I am interested that the Catholic theologian Roberto Goizueta, when he reflects on these distinctions of Gutiérrez, comes to the conclusion that 'a genuine spiritual poverty will necessarily manifest itself in a life of material simplicity'.[33]

The majority of us are outworking our faith in a very different culture from that of Latin America and most of us will not be attempting to embrace poverty in the way that Gutiérrez and others did. Nonetheless, there is a resonance here with discussions that we have touched on and will look at more fully later, discussions around simplicity as a sacrifice and not merely a means to a deeper personal happiness. The strong emphasis of liberation theology on the poor, on justice and on community can inspire us to think differently in our own communities and contexts.

Quakerism and liberation theology are just two of many examples we could have drawn on to show that, while consumerism and globalisation might be contemporary contexts, the Church has a long history and established tradition of Christian simplicity and radical dissent. These are two of the many movements down through church history that form the shoulders of giants upon which we stand in our current desire to find ways of living out our faith in today's culture.

5. Ecclesiology and Christian formation in consumer society

How are Christians formed into disciples of Jesus in consumer culture? In what context will formation take place when church attendance is seen by many Christians as an optional leisure choice rather than as the central event of each week? These and other similar questions are part of a big conversation that is currently going on within evangelical church circles concerning Christian formation and discipleship.

Given what we saw in our previous chapter, this is not surprising. We live in a society that specifically works to form us into consumers. Right from our youngest days, we are 'consumers-in-training', taught to have certain desires and to seek to see them fulfilled in certain ways. And yet the early Church leader Paul said that we are being transformed into the likeness of Jesus Christ, by the working of the Holy Spirit (2 Cor. 3:18). This creates a tension for us in our Christian living. We are like Doctor Dolittle's pushmi-pullyu: a creature with two heads each going in the opposite direction. Consumer values take us in one direction, Christ-centred values in the other.

One of the issues that arises is that of detachment. We have already seen that a key feature of consumerism is that it distances us from the things we consume so that we become detached from the means of production, the producers, and hence the actual product itself. In Vincent Miller's discussion on consumerism and religion – which we touched on in the previous chapter – he extends his treatment on detachment (what he calls 'commodification') to consider its relationship to the Church. Using the lens of such things as the music of Moby (which uses samples of old Negro Spiritual songs), Madonna's use of religious iconography, the general penchant for Tibetan prayer flags (guess which decade he was writing in!) and the celebrity nature of the Pope and the Dalai Lama, he looks at how the symbols and practices of religion, both Christian and other, have been co-opted by consumer culture to serve consumerism's ends, abstracting them from their original referents.[34] In other words, these things, which were originally embedded in religious contexts, have been lifted out of them and used to create pleasing consumer products.

The point for Miller is not just to provide an interesting piece of cultural analysis, but to demonstrate that this directly influences those who profess a Christian faith. Consumerism, as we know, is not just a practice, but a value system that teaches us to view and relate to the world in a particular way, as consumers. Miller's contention is that this is conducive neither to Christian development nor to ecclesiology. The concern is that Christians 'engage religious beliefs and symbols with the interpretive habits and dispositions they use for commercial popular culture'.[35]

The crux of Miller's argument is that abstraction is the enemy of the Christian faith: 'The fundamental problem with the commodification of culture is that it trains believers to abstract religious doctrines, symbols, and practices from the traditional and communal context that give them meaning and connect them to a form of life.'[36] With Baumanesque echoes, these doctrines, symbols and practices thus become like colours on a palette that can be chosen to enhance one's *already constructed life*, rather than being the framework around which one's life is shaped.

A teacher once showed her pupils a jar filled with large stones. 'Is it full?' she asked. She then picked up a handful of small pebbles and poured them into the jar around the big stones. 'Now is it full?' she asked. With her students watching, she went on to pour in a container of sand, and then filled the whole jar up with water. 'Finally,' she said, 'it is full.'

The question, when it comes to Christian formation, is what are the large stones that we will put in our lives around which everything else needs to fit?

Our contemporary society teaches us to see the large stones as being things like a settled job with a secure income, a house, consumer goods, and so on. Those are what we are to get secure in our lives first, and then everything else (church, friendships, time to build relationships, etc.) has to fit around those. The big stones have to go in first before everything else.

The biblical narrative of following Christ, however, tells us that the large stones are quite different: they are about pursuing God's kingdom of justice and righteousness; picking up our calling to serve the wider creation; and living to see our relationships enhanced in all areas. These are what we are to focus on first, and then trust that God will work out the other things and pour them into the jar of our lives too. I do not say that lightly and I am fully aware that it is altogether easier to say this in a book than live it out in practice. My husband Greg has been much better at living in this way than I have, and I have learned a lot from him, often painfully!

What is at stake here is what we might call our 'focal concerns': those priorities around which we orientate our practices. If one of the key cultural traits of consumerism is that it detaches us – from other people, from God, from the wider natural world, from ourselves – then the most effective means of questioning that trait is actively to engage in ways of forming lines of reconnection. Our focal concerns, then, will be all to do with re-engagement and the building of relationships, on all levels.

When we have our focal concerns in place, then we can use many aspects of consumer culture to serve those, rather than the other way round. Technology and the media are good illustrations of this as they play a large role in forming us as people in our current culture. Living in a highly technological society brings its challenges. It can teach us to value the end product more than the work involved, leading us to look down on common labours. It can teach us to need constantly to be entertained, leading us to fear silence and empty time, and it can teach us to expect everything to be fast, new, time saving and focused on ourselves, leading us to become people who are impatient and easily irritated.[37]

Because of this, Christian writing on consumerism can take a very negative approach to technology. The American theologian Michael Budde, for example, contends that the global culture industries have a direct impact on church life and Christian formation, and that impact is distinctly unhelpful.[38] For Budde, it is a 'zero-sum game': 'to the extent that culture industry formation succeeds, Christian formation fails', or, to put it more practically, 'time spent with television, recorded music [etc.] is almost always time not spent being involved in the sorts of things that form people in practices and affections relevant to the radical demands of the gospel'.[39]

There is no doubt that culture competes with church as a location for formation – and often more successfully.[40] Within that, though, I would want to say that the role of technology and the media remains *ambivalent* rather than purely negative, and that an approach such as Budde's is too simplistic.

What is at stake here is to be aware that technology and the media have the potential to form us in ways that run counter to our focal concerns, and so to ensure that we use them wisely. That will look different to each one of us, and what is important for one may not be important for another. I, for example, decided many years ago not to buy glossy women's magazines because I knew that they would feed a negative sense of self-worth and would teach me to conform my understanding of womanhood to societal stereotypes. Other examples of practices we could undertake would be to have periods where we fast from technological screens of all sorts – maybe a prolonged fast (such as no Facebook during Lent) or regular smaller breaks, whereby we ensure that each day we put our screens down and do something different: go for a walk, play the piano, play a game, have a face-to-face conversation with someone, and so on. Being aware and making good choices is the order of the day here. Once we find ourselves missing what someone is saying to us, or not noticing the sunset out of the window, because we are playing Clash of Clans or Candy Crush, we know it is time to sort things out!

This conversation about Christian formation is the final strand of the ecclesiological context within which the themes of this book find their location. It is my contention that the practices which we are beginning to highlight, and which we will consider more fully in Part Three, go a long way towards answering the question of how we can be formed as Christians within our consumer culture. Crucially, we cannot do these practices on our own, in isolation from other people. What is needed is what we might call 'communities of engagement': ecclesial communities that form a counterculture both through retreat and through engagement with public life in all its facets, including the economic and political.

But before we look at all of this in more depth, there is some theological work that we need to do.

PART TWO

Breathing In, Breathing Out – the Theology

Introduction

I have one problem when it comes to public speaking: my voice. (Well, OK, some may say I have quite a few problems when it comes to public speaking, but my voice is the one that troubles *me* the most!) Put bluntly, I do not have a very strong voice, and if I am having to do quite a lot of public speaking I can easily strain it and then lose it, which is not very helpful. Put me somewhere where I am both speaking a lot publicly *and* having to talk to people in a noisy setting, and I've really had it.

Thankfully, that has got a lot better due to the invaluable help of Cathy, the wife of someone I was speaking with at Spring Harvest one year. Spring Harvest (a Christian conference in the UK, held over the Easter holidays) has historically been one of the worst places for me voice-wise, as I have found myself speaking publicly three or four times a day, leading team meetings (which inevitably makes me speak more loudly), praying for people in a loud evening meeting, and then chatting to people late at night in a crowded, noisy bar. By the time I've done that for, say, twelve days in a row, my voice is shot and I croak and whisper my way through my final seminars!

But this wonderful woman approached me one year after hearing me speak in the Big Top in the evening celebration and bravely suggested that I wasn't speaking properly. Would I like her to help me? It turned out that Cathy was a speech therapist and so I gladly accepted her offer.

The next afternoon we met up and she led me out to a large square of grass, bordered along the sides by Butlins chalets, three storeys high. She stood me at one end and told me to speak and make my voice heard by those in the chalets on the other side of the square. Feeling rather self-conscious in front of lots of people generally milling around the area, I spoke as loudly as I could and tried to get my voice to reach as far as it would go. I was pretty pathetic!

Having tried a few things with me, Cathy reached her verdict. The problem, she told me, was with my breathing: I simply didn't do it properly, and that affected my voice (as anyone who has had any vocal training will tell you).

I needed to breathe in fully and deeply: not from my chest as I had thought (it seemed logical to me – that's where my lungs are, after all!), but actually from my stomach, pushing my tummy out with each intake of breath. That way I was really filling my diaphragm and, if my shoulders lifted when breathing, then I knew I was doing it wrong. When I had breathed in that way, then I was able to breathe out from a deeper place and my voice both went further and did not strain my throat.

I'm still not brilliant at this technique, but I know that what Cathy told me that afternoon fundamentally changed how I speak, and I now consciously try to remember when I am speaking to be aware of what I am doing. I have learned how to breathe.

So far in this book we have focused on the context within which we are seeking to live out our Christian faith. We have looked at globalisation – discussed first because of the heightened concern for global issues of social injustice and environmental breakdown that so many of us carry – and then at our consumer-driven culture, a crucial context that most of us live in and are hardly aware of at all, like a fish not noticing the water in which it swims. We then turned our attention to the specific Church frameworks and traditions that are important in helping us think through how we connect our faith to the culture we live in, the broader issues of this world, and how we live our lives.

What is interesting to note is that emerging out of our discussions is a double movement of retreat and engagement: a rhythm of breathing in and breathing out. As we noted earlier, one of the ways of responding to our global and societal context is through retreat and withdrawal: finding ways to reduce our involvement in the system, reducing our expenditure and living more frugally. We can make conscious decisions to give more time to building relationships than to buying and consuming more goods, and create space and stillness in which to deepen our relationship with God. This retreat is not done out of an attitude of abject despair, but as a way to respond to, and resist, our cultural context. We breathe in and retreat.

Breathing in well, though, takes us to a deep place from which we can then breathe out more effectively and engage. Ethical consumerism is one way by which we can respond to the negatives of globalisation, using our power *as consumers* to bring about some benefit and counteract the immense damage done through the global trading system. But we have also seen that building relationships and community in all its different facets (with God, with other people, and with the non-human creation) is key to what we are thinking about in this book. As we do so, we use our life actions positively to bring about change, both within ourselves and in the people and places around us and further afield. We breathe out and engage.

What is important to recognise is that this double movement is a fully theological undertaking: it comes from a particular understanding of the Christian faith and of the demands that such a faith places on our lives. However, it needs to be acknowledged that the desire to embrace the dynamism of this rhythm of retreat and engagement does also carry within it some challenges and tensions. These tensions coalesce around two broad questions: (1) what is the relationship of Christianity with culture? And (2) what is the relationship of the Christian faith with the material world? These questions, while inevitably interlinked, are yet distinguishable. They are also perennial questions, but I believe that the attempt to live more simply provides us with a fruitful way of constructing answers in such a manner that we are enabled to live faithful lives in the midst of global and social contexts that many of us find inherently problematic.

Part Two of this book seeks to excavate the tensions that surround us and consider the polarities that we need to avoid. As with the previous discussion of our various contexts, so too here: simply the act of specifying what those tensions and polarities are brings them to our attention and therefore is a helpful first step in learning how to negotiate them. Chapter 4 will consider two of those extremes: the danger of disappearing into an oppositional enclave, and the danger of sinking into a therapeutic form of Christianity. Chapter 5 will then focus on the critical question of how we develop a Christian approach to money and material goods and will consider the danger of embracing the opposite of a therapeutic form of Christianity: a world-denying attitude towards material goods. Chapter 6 takes us into the heart of our theological journey and uses Thomas Aquinas's understanding of the relationship between the virtues of temperance and justice to help us explore how negotiating these tensions well will help us hold together concern for self with concern for other.

I hope you will stay with me on this journey. It is both a fun and a challenging one that takes us through Anabaptists, the Vineyard movement, early Church Fathers, saints Benedict and Francis, Aristotle and Aquinas. I am not sure they have ever been brought into such a conversation together: a dinner party with them all at one table would make for an interesting evening indeed! However, be warned as before: what these chapters aim to do is highlight the need for continuing discussion, rather than bring the discussion to a close by providing definitive answers.

Chapter 4

Get Thee to a Nunnery?
Unhelpful retreat versus unhealthy narcissism

An oppositional enclave

I sometimes imagine a Monty Python or Horrible Histories sketch based on the Desert Fathers. In it there are numerous men with long hair and unkempt straggly beards, barefooted and wearing unwashed tunics. They are in the desert, where they have fled in order to find silence and solitude, but what they have found instead is lots of other men trying to do the same. In my mind they jostle against each other, trying to maintain an exterior appearance of holiness, but inwardly cross and grumpy, trying to push the others out of their way in order to reach the more isolated parts of the desert before anyone else. Am I the only one to find that image a bit funny?

Of course, it is a send-up of the reality, but, as with all the best send-ups, it retains a kernel – albeit perhaps a very small one – of truth. The Desert Mothers and Fathers were remarkable people who left their lives behind in order to live in the extreme discomfort of the Egyptian desert. They were not the first people to do so. The Egyptian desert in the first centuries AD was already well established as a place where the outlaws went: those peasants, slaves and thieves who were escaping the taxes and laws of Graeco-Roman Egypt. The first Christians began making their way to the desert to escape the persecution brought on by Emperor Decian in AD 249 and thousands took up refuge there during that time.[1]

What began as an escape from persecution turned into an escape from quite the opposite when Constantine converted to Christianity in AD 312 and subsequently pronounced Christianity the official state religion, thereby affording it a host of privileges it had never enjoyed before. This was a shock to those who saw their Christian faith as one of purity, martyrdom and sacrifice and, from the early fourth century onwards, the desert became the place for those who wished to escape this new situation. Living in the desert was seen as a way of continuing the faithfulness of the martyrs which had been such a prominent feature of earliest Christianity. From being a refuge from persecution, it now took on a new identity as a refuge from the values of the present, sinful world, which were seen as a distraction from one's relationship with God. As the Greek theologian Stelios Ramos explains, in the desert 'one remains alone with God – the Other who knows all things – and thus through Him can turn inwards to contemplate and study oneself'.[2]

This was the birth of monasticism (from the Greek *monachos*, meaning 'alone'; our word 'hermit' comes from the description of these first desert dwellers as 'eremites', from the Greek for 'desert', *eremos*), and the desert came to be populated by huge numbers of Christians living in different variations of solitude and community. In fact, at one point, Father Poemen was reported to have said (no doubt in a grumpy Horrible Histories fashion), 'There's scarcely any desert left.' As we will see shortly, that was probably somewhat of an exaggeration, but the point is made.

As we saw in the previous chapter, the monastic tradition has deep resources for us to draw on as we seek to live out our faith in our own, very different context, two thousand years later. But it also brings challenges and extremes from which we should steer away, and one of those – the first of the polarities that we are considering – is the danger of retreating into an oppositional enclave in relationship to the wider society around us.

The roots of monasticism in the Desert Mothers and Fathers are undoubtedly to be found in their desire to separate from the general society. They were well known for uttering apoph-thegms – short sayings that contained nuggets of wisdom – and various collections of these exist. One such is the collection of lives and sayings called *Vitae Patrum*, which was collated by the Jesuit Heribert Rosweyde in the early seventeenth century. In it is a description of the desert of Nitria (which became known as Cellia, 'the desert of cells'):

> To this spot those who have had their first initiation and who desire to live a remoter life, stripped of all its trappings, with-draw themselves: for the desert is vast, and the cells are sundered from one another by so wide a space that none is in sight of his neighbour, nor can any voice be heard. One by one they abide in their cells, a mighty silence and a great quiet among them.[3]

And the sentiment of the Desert Mothers and Fathers is encapsulated in the reply that Arsenius gave to the Abbot Marcus, who asked him, 'Wherefore does thou flee from us?' The old man is said to have replied, 'God knows that I love you: but I cannot be with God and with men.'[4] Arsenius was from a wealthy family and became a prominent Christian leader, but he eventually withdrew into the desert out of a desire to live a solitary life. Because of his former prominence, people sought him out for his advice and so he tried to live in places where he could not be found. When Theophilus, Pope of Alexandria, came to visit him one day with a group of other people, Arsenius said to him, 'I entreat you then that, whenever you are informed of Arsenius's abode, you would leave him to himself and spare yourselves the trouble of coming after him.' Thus, as the Dominican historian Lucien Regnault has put it, 'It is this desire to remove oneself fully from the world's grasp so as to fully belong to God that led the monk to the solitude of the faraway desert.'[5]

The desert dwellers of the fourth century, both anchoritic (those who lived in seclusion from other people – from the Greek *anachoreo*, 'to withdraw') and cenobitic (those who lived in community with others – from the Greek *koinos*, 'common', and *bios*, 'life'), laid the original foundation for Christian monasticism, but subsequent forms did not always follow precisely in their footsteps. As we will see in the next chapter, there are divergent views within monasticism about a proper relationship to the material world, and the same is true in relation to the way monasticism views the relationship to the social and cultural world. So, for example, Augustine – setting up his community in the late 300s or early 400s AD while the desert monastics were still very much a feature of the Christian world – decided not to form that community in the desert but to locate it conspicuously in the heart of the city of Hippo Regius, first at the 'garden monastery' within the church compound and then as part of the bishop's residence, thus demonstrating that the desert approach was not the only one.[6]

St Francis, too, rejected the dominant Benedictine monasticism, precisely because it was based on cloistered communities that separated themselves from 'the world', whereas, as we shall see in the next chapter, his aim was to rid himself of all encumbrances in order to take the gospel of Christ *into* the world.

All of this demonstrates that monasticism's relationship with the world at large cannot be quantified too simplistically and, of course, contemporary monasticism shows this divergence too, from the withdrawal of monks to the remote Mount Athos, to the urban immersion of the Columban Fathers. Nonetheless, the overall tenor of monasticism entails separation from the wider community and this will be at odds with most of us reading this book, living 'regular' lives within contemporary society and seeking to live out our values – our 'focal concerns' – within that society, as teachers, church leaders, parents, charity workers, business people and so on, and the majority of us will not have chosen to live a permanently celibate life. This gives us a closer relationship with the broader society than the monastics, as it is so often through our work and our family situations that our lives overlap the most with the society in which we live. While there is much to learn from monasticism, therefore, its emphasis on the retreat side of our double movement pushes us out to forge our own way through these issues.

Adding to this complexity is the reality that an oppositional enclave does not only emerge from living a cloistered life; it can come simply from our attitude to the people around us, however much we may functionally be a part of them (and monasticism has always recognised that the interior dimensions of one's life may bear little resemblance to the outer circumstances).

There is a very interesting book written in 2010 by the Christian American sociologist James Davison Hunter, in which he investigates the different approaches to culture adopted by American evangelical Christians.[7] It is his contention that American evangelicalism has developed an obsession with the rhetoric of 'changing the world': a rhetoric that has come in as they have grown increasingly concerned with the lack of influence they have on American culture and the increase of the perceived evils of secularism and liberalism through the course of the twentieth century.

Hunter looks at three major approaches to cultural engagement in American evangelicalism, classifying those as 'defensive against', 'relevant to' and 'purity from'. The 'defensive against' model relates to the Christian Right who see the secular liberal American culture – with its divorce, abortion on demand, illiteracy, out-of-wedlock births, crime, drugs, family break-up, gay rights and violence – as attacking traditional Christian values and hence the moral framework of the country. Key figures here include James Dobson and Jonathan Falwell. The 'relevant to' model represents the politically progressive Christian Left. Sharply antagonistic to the 'defensive against' people, they wish to stand up politically for all that the Christian Right has neglected, issues of social equality and environmental care. Key figures here include Ron Sider and Jim Wallis. Standing slightly apart from the 'defensive against' and the 'relevant to' categories are those Hunter defines as 'purity from'. These are what Hunter calls the 'neo-Anabaptists', sharing similar concerns with the Christian Left, but operating within a more separatist model (neo-Anabaptists are people today who would identify with much of the theology and practice of the Anabaptist tradition but do not actually come from a denomination with an Anabaptist link, such as the Mennonites). John Howard Yoder and Stanley Hauerwas are key figures here.

Hunter interrogates each of these approaches in different ways, but of most interest for what we are considering in this section is the main criticism that he levels against the neo-Anabaptists, which is that their response to the wider society is essentially negative. Their theological narrative is based on an early Church that developed independently of the state and in a hostile political environment, and they take their cue for today from that. Therefore, 'opposition was and remains centrally important to the Anabaptist identity and its vision of social and political engagement with the world'.[8]

We saw in chapter 2 that both Christian and non-Christian commentators on consumerism have historically taken an overwhelmingly negative approach, and it is my experience – in listening to people talk about these issues as I have travelled around the country, and in being aware of my own attitude – that people who think and care deeply about these things have a tendency to follow suit and to develop an 'us and them' worldview, in which we can see ourselves as separated from (and superior to) those around us by virtue of our lifestyle decisions.

This was something that came through from the people I interviewed for my doctoral research. One person, for example, talked about seeing 'quite a lot of my friends, where actually their identity is wrapped up so much in fashion trends and in buying things for their children, that you just think, "My goodness, they don't need to have that, they're only tiny"', and she described 'that kind of mentality' as something she was 'kicking against [as] part of simplicity'. This 'us and them' worldview does not fit neatly into the distinction between Christian and non-Christian either, and another person highlighted this in relation to a previous church to which they had belonged:

> We noticed that there were people who just used to do a lot of shopping and we caught the shopping bug from people. We would go to church . . . and we found ourselves wanting to go shopping more often and judging our clothes and we were told, 'wouldn't it be nice to have this', and, 'this looks a bit old and faded and should be replaced'. And I realised we were picking this up from the Christians!

This attitude stemmed from the very real desire not to allow the practices of consumerism to draw them away from a life lived Christianly, and also from a recognition of the damage that is done to many living within a consumerist society. The research participants' attempts to live more simply stemmed partly from the view (as one person said) 'that everyone's burning out, they're working too hard, they're too busy, their lives are too cluttered, consumerism has set in massively, shopping has become an obsession'. However, there is a danger that 'they' becomes a term applied almost sanctimoniously to everyone else *en masse*.

Simultaneously, however, we have already seen that a large part of people's moves to live more simply comes from a desire to build relationships and community – both within and without the Church, and on a local and global level – and this stands in tension to an 'us and them' attitude. There is thus a precarious path we need to tread between a pessimistic attitude towards other people, which leads to a separatist approach, and a positive desire for community and engagement.

In contrast to a rigidly held chasm between Church and world, evidenced in some forms of monasticism, I want to encourage us to seek to walk a *via media* that recognises the many evils inherent within a consumerist system – and refuses to capitulate to them – but does not separate itself off into a disengaged and defensive island, whether physically or psychologically. In doing so we hold together both the 'no' of God's judgement against unjust and oppressive realms and the 'yes' of God's love for the world that he has created.[9] This *via media*, as Bretherton notes, 'implies neither withdrawal nor subcultural resistance but, as exemplified in the stories of Joseph, Daniel, and Esther, it entails combining active investment in Babylon's wellbeing with faithful particularity and obedience to God'.[10]

I have found Robert Markus's articulation of Augustine's concept of the *saeculum* helpful in thinking this through.[11] Markus identifies that within Graeco-Roman culture were two foundational spheres: the sacred and the profane. The sacred 'was what belonged to the gods and to their cults', and the profane (in contrast to how we might define the word today) 'was everything which lay outside the sanctuary, around the shrine: the sphere of ordinary everyday life'.[12] In the fourth century, as the Graeco-Roman cult came into confrontation with Christianity, the profane became a negative term, associated with exclusion: a hostile sphere to the sacred. Into this context, Augustine developed the notion of the secular, which was the sphere that lay in the middle: 'not a third City between the earthly and the heavenly, but their mixed, "inextricably intertwined" state in this temporal life'.[13] That sphere was not so much neutral as ambivalent.

It needs to be stated that we are here peeping into an immense theological discourse around Augustine: his notion of the two cities (the City of God and the earthly city), how they relate, and what that means for our own understanding of the kingdom of God, the Church, the state, culture, politics and so on. Our point is not to enter into that fray but to see how we might profitably appropriate these spheres for our own understanding of how we approach the society in which we live. Markus makes the interesting statement that 'the idea of the secular is present within the Christian tradition from the start but takes on a very different meaning according to the historical circumstances in which it is applied',[14] and I think we can apply this idea to our own circumstance.

The sacred is that which is 'roughly coextensive with the sphere of Christian religious belief, practices, institutions, and cult', and this is where we locate ourselves; living out a Christian life centred around our relationship with God and focused on care of local and global neighbour and of the wider creation.

The profane is that which is 'close to what has to be rejected in the surrounding culture, practices, institutions'. This is all that is evil within the structures of our globalised, consumer-driven culture, what Bretherton would call 'the imposition of instrumentalizing and commodifying logics upon social existence by state and market procedures'.[15] It is right to see these two spheres as essentially antithetical.

But in between these two spheres is the secular, that which 'does not have such connotations of radical opposition to the sacred; it is more neutral, capable of being accepted or adapted'.[16] In this sphere lies the tension of our relationship with consumer society and, in particular, here is where we can locate the many people (Christian and non-Christian) who are deliberately not immersing themselves indiscriminately into consumer culture, but are attempting to live their lives as best they might, carrying out their daily duties, managing their relationships to the best of their abilities and living in all the complexities of modern-day families.

This understanding of the *saeculum* helps us to stand in the middle between a full acceptance of consumer culture that collapses the values of the Christian faith fully into the values of consumerism, and an alienating rejection that sees nothing of any worth in the culture in which we live. It is my contention that this understanding provides a balance for the rhythm of retreat and engagement that we drew out in the introduction to this second part of the book. As it does so, it encourages us to see that in Christ it is possible to bring redemption rather than outright condemnation of different areas of society and thus helps us as we look to be witnesses within our different contexts.[17]

Therapeutic Christianity

Southampton Central train station was a memorable place to be on the day Southampton FC were promoted to the Premier League. I happened to be changing trains there that particular Sunday afternoon, a little while after the deciding match had finished, and found myself in the middle of a throng of people, all celebrating the team's success (I have no idea who Southampton had beaten – the losing side's fans were presumably keeping very quiet in a corner somewhere). Normally a somewhat subdued place to be, with people waiting around not saying very much to one another, this afternoon could not have been more different. All the platforms – and then the train I boarded – were full of men (predominantly) with their arms round each other or up in the air, singing at the tops of their voices. It was quite something!

Singing songs seems to be an essential part of our make-up as human beings. Wherever you go, in whichever culture, at whatever time in history, you will find singing. As human beings, we simply cannot stop ourselves singing. And that, of course, has been the case all through the history of Christianity, reaching right back into our Jewish roots, as far back as Miriam singing her song of celebration when the Hebrews made it safely across the Red Sea (Exod. 15). For as long as we can remember, we have sung songs praising God for who he is and what he has done. The very word 'hymn' (from the Greek *hymnos*) simply means 'song of praise'.

It is so much a part of our church culture that I sometimes wonder if we really think about what we are singing. If you are a churchgoer, how much notice do you take of the hymns and songs that you sing there? Are you aware of the words and of how much you may be absorbing the theological understandings that they contain and implicitly teach us?

Last Sunday, we sang three songs at the meeting I attended. The first, 'I Walk By Faith' (Hillsong), is a song of declaration, simply declaring that I will walk and live by faith and put my trust in God. The second was 'Oceans' (also by Hillsong), a song with the same theme of putting our trust in God whatever deep waters we find ourselves in. The third song was 'You Are The Way' (from Worship Central), written as a bit of a party song, to celebrate Jesus' statement in John 14:6 that he is 'the way, the truth and the life'. All three are good songs, declaring or celebrating important aspects of the Christian life, and I do not want to be unduly critical, but none of them could be considered particularly high in content in comparison to a song such as Stuart Townend's 'How Deep The Father's Love For Us' or 'In Christ Alone'.[18] Taken together as the only songs sung that morning, I left with the impression of having fed on a nice but small and unsatisfying snack rather than a substantial meal.

The singing of these and other such songs in church reflects the impact of the charismatic movement: a new movement that hit the British Church in the 1960s. It had its roots in the Pentecostalism that had begun in the USA and from there spread throughout the world, and it brought the practice of spiritual gifts into the mainline denominations, both Protestant and Catholic. At the same time that the effects of the charismatic movement were expanding across, and being resisted by, various sectors of the established Church, so also was being born what were first known as 'house churches' but are now referred to as the 'New Church movement'. (Although I was brought up as an Anglican, it is this part of the Church that has been my own home for the duration of my adult life.) With its large-scale non-denominational gatherings and programmes, the charismatic movement effectively changed the face of the British – particularly Protestant – Church and its impacts continue into the present day and no doubt will continue for some time yet.

Many of the values of the charismatic movement have become ubiquitous throughout the Church in the UK – and indeed throughout the Western world – and there are some key theological traits that are pertinent to our discussion and that lead us into a consideration of the second danger inherent within attempts to live more simply: the danger of a therapeutic Christianity.

A useful gateway into this discussion is the treatment that Martyn Percy gives of what was one of the most influential figures and groups in the charismatic movement: John Wimber and the Vineyard churches.[19] One of the things Percy does is to analyse Vineyard songs from the 1980s (it would be fair to say that Vineyard was to the 1980s what Bethel and Hillsong are to the contemporary worship scene).[20] He notes particularly the distinctly personal and individualistic nature of the songs, so much so that just under half of them have 'I' in the first line. In years gone past, one of the main functions of hymns was as a doctrinal teaching device, particularly in the days when literacy was not near-universal as it is today. However, rather than teaching doctrine, the songs Percy looked at functioned instead to provoke experience, by the participant, of God. An analysis of the songs showed that this experience consisted predominantly of two things, God's power and God's love, both of which are depicted as being there to heal the participant's afflictions, whether they be physical or emotional.[21] This understanding forms the basis of what we might call a therapeutic Christianity.

All hymns and worship songs function with what can be called a 'theological imaginary'. That theological imaginary might, for example, be of a God who is distant and like a judge, threatening people with terror or hell; or it might be of a God who is engaged in a spiritual battle and calls his people to fight for him. Different types of songs reflect different understandings of God and of ourselves. Percy notes that the theological imaginary with which these Vineyard songs work is of a God who 'is personal, known, intimate and present, forever ready to show his love by meeting the needs of those who communicate with him'.[22] While not wishing to distract you too much, next time you are in a church meeting or service you might like to think through what understanding of God and of ourselves (and of the wider creation too – but that is a further issue[23]) is being put forward by the songs you are singing.

It is interesting to note that this observation about the individualistic character of worship songs is nothing new. Indeed, even in 1897, an article in the *Church Times* called for all hymns that started with a capital 'I' to be dropped, deeming them too subjective and sentimental.[24] It needs to be said, too, that Percy's analysis relates to songs that reflect the Vineyard of three decades ago or more, and would not necessarily be a fair representation of songs sung by churches within the Vineyard or wider charismatic movement. There has been much more emphasis in recent years on writing and singing songs that reflect a mixture of confession, reflection on Christ's sacrifice, an awareness of dark times, a call to justice and so on. Having said that, though, a look at the top five songs in the US Billboard chart of 'Hot Christian Songs' at the time of writing shows songs that are entirely focused on the writer's feelings and emotions, with little doctrinal content (remembering that doctrinal content is different from theological content since the words reflect the theological understanding of the songwriter).[25]

The point of this is not to criticise these songs as such. I am not advocating songs that are full of doctrinal content alone. We are, after all, humans with feelings; the Christian faith is a mixture of belief and experience, and we need songs that reflect the experiential, subjective side and are not focused on the mind alone. The point is that worship songs of this sort have been foundational in laying a contemporary theology that interiorises and individualises Christian faith. Crucially, they operate with a theological imaginary that sees a relationship with 'the Lord' as the gateway to having one's needs met. Allan Anderson has written extensively on the history and theology of Pentecostalism and makes the point that 'Pentecostals and Charismatics relate the gospel directly to their troubles and the process of understanding the gospel essentially begins in the context of felt needs.'[26]

Pete Ward has picked up this discussion in his exploration of the relationship between sung worship and British evangelicalism since the 1950s, tracing the rise of charismatic worship to the point at which he can state that it 'has become the default setting in most evangelical churches in Britain', and he agrees with Percy that 'the contemporary worship song occupies a particular space in charismatic spirituality: it is the means to a personal encounter with God'.[27] Ward looks at hymnologist Lionel Adey's classic categorisation of hymns into three types. The first – the objective – is hymns that give an account of a biblical event or theological theme. The second – the subjective – refers to those hymns that have similar content but also include the relevance of this for the participants. The third – the reflexive – are those hymns which focus on the act of worship itself and on what is happening to the worshippers as they worship. It is this final category that Ward notes has become predominant over recent decades.[28]

From where does this turn to the inner self come? The history of this is complicated, with many interweaving strands, but Anderson, in his analysis of Pentecostalism, traces it back to the nineteenth-century Holiness movement, which in itself drew on German Pietism that began in the seventeenth century.[29] The Pietist movement reacted against the formalism of the established Church and emphasised the importance of a personal experience of God, evidenced through 'new birth' by the Holy Spirit. This stream came into contact with revivalism in America in the eighteenth century, which 'stressed the role of the emotions in changing lives'.[30]

The relevance of this to what we are looking at becomes apparent when we consider that the roots of this ecclesiological context are located in the same historical period as, it is argued, the roots of contemporary consumerism. Colin Campbell's ground-breaking work on the history of consumerism, *The Romantic Ethic and the Spirit of Modern Consumerism*, contends that it was aesthetics and the Romantic movement that transformed the Protestant work ethic into a consumer ethic.[31] He makes the interesting point that although 'consumerism justified everything which Puritanism condemned', what is most remarkable is that the consumer revolution was carried through precisely by those sections of English society – the middle classes – that had the strongest roots in Puritanism and so should have been those most likely to disapprove of the new demand for 'luxury goods' and 'pleasurable indulgencies'.[32]

Campbell's key points build on his understanding of the development of a modern form of hedonism that differentiates from traditional hedonism by way of being focused predominantly on the emotions and the imagination (Campbell has much to say about the role of daydreaming and fantasising in consumerism[33]), rather than on bodily, tactile pleasures.[34] Campbell's view is that this modern form of hedonism arose from a disenchantment with the Calvinist doctrine of predestination and led to a more individualistic approach to life and the development of what he has called 'the Man of Feeling'.[35] He traces the rise of consumerism from Puritanism, through Sentimentalism and into Romanticism, and sees consumerism as the attempt to bring to reality that which is fantasised about in the act of daydreaming.

Campbell's work is very involved and the details of it do not need to detain us here.[36] What is germane to our discussion, though, is that the rise of modern charismatic evangelicalism, which has had such an impact on the Church throughout the Western world, takes place at the same time as the increasing introspection of the modern individual. We must be careful here not to posit too close a relationship between evangelicalism and Romanticism. David Bebbington, in his classic exposition of modern-day evangelicalism, argues rather that evangelicals were influenced more by the Enlightenment (such as the emphasis on rationality rather than mystery, and a view of nature that saw it as there to be mastered).[37] Nonetheless, Campbell has shown that there was a counter-side to the Enlightenment and its 'age of reason' as 'the process of disenchanting the world served both to permit and to prompt the accompanying voluntaristic re-enchantment of experience'. Reflecting the seminal work of Karl Polanyi, all movements have their counter-movements and so it is here too, with the result that 'the Age of Reason was also necessarily the Age of Sentiment'.[38] With its tendency to absorb and reflect the culture of which it is a part, it would not be unexpected to see evangelicalism following suit as the Protestant work ethic became the consumer ethic.

What does all of this have to do with the desire to live more simply? Well, we find ourselves in a situation today in which 'the increasing self-absorption displayed in a rights-governed and consumer-oriented liberal culture' poses a distinct danger to those of us wanting to live more simply as an outworking of our Christian faith.[39] The danger is that the pursuit of a more simple life can stem from a therapeutic understanding of Christianity that sees faith as being there to meet our needs, and so such lifestyle decisions can arise solely from the desire to construct a more self-fulfilling life for oneself, to the detriment of the wider concerns that we have looked at throughout this book.

This danger is not purely theoretical and can be seen in a number of popular-level Christian books that have been written in order to encourage people to adopt a more simple life as an antidote to consumerism. I think of one book, which I shall leave anonymous because the author is a friend. The book, overall, is excellent. My one criticism, though, is that it has virtually no mention of broader, global concerns and focuses almost exclusively on the personal effects of living in a consumer society. I think it is fair to assume that the author wants to avoid a guilt-inducing focus on individual complicity in global problems and strike a more positive and life-affirming note, and this is an understandable goal to reach for. But the problem is that not having this focus at all leaves him open to the charge of writing a book 'against' consumerism that arises from the same foundations upon which consumerism itself is built: namely, the search for personal fulfilment.

We have already seen that this is an area of some tension for those of us wanting to live differently in a consumer society. In chapter 3 we noted that while it could result in an increased quality of life (remember the words that my research participants used, words such as 'freedom', 'joy', 'light', 'abundant' and 'rich'), it also brought significant challenges. One of the key challenges is the recognition that the increase in a sense of personal well-being may well need to be balanced with an understanding of sacrifice, as limits are imposed on ourselves in order to live lives that are less damaging environmentally and socially. The reality is that if we are to live in a way that seriously responds to the global challenges around us – a vital component of which will include reducing our resource consumption significantly – then that may well lead to us needing to live life below a level that some of us might find acceptable. This is not to say that it is wrong to want to live more simply as a part of increasing our well-being, in the face of a time-poor and pressured society. It is, though, to make the point that we must hold the desire to build a better life for ourselves, away from the trappings of 'stuff' (the notion of a therapeutic underpinning to simplicity), with the desire to respond to injustice and environmental breakdown, which will of necessity lead to a less materially comfortable life. What is the relationship between these two desires? Are they mutually exclusive, or can they be reconciled and, if so, how?

These are questions we need to grapple with, and they are the focus of chapter 6. Before we reach that stage, though, and in order to lay some further foundations for that discussion, we need to consider the danger that comes from moving too far *away* from a therapeutic Christianity into an attitude towards material goods that leads to a world-denying approach.

Chapter 5

In Plenty or in Want
How to think about wealth

When I was eighteen I went to Malaysia, for part of my gap year. For five months I volunteered at a home for children whose parents had leprosy.

Leprosy is a disease that has had a fearsome reputation. We know it from the Gospel accounts of Jesus encountering lepers who had to live in colonies away from human society. It leads to the deadening of skin and nerves and from there to the deformation and loss of limbs. It conjures up images of people with dirty bandages wrapped around their faces, and stumps where hands and feet should have been.

Nowadays, it is actually easily treatable with antibiotics, which, if used early enough, can not only prevent the disease ever reaching those awful advanced stages, but can actually cure it. (As with all these things, though, access to the medication and the ability to afford it are key, which is why, in poorer countries, leprosy can still be a horrible disease.) Despite the fear that surrounds it, it is also not highly contagious. You are more likely to catch a cold than leprosy, should you encounter a person suffering from both! But it is contagious if people are exposed to it over long periods of time and so the children I was with in Malaysia had to live separately from their parents (who lived in a special village), and they would go back and visit them periodically.

The home was an hour or so from Kuala Lumpur, in a little village, and my living quarters were very basic. I had a room with a bed, some drawers and a table and chair. The bathroom was a squat toilet, a cold-water tap and a bucket, which you used to throw the water over you to wash. I think there might have been a sink but I cannot remember. What I do remember is that I shared my room with a tree frog, which had a very regular routine. Each evening when I went to bed it had gone, no doubt on its nightly jaunts, looking for food or a mate. I guess it never found a mate because each morning when I woke up, there it was, back in its same place in the top corner of the room. I loved my little tree frog and it gave me some sense of reassurance and companionship when I missed my family and friends back in the UK.

That room became home to me and I was ever so content there. I had almost nothing: no computer or phone, just a handful of clothes, a few toiletries, some books and a Bible. I spent my days with the children in the home, eating with them and helping with the chores, and did not really need anything else.

Now, as I sit here writing, I look around me and see a house filled with stuff. Yes, a lot of it has been given to us and not much of it is the 'latest'. But still, it is a far cry from that basic room many years ago. And I have a lot more money than I did back then too. As a married couple, our income has been quite erratic as I have been freelance for the majority of the time

while bringing up the children, and Greg's income has fluctu-
ated as he has pursued his vision for fairtrade jewellery.[1] That
fluctuation continues and our financial future often looks quite
uncertain, but still we have more money in the bank than I did
all those years ago.

The poet and hymnwriter Dorothy Frances Gurney
famously wrote, 'One is closer to God's heart in a garden than
anywhere else on earth', but the question I ask myself is this:
was I closer to God in my room in Malaysia, where I had very
little, than I am now, in my life where I have much? In other
words, what place do money and possessions occupy in the
Christian's walk with God? Is it the case, *de facto*, that having
fewer things and little money will lead to spiritual enhance-
ment in our relationship with God, or should we see such
things as signs of blessing and rejoice in them?

It is these questions that are the focus of this chapter. In Part
Two of this book we are looking at theological issues around
living more simply, and in particular thinking through some of
the tensions that need to be lived in and the polarities that need
to be avoided. In the last chapter we looked at the danger that
simple living can bring of retreating into an oppositional
enclave that works with too rigid an 'us and them' approach.
We then also looked at the other, separate, danger of embracing simple living out of a therapeutic understanding of
Christianity, that sees the benefits of simple living in purely
selfish terms, as allowing us to build a more fulfilling life for
ourselves.

However, it is not enough to leave the discussion there and so
we continue it into this chapter. While it is inadequate to base
our desire to live more simply on selfish grounds alone (as will

become clear in chapter 6), it is important also that we avoid the other extreme: an approach that is self-abnegating and world-denying. It is this extreme that we will consider briefly in this chapter, leading us then to consider more broadly how we should view money and possessions as followers of Jesus.

Asceticism

We have seen already that there is a fresh interest in monasticism and in what its traditions can teach us. Its ancient practices can help anchor us when we feel out of our depth in the pressures and demands of our society, and we can draw on its emphasis on retreat and withdrawal to fuel the decisions we make in our own lives to breathe in and retreat away from the negative aspects of consumer culture. However, we have also seen that while there are aspects of it we would want to embrace, for those of us seeking to live well in consumer society in contexts that involve dependent families, mortgages, jobs and so on, it has its limitations too. In this section I want to look at the deep tradition of asceticism and consider whether it might have anything to offer us.

Asceticism comes from the Greek *askesis*, which means 'exercise', 'training' or 'practice', undertaken with a particular goal in mind. Its precise definition beyond that is controversial and it is one of those terms that is notoriously hard to pin down, particularly because it is given different nuances in different religions and spiritualities. However, it is generally taken as referring to the abstinence from something that is needed for physical survival in order to bring a person closer to the divine.

Within Christianity, it has come to be associated with the Desert Mothers and Fathers. They lived a very particular way of life that was focused on renouncing the world and its 'temptations of the flesh' in order to focus on their relationship with God. Anthony (c. 251–356) is one of the most well known of the Desert Fathers, and the account of his life by Athanasius gives lurid details of the demons who came to tempt him and of the deprivations he went through in order to fend them off. He finished his days by the Nile, enclosed in an old fort, where people passed him food and water through a gap in the walls.

The Stylites made up probably the most extreme form of ascetics in the desert. They were solitary monks who spent their life living on the tops of pillars (from the Greek *stylos*, 'pillar'), the most famous of whom was Simeon Stylite (c. 390–459). He lived on top of a pillar fifteen metres high, exposed to the elements at all times, attached to a pole to stop him falling off when asleep!

During the medieval period, these – and less extreme – practices developed into a more formal theology that used the metaphors of steps on a ladder or stages in a journey to document the path that a person took towards God. There were seen to be three stages in the quest for perfection: purgation, illumination and union with God. Ascetic practices were seen as being particularly important for the first stage of purgation (i.e. the purification of the soul).[2]

The history of Christian asceticism has tended to be rooted in a theology that comes from a Platonic, dualistic understanding which separated body from soul and saw the body as that which got in the way of the soul's progression towards the divine, and hence as something to be abandoned.

This way of thinking is reflected in the consultation on monastic spirituality that came out of the World Council of Churches, the largest global ecumenical grouping of churches, founded in 1948. The report describes the monastic life as a life of conversion, but characterises this conversion as involving 'both asceticism, in which [the monks] leave behind the flesh, which is subject to the powers of evil in this passing world . . . and also a movement of their whole being towards Him who invites us into His Kingdom. Monastic vows evidence this dual process of leaving behind the world and responding to the divine invitation.'[3] Asceticism here is explicitly seen as being about a rejection of the world and the body (the flesh), both of which are seen as being evil. This is, indeed, the opposite of the therapeutic Christianity we saw in the previous chapter, which focused so much on seeing God meet one's current needs, including emotional and physical healing. It also stands in sharp contrast to a theology that affirms the goodness of the created order, including the goodness of the bodies that God has made such an integral part of who we are as human beings.

It is because of asceticism's association with extreme practices and with such a dualistic theology that the New Testament theologian John Ziesler makes the case that, despite its practise by Christians through the centuries, it is not actually in line with biblical theology.[4]

He distinguishes asceticism from renunciation *per se*. In his discussion of the three 'classic' renunciations – sex, property and food – he states that such renunciations may happen for a number of different reasons (such as choosing a poorly paid job out of a sense of calling, or forgoing a meal as an act of solidarity with others). Asceticism, however, he sees as being purely that renunciation that is undertaken 'due to a concern about one's relation with God'. The New Testament scholar Mary Ann Tolbert describes this as 'self-inflicted discipline for the betterment of the soul'.[5] Ziesler then states that there are two primary motivations for asceticism, the first arising from the dualistic worldview just mentioned, which believes that 'the body and all physical things are in themselves evil, imprisoning, and obnoxious', and the second coming from Roman Catholic ascetic theology, which sees renunciation as an essential discipline in the search for union with God.[6] Ziesler's view is that neither has a basis in biblical theology and so he would see asceticism as an unhelpful concept for the Christian.

However, it might be that we do not need to restrict asceticism in this way. Kallistos Ware, the Eastern Orthodox bishop and theologian, advocates a broader understanding. He sees asceticism as that which 'leads us to self-mastery and enables us to fulfil the purpose that we have set for ourselves, whatever that may be. A certain measure of ascetic self-denial is thus a necessary element in all that we undertake, whether in athletics or in politics, in scholarly research or in prayer.'[7] Asceticism, on this understanding, does not need to be based on a worldview that sees the body as evil and needing to be conquered or escaped, but rather on a recognition that discipline and commitment are always needed if we want to reach goals that we set for ourselves. This can emerge from an understanding of the world and of human beings as both created good, and so not to be rejected entirely, but also as bearing the marks of sin, which is why such discipline and commitment are so often needed in order to reach our aspirations.

One interesting way of reading the development of asceticism within the Christian tradition is from a sociological angle, which considers how the development of ascetic practices functions within networks of human relationships. Vincent Wimbush is one of the key academic writers in this area, and in his analysis of asceticism in the Graeco-Roman period he comments that 'ascetic behavior represents a range of responses to social, political, and physical worlds often perceived as oppressive or unfriendly, or as stumbling blocks to the pursuit of heroic personal or communal goals, life styles, and commitments'.[8] The Greek Orthodox spiritual director and academic Richard Valantasis says something very similar. Thinking in terms of social scientific theories of power, he defines asceticism as 'performances within a dominant social environment intended to inaugurate a new subjectivity, different social relations, and an alternative symbolic universe'.[9]

In other words, ascetic practices can be a means of a person responding to a social life context that they find to be hostile and alienating and where they feel they have little power. Such practices can be a means of attempting to bring about an alternative model for life.

I believe both the broader definition of asceticism that Ware provides and this social scientific approach are helpful in looking at where and how we can appropriate asceticism into our own lives. For many of us, the desire to live more simply involves a form of renunciation: we want to get rid of any 'stuff' that impedes our communion with God and his human and non-human creation. As with Ware's assertion, we do this in order to achieve a larger purpose. But there is also something in recognising the subversive, socially resistant nature of asceticism as we reflect back on chapter 2 on consumerism and see simple living as a key part of how we endeavour to withstand the dominance of consumer culture. Ascetic behaviour can be a way of maintaining some sense of control in a society that appears to have let its consumer habits run out of control. In this way, Mary Ann Tolbert might be right to see the contemporary, widening use of the term 'asceticism' to describe such practices as reducing the hours spent watching television as 'a metaphorical use of asceticism that draws the power it has from the concrete, historical phenomenon of ascetic practice'.[10]

Reflecting on the place of asceticism in the Christian life thus takes us to the heart of the issues as we think through the importance of avoiding an approach to simple living and our consumer culture that is rooted in a rejection of this world and a denial of the needs of our bodies. As we consider the chapters on globalisation and consumerism and the immense problems we face – the tragic injustices, the poverty, the inequality, the desecration of the natural world – we know that we must respond with our lives. Living simply is about more than getting rid of a bit of clutter so we can feel better about ourselves (therapeutic Christianity): it is about taking seriously the problems of our world and responding in like manner. If we are to do this in any meaningful sense, it will inevitably involve a certain level of hardship and deprivation in comparison to how so many of us currently live. We will have to make hard choices: choosing to do things that we might find uncomfortable or inconvenient, or choosing *not* to do (or have) things that we would actually really like. Material sacrifice will become a part of our lives, if it is not so already.

And yet we must be careful to recognise that such choices come not from a view that sees material goods as negative in and of themselves. As we saw in the Introduction, we believe in a God who created material things *good*. And our choices should not lead us to a life that is destructive of our bodies, again because we believe that God has created our bodies and breathed his life into them (it is interesting in this regard to reflect on Paul's words to the Colossian Christians in 2:23 that they should not go along with practices that lead to 'self-abasement and severe treatment of the body', NASB). Rather, such choices come from a desire not to be controlled by the things around us but instead to live in a way that responds to the many injustices of our world and seeks actively to restore right relationships.

So then, in our Christian living we should endeavour to live out an approach that does not sink into a self-indulgent, therapeutic faith but at the same time does not then react and go to the opposite extreme of negative self-denial. A crucial component of this whole discussion is the place of money and possessions in the Christian life. It is to this that we now turn for the rest of the chapter, focusing first on what the Bible has to say on this matter. We will then see the different attitudes to money and material goods exhibited by the Christians of the first period of the Church (i.e. the pre-Constantinian era), and then by two of the key influencers within the monastic movement, St Benedict and St Francis.

The M-word

It might seem odd to start our consideration of the Bible's view on money and possessions with a passage that mentions neither, but, as with the Introduction so here too, our starting point is with God's creation of the world in Genesis 1 – a world that he pronounces *very good*. It is so important that we start here. I am constantly in conversations and meetings that remind me how much we are inheritors of a tradition that has viewed the material world in a negative way. We must always remember that we worship not only the God who is Saviour, but also the God who is Creator, who has created a material world that contains God's life-breath. Human beings were put in the world with the serious role of taking care of the rest of what God had made, but this was a blessed role: the first garden was a fertile and abundant place that would have been wonderful to live in. The bottom line, therefore, is that material things are good, and we can use them and enjoy them.

There is also an assumption that part of the using and enjoying is developing. Tilling and taking care of the garden (Gen. 2:15) implies change and, in some sense, improvement. No garden is ever static and a good gardener does far more than simply maintain what is already there, however beautiful it might be. We have been created to image God and reflect him, and I believe that God created us with all sorts of ingenuity, cleverness and resourcefulness so that we would be equipped to do the job he gave us to do. God has created a bountiful world and we may use that world not simply to subsist but to live bountiful lives, in peaceful relationship with others (as Deut. 8:18 reminds us, God has given us the ability to produce wealth[11]). Although not the main concern of our thoughts here, it is worth pointing out that this approach leads also to a high view of work.

So we start with a positive appreciation of this world and of our ability to live in it in such a way that benefits us and is enjoyable. This is continued into the story of the Israelite people as a nation. Financial prosperity for Abraham, and then for the people with whom he comes into contact, are key signs of God's blessing and favour on him. The land that God gives to Israel is an abundant land, flowing with milk and honey, and it is expected that they will live in it bounteously and produce wealth. This is emphasised at the end of the Old Testament too, in the pictures the prophets paint of a life lived well, within the context of a nation blessed by God. Micah gives the wonderful hope of a time when everyone will be able to sit under their own vine and their own fig tree. It is a picture of contentment, of security, of having plenty (I am writing this just as my own vine is coming into fruit and, from my table, I can see that the vine is laden).

However, one cannot read the Old Testament without noting its highly ambivalent attitude towards wealth and, indeed, the history of Israel shows the great tendency of money to corrupt and lead to evil. Joseph's prosperity, for example, given to him that he might be the means by whom God's promises to Abraham would be continued, ended with him putting the people of Egypt into slavery (Gen. 47:20–21), and both David and Solomon misused their wealth in all sorts of unsavoury ways. Moreover, the fact that there were certain individuals in the story of the Israelite nation whom God blessed financially does not mean that we should expect God to do the same for all Christians, and there is nothing in the New Testament that would lead us to expect that.

While the land that God provides for his people is fertile and lush and contains all they need, God also makes it very clear that it will only remain so if they follow his laws and live righteously. In particular, that righteousness is to be demonstrated through how they treat each other and how they treat the land itself. The laws of the Sabbath and the Jubilee in Leviticus 25 are particularly interesting. One day a week is to be a day of rest, when no work is done. For one year out of every seven the land is to lie fallow and be allowed to rest, along with domestic animals. The people will have to trust that the land will produce enough of its own accord to meet their needs. Then the fiftieth year (the year after seven lots of seven years) is to be a Jubilee year, when all debts are cancelled, slaves are set free and land returned to its original owners.

This is radical stuff! I was recently part of a small gathering of Christian landowners who were meeting to look at how they might manage their land (some of them owning thousands of acres) along Christian principles. We considered the Jubilee and Sabbath laws and talked about what it would actually look like to put these things into practice (and we do not know if Israel ever actually did this themselves; it is more than likely they did not). Lots of weeds and cows with sore udders were some of the things we mentioned!

What these laws did, though, is vitally important: they put work, money and goods firmly in their place, subsumed under the overriding concern of good relationships and appropriate rest, reminding the Israelites that everything they owned was not actually theirs, it belonged to God. It would have led to a fundamental reordering of society every fifty years, as land was returned and families were enabled to start again. Relationships with other people, with the land and with the animals that share that land are more important than building up your own financial security.

If Abraham's financial prosperity was seen as a blessing from God at the start of the story of the Israelite people, by the time we reach the prophets at the end of the Old Testament we find a very different story, and wealth is roundly denounced. Why? For two key reasons. First, because it is seen as having come at the expense of other people who have thereby been left in a poorer state, and therefore it has meant that the practice of justice, love and compassion has been neglected. Second, because it has led those who are wealthy to forget about God, to be deaf to his voice and to put their trust instead in their riches.

The prophets have *very* strong words to say against those who are living lives of luxury and not only ignoring the plight of others, but actually profiting from them through dishonest trading standards. They were, of course, speaking explicitly into the problem of poverty within the nation of Israel, rather than taking a more global perspective.[12] Nonetheless, certainly I cannot read those words without recognising that my life is luxurious in comparison to so many others around the world, that I consume far more than my fair share of the world's resources, and that I am enabled to live how I do because of an unjust economic system.

When we leave the Old Testament and move into the Gospels, we will be disappointed if we hope to find Jesus primarily concerned with issues of individual piety. The fact that giving is as important to him as praying and fasting, and that he talks more about money than about anything else apart from the kingdom of God, should make us sit up and take note of how crucial this issue was to him.

Commentators differ over the socio-economic and political context into which Jesus was speaking. There is disagreement

over how economically prosperous Galilee itself was, and opinions based on archaeological research vary from seeing Galilee
as a place of poverty to viewing it as a place of egalitarianism
and prosperity due to manufacturing and trade.[13] Whatever the
exact situation, there is no doubt that the nation of Israel as a
whole was under foreign occupation and was suffering as a
result. The Romans were their oppressors and they ruled them
tightly, with a heavy taxation system (think how hated the tax
collectors were in the Gospel stories). Although there were
winners in this situation (i.e. those who collaborated with the
Romans), there were many more losers, and the Gospel narratives portray a context where many people were struggling to
meet their daily needs.

Jesus, therefore, has some very robust words to say about
money and about its dangers.[14] He describes riches as being a
strangler and a worry. Money can blind us from the eternal
realities of life, and – strongest of all – money can actually be a
curse for us.[15] Reflecting the Old Testament prophets' condemnation of those whose wealth both came from and led to injustice, and those whose wealth led them to forsake their God,
Jesus speaks harshly against those who are rich in this life.
Bearing these things in mind, it is no surprise that Jesus tells
his disciples that it is very hard for a rich person to enter the
kingdom of heaven.

However, it is not impossible and, as Jesus says, 'with God
all things are possible'. When the rich young man comes to ask
him what he has to do to inherit eternal life, Jesus replies that
he needs to sell all his possessions and give the money to the
poor. But it seems as if this is not an instruction that all his
disciples are to follow. We know that there were wealthy

women who supported his ministry, and Joseph of Arimathea had evidently not sold all his possessions, else he could not have offered his tomb for Jesus' body to be laid in.

One rich person whose life was turned upside down by an encounter with Jesus was Zacchaeus.[16] He was a person, we assume, who put his trust and value in his wealth. Martin Luther once said, 'Every person needs two conversions: one of the heart and one of the wallet', and in Zacchaeus we see a person demonstrating these two conversions working together. Zacchaeus's money was earned at the expense of the people in Jericho and he knew that the only appropriate response on meeting Jesus was to give back all the money he had wrongfully taken – four times over! As he gave away half of his possessions to the poor and then paid people back four times, we can only guess at the financial effects that had on him. It is unlikely he would have been rich after that. Here was no giving away of his surplus in order to feel better: this was a radical outworking of the Jubilee principle.

Jesus' most well-known saying, of course, is that one cannot serve both God and Mammon (Money). This reflects the first commandment in Exodus 20 that the people of Israel were to have no other God except Yahweh. We saw in the Introduction that this was fundamentally an issue of trust and security: would the Israelites trust Yahweh to look after them or would they look elsewhere? And Jesus raises this question here too: in what or whom will we put our trust? Will money be our god – that which we spend our lives searching after – or will God be the one we live our lives for?

In this passage in Matthew 6, Jesus then gives us the more positive side to his negative words about money. The reason we should not be preoccupied with money is because we should instead be preoccupied with seeking the kingdom of God. Jesus challenges head on our obsession with material things (our 'treasures', our clothes, our food), and instead challenges us to put the kingdom of God first, and trust God to provide us with all we need as we do so.

For Jesus, this attitude is a necessary part of being his follower. For the first disciples, following him meant leaving everything behind – family, business, possessions – and living a life of sacrifice. Jesus makes it clear that a person should count the cost and consider carefully whether they are really able to make such a choice, before saying 'yes' to following him. Jesus' disciples were not drawn from the bottom rungs of society: Matthew was a tax collector; James and John had a successful fishing business; Peter's house in Capernaum seems to have been large enough to act as a base for Jesus and the twelve. So giving everything up in order to follow him was a genuine choice. But the rewards of doing this are great: receiving a hundredfold what has been given up; gaining the kingdom; finding their lives; finding a new family.[17]

One particular incident in Jesus' life that is worth mentioning here is his observation of the widow who gave her two very small copper coins. In contrast to all the wealthy people who were also putting their gifts into the temple treasury, Jesus declares that 'this poor widow has put in more than all the others' (Luke 21:3). We see here how different the values of the kingdom are from the values of society. In our world (as was no doubt the case then too), it is size and numbers that count; we are praised for the amount we give. In Jesus' eyes, what matters is how much we have left afterwards and the sacrifice we have been prepared to make.

Jesus was speaking into a situation in which he foresaw massive social upheaval and dislocation. He knew that following him would take disciples along a collision course with the authorities and that losing family and possessions – and lives – was a probable outcome. And so in this sort of context, a radical attitude to money was needed.

How does that translate into the period immediately after Jesus? As we move into the time of the early Church, we meet a mixed context of itinerant missionaries spending and giving their lives for the gospel; a rapidly expanding movement; persecution and hostility from the religious and political leaders; people from all sectors of society believing in Jesus and getting baptised; and some sort of settled Christian faith beginning to emerge as fledgling churches took their first steps in this new faith, generally based around people's homes.

The first indications we are given of how the early Church took on Jesus' economic ethic are the pictures drawn in the early chapters of Acts. The influential New Testament scholar Martin Hengel has described the life of the very first Christian communities as being a sort of 'love communism'.[18] It seems that what is envisaged here is not communal living with the abolition of private property (clearly, people throughout the early years of the Church owned their own houses, fields and businesses), but a community that put other people's needs before their own, and where members were prepared to give of their own possessions and money in order to see those needs being met. It is a truly remarkable picture.

In the letters of Paul, we see the early Church reaching increasingly into the middle and upper echelons of society, as well as evidently attracting many who had little money. This mixed economy in the Church brought with it distinct problems and, particularly in his letters to the Corinthian church, we see Paul speaking very strongly into this scene. His words about how to conduct the Lord's Supper reflect a situation where those who were wealthy were able to eat their fill of the meal (and remember it would have been a full meal, not a wafer or piece of bread and sip of wine), leaving little left for those who arrived later because they were working, and who therefore went hungry. Paul castigates those who, in this way, were 'humiliating those who have nothing' (1 Cor. 11:22).

But he has more positive words to say to the Corinthians when he encourages them to be generous and faithful in their giving. It is interesting that his words to them in 1 Corinthians 16 are the most specific advice given on this subject in the New Testament letters. It would appear that the Jewish practice of tithing was not continued. (Of course, the 10 per cent figure often quoted was actually the very minimum and there were multiple tithes, bringing the percentage nearer to 23 per cent.) Instead, Paul advocates that people should give regularly (on the first day of each week) and should give according to their means. In 2 Corinthians he adds the important principle of generosity. These are very helpful principles still for us today, and I will unpack them further in Part Three.

It is in Paul's words to Timothy that we have perhaps the most misquoted sentence in the Bible: 'the *love of* money is *a* root of all kinds of evil' (1 Tim. 6:10, italics mine). Timothy is clearly in a church context where quite a few members are rich and Paul is concerned that the evident wealth does not turn Timothy's head. Paul here speaks of the need for contentment, because trying to get rich can lead to many traps (Heb. 13:5 says similarly, 'Keep your lives free from the love of money and be content with what you have'). He then encourages those who *are* rich to make sure they keep their trust in God and are generous with what they have. It is notable that there is nothing in Paul to suggest that believers should give all their money away; rather money should not be the focus ('I have learned the secret of being content in any and every situation, whether well fed or hungry, whether living in plenty or in want', Phil. 4:12).

When we look at what James has to say about money, we get the impression that he is writing to churches that are seriously messed up! They are taking each other to court; talking lots but doing little; showing favouritism to those with money; gossiping and cursing; fighting and quarrelling; and living in luxury and self-indulgence while others live in poverty. It is quite some list. And so James has harsh words to say in this context, pushing his hearers to live lives that are full of wisdom and good deeds. There is no positive view of money given in the letter from James.

The New Testament after the time of Jesus thus presents us with a picture of churches with people from all sorts of economic backgrounds. No doubt there were many who were poor, but there were also others who were business people, some who owned large houses, some who were evidently very rich. While there is a certain acceptance of the presence of wealthy Christians, the early Church leaders we see in the New Testament have nothing positive to say about having money. The constant theme is to beware favouritism, beware division, beware putting your trust in money, and be generous with what you have.

Moving beyond the immediate context of the New Testament Church, what is most striking is the outstanding care and compassion undertaken by the Church in the first centuries of Christianity. Indeed, it is so striking that both Christians and pagans wrote of this particular feature of the early Church, with even the pagan Emperor Julian acknowledging towards the end of this period that 'the impious Galileans support not merely their own poor, but ours as well'. Can't you just hear how grumpy he is when he says this? The early Christian philosopher and apologist Justin, writing towards the beginning of the second century, provided this moving description of a local Christian assembly:

> On the day which is called the day of the sun [they meet] to pray and read and to celebrate the Eucharist, at the conclusion of which the deacons take the Eucharistic elements to those unable to be present, presumably through reasons of sickness or imprisonment, whilst the rest of the congregation . . . give what they will, each after his choice. What is collected is deposited with the president, who gives aid to the orphans and widows and such as are in want by reason of sickness or other cause, and to those also that are in prison, and to strangers from abroad; in fact to all that are in need, he is a protector.[19]

I find it fascinating that this description of an early Church service or meeting has these basic elements at the heart of what they do: praying, reading (presumably the Bible or some sort of apostolic instruction), celebrating the Eucharist together and sharing their money. What a beautifully simple picture and a demonstration, again, of how central to the Christian faith is the principle of sharing our money with people in need.

Overall, the impression is gained of a Church very involved in caring for the extensive needs of those around it, both within and without its boundaries. However, as the Church increasingly reached into the upper echelons of Greek society, the impression is also given of a struggle to determine the place of riches within the Christian life. On the one hand, there was the acknowledgement, even from as strident a person as Tertullian, one of the foremost early Christian theologians, that God can 'grant riches', because 'with them many works of righteousness and philanthropy can be achieved'.[20] Indeed, the amount of care provided by the Church presupposes a certain amount of disposable private property.

On the other hand, there was the recognition that wealth brings many dangers and can blind one to the needs of the poor rather than being a means of alleviation. The Archbishop of Constantinople and leading Church Father John Chrysostom is famous for preaching against the 'greed and the arrogance of the rich', but he was far from being a lone voice in the early centuries of the Church.[21] The ubiquity of this theme through such well-known writings as the Didache, the Shepherd of Hermas, Clement of Alexandria and the Cappadocian Fathers testifies to the presence of wealthy Christians who were precisely *not* living according to the ideal set out in Acts 2 and 4; something which was distinctly problematic to the early Church.

Among the many different writings on the question of riches throughout the period of the early Church, two themes clearly emerge, both of which are important for what we are thinking about here. The first is that material goods and riches are not evil in themselves. This theological position was crucial to the combating of Gnosticism, illustrated in Clement of Alexandria's writing on wealth. A strong doctrine of creation mitigated against the world-denial of the philosophical ascetics and meant that physical, created things were viewed as good and to be valued, not discarded.

Writing about the 'rich young ruler' in Matthew 19:16–30, Clement of Alexandria (a key theologian who died in AD 215) is at pains to distance himself from such asceticism, asserting that Jesus 'does not, as some conceive off-hand, bid him throw away the substance he possessed, and abandon his property; but bids him banish from his soul his notion about wealth, his excitement and morbid feeling about it, the anxieties, which are the thorns of existence, which choke the seed of life'.[22] This does not mean, though, that wealth itself is unimportant; rather, it is to be seen as a tool which is 'itself destitute of blame . . . Are you able to make right use of it? It is subservient to righteousness. Does one make wrong use of it? It is, on the other hand, a minister of wrong.'[23]

Thus the second theme is that, while wealth and material goods are not in themselves evil, the imperative is that they are only given for the sake of others: 'Owners of property or wealth should use for themselves only enough to meet their needs. What surpasses the measure of sufficiency is superfluous and should be shared with others whose primary needs are not being met.'[24]

In his evaluation of the Christian communities of the second and third centuries, Hengel makes the perceptive assessment that 'possessions acquired a contradictory aspect. They were regarded simultaneously as a dangerous threat and a supreme obligation.'[25] Despite its attraction, the 'love communism' of the very earliest days was not something that was able to be continued in the regular life of the Church.[26] At the same time, Christianity's rootedness in the Jewish doctrine of creation and the necessity of counteracting the dualism of the Gnostic threat ensured that material goods and private property earned a legitimate – if uneasy – place. Compromise, therefore, was sought in an understanding of 'proper usage': a concept to which we shall return in our consideration of Aquinas.

Before we turn to our next chapter and Aquinas, let us bring our discussion full circle and return to the monastic tradition, out of which asceticism has developed. The contradictory aspect of money that Hengel identifies is something I believe to be a constant struggle for the person wanting to live well as a follower of Jesus, whatever century they might be living in. We have seen this in the early Church and we can see it too in the different understandings of material goods brought into operation by St Benedict and St Francis, two of the most influential figures within monasticism.

St Benedict

Although the Desert Fathers and Augustine had ensured that monasticism was already well established by the time of Benedict, it is his Rule – and the Order that arose from it – that is widely regarded as the most influential in the Western tradition. Two features are of note for what we are thinking about in this chapter. The first is that one of Benedict's aims was to bring moderation into the monastic way of life that had been founded on the extreme rigorisms of the Desert Fathers. As he said, his aim was to 'establish a school for the Lord's service' and to provide guidance that was not 'harsh or burdensome'.[27] His was not the way of harsh austerities and bodily deprivations: instead he prescribed what he saw as being sufficient clothing, food and sleep for the monks. Benedict's definition of 'sufficient' appears severe in a contemporary context (such as only having two tunics), but the likelihood is that it would have resulted in conditions that were not much harder than the daily experience of many entering his communities.[28] This sense of moderation is encapsulated by Dom Butler, who describes Benedictine virtue as 'that keeping of the happy mean between rigorism and laxity'.[29]

At the same time, however, Benedict's views on private property were uncompromising: 'Those in monastic vows should not claim any property as their own exclusive possession – absolutely nothing at all, not even books and writing materials. After all they cannot count even their bodies and their wills as their own, consecrated, as they are, to the Lord.'[30] Benedict based his commands on his particular understanding of the 'love communism' of the early Church in Acts that we saw earlier, seeing the phrase 'and they held all things in common' as teaching against personal ownership. Instead, ownership resided in the monastic community, which would thereby supply 'everything they need in their lives'.[31]

The difference between this and the Franciscan view of poverty is helpfully illuminated by Butler's reminiscence of the late Bishop Augustine O'Neill's insight into Benedictine poverty. He talks of how the different phases of Christ's life lead to different kinds of poverty:

> There was the utter destitution of Calvary; there was the poverty almost as great of Bethlehem; there was the poverty of the public life, when at times He had not where to lay His head; and there was also the poverty of Nazareth. Calvary is the type of Franciscan poverty; but Nazareth is the type of Benedictine poverty. It was not the poverty of beggary, but the poverty that obtains in the household of a carpenter or other skilled artisan. It is simplicity and frugality, rather than want.[32]

St Francis

St Francis had a very different approach to money and possessions. Where the early Church, as we have seen, considered it appropriate to have personal property, so long as it was used to meet the needs of others, and Benedict considered communal property appropriate, but not private property, Francis believed that there should be no ownership whatsoever: all ownership was wrong, whether private or communal. Theologically, he based his views on the kenotic poverty of Christ expressed in, for example, Philippians 2:5–11 and 2 Corinthians 8:9. Christ's homeless poverty, Francis believed, was an example that should be followed literally, as were Jesus' instructions to his disciples to take nothing with them when they went out to preach.[33]

Francis came from a very wealthy, privileged background and so he rejected not only the familial wealth of his upbringing but also the traditional monastic life in order to renounce material goods altogether and identify his life (and therefore the lives of his followers) with the kenotic Christ. It is important to note, however, that these actions were not so much seen as arising from a world-denying asceticism as from the desire – once again following Christ's example – to see the salvation of others, particularly the economically marginalised.[34] Contrary to the early Church – and of course living in a very different time; one that was witnessing the rise of the money economy[35] – Francis saw wealth and money as nothing but a hindrance to that goal.

In looking at the early Church and at Francis and Benedict, we see three different attempts to live out an understanding of the Bible's view on money and possessions, and what becomes evident is that this issue has been wrestled with by the Church since its earliest days. The challenge for us is to steer away from a world-denying anti-materialism, while at the same time avoiding the other extreme of embracing material goods uncritically. The examples we have considered provide us with instances of the paths that others have chosen to take.[36]

Like St Francis, we all seek to locate our views in some way or another in the life of Jesus, although we might come to different understandings as to how far Jesus' lifestyle and words are to be followed literally today. Like St Benedict, we have identified that there is a need to find a middle way between 'rigorism and laxity', although most of us reading this will have no qualms about private property. And, like the early Church, we would want to emphasise the importance of using material goods well, for the benefit of others (and we would want to extend our understanding of the other to include the wider creation).

Conclusion

So what sort of a conclusion can we reach as we think about this crucial topic of a Christian attitude to money and material goods? The Bible overall has a huge amount to say on this issue and there is more depth into which we could have delved, had space allowed.[37] And over the course of its writings the Bible covers a wide variety of different contexts, all of which need to be borne in mind before we attempt to provide neat formulas.

I find Andrew Perriman's assessment very helpful, in his report for the Evangelical Alliance on the Word of Faith and Prosperity movements.[38] He suggests that we can see two approaches to wealth coming through from the biblical material, which correspond to two modes of discipleship.

On the one hand is what he calls 'an unsettled discipleship of the road'. This is the sort of discipleship shaped by Jesus' ministry and the missionary work of the early Church. It 'requires the abandonment of previous securities, a radical trust in God to provide for material needs'.[39] It is a form of discipleship that is often set in a context of persecution, suffering and instability. In that sort of a context, 'a theology of material prosperity appears irrelevant; wealth is likely to be a hindrance or distraction'.[40]

On the other hand is what Perriman calls 'a settled discipleship of home and workplace'. This is the sort of discipleship more appropriate to a 'community with more or less reliable means of income and potentially a high standard of living', a setting in which the threat of persecution is not so prevalent.[41] In this sort of a context, the emphasis will be more on recognising the blessings of material goods and the imperative to use them to bless others: working to alleviate poverty and oppression and seeing financial prosperity 'less as a product of a worldly economic system or a measure of personal success and more as a gift of grace, given for enjoyment and well-being of the people'.[42]

What I find helpful with these models is that they give full weight to the question of context. I would argue against attempting to formulate one tightly drawn 'theology of money'. Instead I would argue that different approaches are appropriate for different callings and life situations. We may well find ourselves oscillating between the two models as we go through life and obey the leadings of God. That has certainly been my experience. By taking this approach we can avoid the guilt that can so easily come on us when we think about these questions.

What Perriman does not draw out, and what I would want to highlight, is that these two models should be brought into continual interaction with each other, so that when we find ourselves living more in one model, we should interrogate ourselves with the other. For those of us living the unsettled discipleship of the road, we might want to ask ourselves whether the calling God has placed on us and the life we have chosen to live has led us to take too negative a view of material goods. Has our abandonment of luxury for the sake of the gospel been too harsh? Has it led us to look judgementally at those who are not living in the same way as we are? Are we willing to receive abundance from God – in whatever way that might come – should he choose to give it to us? Can we acknowledge and thank God for those who are blessed financially and are using that to give to others? Are there family responsibilities we have neglected for which we need to take more responsibility?

And for those of us living the settled discipleship of the home, we might want to ask ourselves whether the life we are living has led us to embrace material comforts too readily. Are we using this model as an excuse to live with more luxury than is appropriate? Are there areas of our life that have become too settled, where God is prompting us to step out and take some risks? Are we truly using our money to bless others as fully as we can, or are we just doing that to a certain extent and mostly using it to bless ourselves? As we seek to make our future secure, are we storing up more money in our pensions and savings than we should be?

Bringing these two models into conversation with each other, wherever we might find ourselves on the spectrum between the two, can be a very useful way of helping us chart the choppy waters of living well in this crucial area of money and possessions.

Recognising that there might not be one 'theology of money' given in the Bible does not, however, mean that anything goes. To conclude this chapter, let us outline the clear principles that have emerged from our discussion, that are helpful always to bear in mind.

1. Material goods (and hence money) are not evil in and of themselves. They are part of a good creation coming from a good Creator.
2. God's intention is for good, for all his creation. His desire is for blessing, abundance and *shalom*.
3. If we do receive increased finances and material goods, they should be received humbly and as a sign of God's generosity

(even in giving us the talent or the social placing to earn that money in the first place), not of our own success. Therefore they should not lead to boasting or self-congratulation, or lessen the need to trust him.

4. Money and possessions can all too easily distract us from following and worshipping God as fully as we should, and we should always ask ourselves what or who it is that we are pursuing. Contentment is thus an important characteristic to develop.

5. While money and possessions are good, they should never be gained at the expense of other people or the wider creation. Given our current economic system, this, perhaps, is the most difficult principle to wrestle with.

6. If we are ever blessed, it is always so that we might also share that blessing with others and help those in need, including the non-human parts of creation. Generosity is a key principle for us to be living out.

Chapter 6

Temperance, Justice and Human Flourishing

A deeper look with Thomas Aquinas

It is my belief that living well as Christians in our contemporary culture is about maintaining a double movement – a rhythm – of engagement and retreat, embrace and rejection, breathing out and breathing in. As we do so we hold a number of key tensions together and seek to maintain a middle way between them all: between a wholesale immersion in consumer culture and an unrelenting abandonment; between the extremes of a therapeutic narcissism and sacrificial self-abnegation; and between a world-denying asceticism and an unqualified embrace of material goods.

In this chapter we will explore a theological framework that can help us make sense of these things and understand more fully what we have been talking about so far. There are different places we might have gone for this, but in my thinking around these issues I have found myself drawn to Aristotle and Thomas Aquinas and the notion of the 'golden mean', or *via media*, as a helpful way of giving a deeper voice to our attempts to steer a pathway through the tensions articulated previously.

What becomes clear very quickly, though, is that the concept of the *via media* only makes sense within a broader set of questions that Aristotle and then (more fully) Aquinas are seeking to answer. These questions focus on notions of the good life and the life of virtue – notions that reflect a large part of what we have already been discussing.

In essence, this chapter explores what I call a justice-orientated eudaimonist ethic. It will become clear what this is as the chapter unfolds. We will chart a path through Aristotle and his understanding of 'the good' and of *eudaimonia* ('happiness'), and then devote the rest of our time to how Aquinas takes on and develops this understanding from his more specifically Christian perspective. This will take us into Aquinas's thinking on the virtues, and specifically his understanding of how the virtues of temperance and justice relate together. We will also see something of his view on money and possessions, which will help our continued thinking on this topic.

What we will look at is hugely relevant and helpful for us as we try to live faithfully with Jesus hundreds of years after Aquinas did his thinking. There are riches here to be drawn on, but they take some committed excavating to reach, so, as I said earlier, if this chapter is too much then you are welcome to skip it and move on to Part Three, where we see the practical outworkings of these strands of thought.

Aristotle and the golden mean

The Greek philosopher Aristotle, born in 385 BC, is one of the giants of the intellectual world, having studied under Plato, who in turn was a student of Socrates. Aristotle was the tutor of Alexander the Great. His writing and thinking covered a vast range of areas across philosophy, science and mathematics, and even theatre and dance. His writings were prolific and we know from others that they were very much admired and that he had a vivid rhetorical style, but sadly these are lost to us and what we have left are his lecture notes (although these are detailed and thorough and not what we might think of as lecture notes today).

One set of lecture notes was on ethics and became the treatise known as *Nicomachean Ethics*. Originally these were written on ten scrolls and they were then edited into their final form, which consists of ten books (edited probably by his son, Nicomachus, although the treatise may simply have been dedicated to him; we cannot know for sure). Although there is another treatise called *Eudemian Ethics*, this is generally thought to represent Aristotle's earlier thinking, and it is in *Nicomachean Ethics* that we have his most mature thinking, which has influenced Western philosophical thought down through the centuries.

Nicomachean Ethics opens with the statement, 'Every sort of expert knowledge and every inquiry, and similarly every action and undertaking, seems to seek some good. Because of that, people are right to affirm that the good is "that which all things seek"' (1094a1–3).[1] Aristotle's view was that every action is undertaken with a particular goal or end in mind – a *telos*. He saw that there are many different ends in life, related to many different activities (I boil a kettle with the goal of making a cup of tea; I switch on my computer with the goal of spending some time writing: making a cup of tea and writing are 'ends'). These ends are what Aristotle calls 'practicable' (1097a24). But all these practicable, 'mini' ends are ultimately working towards one ultimate, overarching end. This end is what Aristotle calls 'the good', and his ethics are based on finding out what that good is in life and then how that good might be pursued. He wanted to find that which is 'complete' and 'worth pursuing for itself' (1097a30–31). In other words, is there one thing for the sake of which all other things are done (1097a19–20)?

The answer Aristotle gave is *eudaimonia*: 'happiness seems most of all to be like this; for this we do always choose because of itself and never because of something else' (1097b1–2). Everything we do is, finally, done because we are working towards the ultimate goal of happiness. It is important to understand this concept of *eudaimonia*. Although most commonly translated 'happiness', this is not entirely satisfactory as it does not quite match our contemporary understanding of happiness and has a fuller sense of well-being, flourishing and completeness of life. Because it is so hard to translate in its fullness (a bit like trying to translate *shalom* adequately), unless using a direct quote, I will maintain the usage of the Greek *eudaimonia* rather than translating it.

Eudaimonia is thus seen by Aristotle as being the 'chief good' and the ultimate end of life. What that means more precisely is to be found in discovering what is 'peculiar to human beings', as opposed to what is shared with all other animals (1098a1). Aristotle identified this as the human capacity for reason, and so 'the function of a human being is activity of soul in accordance with reason' (1098a8–9): our aim in life is to realise our full potential as rational beings, to use reason well. Using reason well in our lives is what will lead to *eudaimonia*.[2]

Aristotle believed that when we undertake an activity, we want to do it at the best level we can, and that is the same with life in general: we want to live it at its best. 'The human good turns out to be activity of soul in accordance with excellence' (1098a16–17). It is important for Aristotle that this activity takes place over a lifetime; a one-off or irregular practice of reasonable excellence will not 'make a man blessed and happy' in the same way that 'a single swallow does not make spring' (1098a18–21). Although important and controversial qualifications are brought in later in Book X, at this foundational stage of *Nicomachean Ethics*, *eudaimonia* is thus defined in very active terms, as 'a sort of living well and doing well' (1098b22). It is knowing what the good life is so that it can be lived better.[3]

The concept of excellence is very important to Aristotle's understanding of the good life, which is to be found not in the pursuit of amusement, wealth or power, but in the pursuit of being the best a human being can be in their capacity as a human being. The Greek for excellence, *arete*, can also be translated as 'virtue' and is where we get our ideas of the virtues from. The virtues allow a human being to reach that purpose (1106a15–17). Aristotle categorises the virtues into two sorts: 'the one intellectual and the other of character, the intellectual sort mostly both comes into existence and increases as a result of teaching . . . whereas excellence of character results from habituation' (1103a15–18). So intellectual virtues are things that can be learned through teaching, and include scientific knowledge, technical skill and what he calls 'practical wisdom'. The moral virtues are things such as courage, temperance, truthfulness, patience, humility and friendliness. The importance of action is again stressed, for it is through a person's actions that dispositions to behave in a certain way, whether good or bad, become settled in that person's life (1103a23–1103b26). Both sets of virtues are needed: the intellectual virtues help one to know what is right and the moral virtues help one to act in the right way.

How then should one act in order to live well? Aristotle shies away from being prescriptive because he recognises that he can only deal with such issues with a 'rough outline' rather than 'with precision' (1104a2–3). This is because people's situations vary: 'things in the sphere of action and things that bring advantage have nothing stable about them . . . for it does not fall either under any expertise or under any set of rules – the agents themselves have to consider the circumstances relating to the occasion' (1104a1–1104a10). What he can offer, though, is his principle of the 'mean' of an action, since 'the sorts of things we are talking about are naturally such as to be destroyed by deficiency and excess' (1104a12–14).

According to Aristotle, a virtuous activity is that which lies in an intermediate position between what he calls 'two bad states, one involving excess, the other involving deficiency' (1107a3–4). So the excess of courage is foolhardiness and its deficiency is cowardice; the excess of humility is self-debasement and its deficiency is pride; the excess of friendliness is a fawning obsequiousness and its deficiency is surliness, and so on. The two virtues that stand apart in the sense of not being a mean are wisdom and love, neither of which have an excess, only a deficiency: foolishness and malevolence respectively.

In talking about the mean, Aristotle is not referring to a mathematical mean.[4] Rather, and using the analogy of diet, Aristotle stresses that the mean is relative '*to us*' (1106b8); in other words, it is 'determined with reference to the particular capacities and limitations of the person undertaking any given action'.[5] Thus there is no tight prescription as to what a virtuous action may look like in any particular situation, and indeed it may well veer more towards one extreme than the other. Aristotle is consequently aware that finding this mean of excellence is difficult to achieve, 'as for example finding the centre of a circle is not a task for anyone, but for the skilled person' (1109a26–27), and he advises that a person try to steer away from the extreme they think is most attractive to them. 'One should sometimes incline towards excess, sometimes towards deficiency; for in this way we shall most easily hit upon what is intermediate, and good practice' (1109b25–27). The virtue of wisdom, Aristotle says, is what finally enables a person to determine the intermediate (1107a2).

For Aristotle, *eudaimonia* is not to be equated with pleasure as such, but with living a life of excellence, i.e. a virtuous life. Nonetheless, *eudaimonia* and pleasure are closely connected. Aristotle states the issue as being 'whether we choose living because we want pleasure or pleasure because we want to be alive' (1175a18–19). As he debates this (and commentators differ as to how satisfactorily he does so[6]), he attempts to hold his ground in the face of two opposing opinions: first, that pleasure is an end in itself (in 1172b9–1173a13 he refutes the hedonism put forward by the mathematician Eudoxus), and second, that all pleasure is wrong (1172b36–1173a14). Aristotle holds pleasure to be good, although he stipulates that such pleasure should derive from worthy activities, rather than from frivolous amusements (1175b24–1176a29).

Overall, however, there is a tension at the heart of Aristotle's ethics over the place that pleasure occupies in his understanding.

This tension is carried into his final conclusion that in the end, and having spent so long on the life of virtue, it is actually a life of philosophic contemplation that is the 'complete happiness' (1178b9), with a life of ethical virtue carrying the status of 'second happiness' (1178a9).[7]

This initial exploration of the notion of *eudaimonia* is helpful in relation to the discussion that has arisen at various points in the book concerning the search for happiness. A key issue for us as we seek to lead lives of Christian excellence today is how to hold together personal well-being and notions of sacrificial living – an issue which is prompted by the problems generated by globalisation and consumerism. With this in mind, we will turn now to Thomas Aquinas, the immensely influential thirteenth-century theologian and philosopher, to see how he might help us with a more properly theological understanding. A brief word of caution needs to be sounded here. Aquinas's theology and works are vast and the aim here is in no way to attempt any sort of overview or comprehensive understanding of his theological schema. Instead, I want to use him as a conversation partner and bring him into dialogue with what we are thinking about in this book, because there are themes within his thought that are useful to us in this regard.

This next section looks at how Aquinas develops Aristotle's understanding of *eudaimonia*, giving it a more explicitly Christian framework. We will see that Aquinas's theological appropriation is helpful for us because of the positive note we have identified in relation to living more simply. As we saw in our earlier research, a life lived in this way is identified as being personally beneficial – a life that brings joy and lightness. This is a good antidote to the more 'doom and gloom' approach that can result from focusing on problems of global injustice and environmental destruction. The concept of *eudaimonia*, with its emphasis on notions of well-being and happiness, keeps us rooted in that affirmative attitude.

At the same time, however, the very idea of *eudaimonia* contains within it the debate that has been coming to the fore through the course of this book: how to hold in tension one's own well-being with that of others. As we have seen, there is a drive within the simplicity movement towards a particular reading on self-realisation. This is not wholly bad and, as discussed in previous chapters, is not to be discarded wholesale. But my contention is that taken by itself it is not ultimately Christian, because the Christian is called to be focused on the other as well as on the self.

Therefore, we will begin with a brief overview of Aquinas's understanding of *eudaimonia* and of the necessities of the virtuous life. We will then draw on his thinking about the virtues – particularly those of temperance and justice and their relationship to each other – to reframe this discussion and help us find a way forward. This will include a brief consideration of Aquinas's position on wealth and possessions, picking up on the discussions of the previous chapter.

Aquinas

Aristotle laid crucial foundations in his thinking about the eudaimonist life. Aquinas began to use this thinking fifteen centuries later, as part of a general rediscovery of Aristotelian thought that had been taking place in the twelfth and thirteenth centuries, when Aristotle's works were translated into Latin and hence became more available. Aquinas came from a very different cultural situation and from a radically different theological background (Aristotle, of course, was pre-Christian), yet he found much in Aristotle that was helpful as he developed his own answers to the question, 'Of what does life consist?'[8]

Aquinas bases his thinking on Aristotle's logic that focuses on people's actions, and he agrees that all actions are aimed at particular ends. In his own commentary on the *Nicomachean Ethics*, for example, he follows Aristotle in stating that there are 'different goods aimed at in the different activities and skills. The good aimed at in medicine is health, the good aimed at in military arts is victory, and in every other art some other good.' All these activities have their own good, 'for the sake of which everything else is done'. It is these goods that are properly called 'ends'. But, again following Aristotle, he states that there must be one end to which all things are directed: 'for there must be one last end of the human being as a human being, because there is only one human nature'.[9] This 'last end' is identified by Aquinas as 'human good, or well-being'. This good is the most complete good: 'that which is so desired for its own sake, that it is never desired for the sake of anything else'. Although Aquinas mentions the seeking after 'honour, and pleasures, and thought, and virtue', all of which he believes are chosen for their own sake, he concludes that they are also chosen 'for the sake of well-being, in that we think that through them we will lead a life of well-being. Hence we are left with well-being as the most complete of goods, and hence as the last and best of ends.'

In what does such *eudaimonia* (or *felicitas* or *beautitudo*[10]) consist? On one level, Aquinas continues with what we have already seen in Aristotle, basing his view on what he calls the actions that are 'proper to man' and locating *eudaimonia* with 'performance according to excellence'.[11] However, he then introduces his own significant interpretation of *eudaimonia*, drawing on his Christian heritage. For Aquinas, 'man's natural desire can in no other way be satisfied except in God alone'. At this deeper level, then, it is only God – what Aquinas calls 'the beatific vision' – that can give a person their 'ultimate perfection, which is the perfect happiness of man'.[12] In Aquinas's schema, God alone is the perfection of all that is and all things can only find their being in relationship to God.[13] Thus humanity's aim is 'movement into God'.[14]

Aquinas transforms Aristotle's concept of *eudaimonia* (which Aristotle viewed as being achievable in this life and through one's own rational contemplation) by putting forward the notion of there being two kinds of happiness. Clearly, 'perfect happiness can consist in nothing else than the vision of the Divine Essence' (*ST* I–II.3.8). But he does also stipulate that some sort of happiness can be reached in this life too (I–II.5.5) and so he introduces the theological distinction between 'imperfect' and 'perfect' happiness.

This imperfect happiness consists in the operation of the virtues (I–II.5.5) and is akin to Aristotle's 'second happiness', but Aquinas draws on Christian tradition and the Scriptures to develop the presence not only of the two sorts of virtues of which Aristotle spoke (the intellectual and the moral/cardinal), but also of a third category, the theological. The intellectual virtues do not need to concern us here, but the moral virtues are those that are needed for a good or happy life in the present: they are predominantly the virtues of temperance, courage, justice and prudence, and they can be acquired through the practice of good habits. In this sense, 'human virtue directed to the good which is defined according to the rule of human reason can be caused by human acts' (I–II.63.2). These virtues are thus 'acquired', in that they can be gained through human action, in a similar sense to Aristotle's.

However, Aquinas recognises that these virtues have their limitations, because 'the power of those naturally instilled principles does not extend beyond the capacity of nature'. Because human nature is fallen, we will not be able to live out these virtues purely through our own attempts. A person therefore 'needs in addition to be perfected by other principles in relation to his supernatural end' (I–II.63.3). These other principles are twofold. They are, primarily, the theological virtues of faith, hope and charity: virtues that are 'infused', in that they come from God alone and not through any human effort, and are fully directed to the supernatural end (I–II.62.1). Secondarily, both the intellectual and the moral virtues can also be infused when their end is directed towards God as opposed to that which is purely natural (I–II.63.3–4).

This understanding of *eudaimonia* and the virtues lays the foundation for the rest of our discussion concerning Aquinas. Aquinas gives us a properly Christian framework within which we can explore the question that underlies this book: how does one live well as a Christian in contemporary consumer society? The notion of well-being, or happiness, is an apt one for us, but Aquinas demonstrates that it only functions when subsumed into a larger whole: that of life with God. In this way, Aquinas shows that happiness in the present is possible, but it is only possible through a life of grace-filled virtue, and it is through such a life that a person is enabled to move towards life in the divine. If we want to look not only at how we can respond to issues of social inequality and environmental breakdown, but also at how we do so within a specifically Christian framework, then this understanding is vital.

Jean Porter is Professor of Theology at the University of Notre Dame and one of today's leading Thomist commentators. Her discussion of Aquinas's understanding of *eudaimonia* is very helpful. For her, there is a distinction to be made between 'well-being' and 'happiness'. Well-being, for Porter, is 'the general normative ideal of human flourishing . . . analogous to the normative ideal of flourishing proper to any other kind of creature, and as such, it will include all the components of a humanly desirable life, including life itself, health, security, and participation in a network of family and social relations'.[15] Happiness, on the other hand, is 'the distinctively moral ideal specifying and qualifying' this well-being: that which specifies 'the best or most appropriate way in which men and women can attain and enjoy the activities constitutive of well-being'.[16] Porter wishes to assert that the two are not coterminous: one cannot simply equate well-being with happiness. Simultaneously, however, it is insufficient to profess that 'true happiness (authentic human existence) is not a matter of animal well-being' at all, so the two should not be divorced too far.[17] As we have noted, when we look at Aquinas we see that his emphasis on the beatific vision does not negate the possibility of 'a form of happiness which is connatural to the human being considered as a specific kind of creature'.[18] Nonetheless, he locates that happiness in a life rooted in the virtues, both acquired and infused, because it is just such a life that orientates a person towards God.[19] As the Dominican priest and philosopher Fergus Kerr beautifully expresses it, 'Thomas offers a moral theology, a Christian ethics, which is centred on one's becoming the kind of person who would be fulfilled only in the promised bliss of face-to-face vision of God.'[20]

For Porter, the notion of virtue is richer and more comprehensive than that of well-being because it places life's focus elsewhere. Well-being and virtue do not need to be entirely separated from each other, but nonetheless, virtue 'can take forms which seem, at least at first sight, to renounce aspects of the more basic ideal – the obvious example being the monastic ideal of poverty, celibacy, and obedience, explicitly defended by Aquinas and his contemporaries as a life of praiseworthy renunciation of fundamental human goods'.[21] Thus the ideal of virtue allows for a life that is not solely preoccupied with pursuing well-being.

The relevance of this for us is clear. It articulates a recognition that a life rooted in the virtues might actually reframe our understanding of what constitutes well-being. As we think through matters of human inequality and suffering, and ecological problems, as well as our struggles with the extent to which the motivation for living simply is self-fulfilment, this reconstituting is vital. Reflecting on the virtues thus opens up the possibility that, as Porter says, 'the happiness proper to virtue may be consistent with ways of living which involve the deliberate renunciation of some aspects of well-being'.[22]

There are two virtues that are of particular significance to our discussions in this book, namely temperance and justice, and we turn now to a brief consideration of them. Let us think first about temperance.

If virtue is simply 'a stable disposition to act in ways that are good',[23] then temperance is about having a stable disposition that leads us to act in ways that are good in relation to our appetite – our desire – for material goods and pleasurable experiences. Temperance is, for Aquinas, 'a certain disposition of the soul that imposes the limit on whatever passions or operations, lest they be carried beyond their due' (I–II.61.3). It is important to highlight that Aquinas here is not just adding a Christian gloss to an Aristotelian structure: although primarily related to the things that are 'natural to man', temperance has 'excellence' as its focus, an excellence that is related to the Divine Law and has the goal of ultimate fulfilment in God (II–II.141.2).[24]

Temperance has as its aim both the more exclusively physical goal of being, 'to ensure that one's desires for, and one's use and enjoyment of, food, drink, and sexual relations are consistent with the preservation of the individual and the species', and also the wider goal of ensuring 'that one's engagement with these sensible goods exhibit moral and spiritual beauty or honour'.[25] Drawing on Aristotle's doctrine of the 'mean', temperance is thus seen as a *via media* between a self-indulgent love of sensory experience and an improper indifference towards such experience, reminding us of the tensions we have been looking at in Part Two of this book.[26] As we saw in relation to Aristotle's understanding of the mean, the practical outworking of temperance changes as befits an individual's situation and the circumstances within which they stand.

What becomes clear on reading Aquinas is that, for him, temperance is not to be equated simplistically with saying 'no' to things and renouncing pleasure. Although arising partly from a fear of the consequences of 'man's appetite [being] corrupted chiefly by those things which seduce him into forsaking the rule of reason and Divine law' (II–II.141.2), temperance also stems from a desire to use rightly those things that are pleasurable. Pleasure is wrong when it threatens the rule of reason, but pleasure is not wrong intrinsically. What is important is having one's appetites rightly ordered and acting accordingly. I love the summary of Thomistic temperance that theologian Diane Cates gives when she expresses it as being 'best construed as a habit of being consistently moved and pleased in a beautiful and honorable manner by attractive objects of sense experience'.[27]

Having said that, however, while the positive is there, the dominant note in Aquinas's discussion on temperance is restraint – if only because he presupposes that the primary extreme towards which humans tend in relation to 'the things that especially attract man' (II–II.141.2) is one of excess rather than deficit.[28]

Nonetheless, a Thomist account of temperance moves us away from the dangers of the world-denying asceticism we have discussed, into an appreciation of what it means to use pleasurable things rightly. As we have seen, such an understanding for Aquinas is always determined teleologically, i.e. through a consideration of the end to which pleasurable things are to be used. That end is twofold. First, there is the immediate, proximate end, which is whatever 'the need of this life requires' (II–II.141.6). We will explore more fully below what

Aquinas understands by this. Second, that proximate end is subsumed into the ultimate end of all virtuous living, namely what Aquinas calls *beatitudo*.

Temperance is thus undertaken not just for the sake of the well-being of one's body, but in order to direct one towards God. The desire for pleasurable things, therefore, while not wrong in itself and indeed capable of directing a person to God, still has a limit and should be pursued only to the point where the need is met.[29] The notions of limit and restraint are undoubtedly strong in Aquinas's exposition of temperance, but again they are to be understood teleologically: 'for Aquinas, temperance is a form of purposeful limitation: limiting the pursuit of one good for the sake of a greater good'.[30]

Although Aquinas focuses his attention on the appetite for food, drink and sex, I believe we can remain faithful to his thought in broadening the remit to include the wider spectrum of material goods on offer today, for which we might have a desire – things such as type of house, car, clothes and technological equipment, as well as financial income.

The conclusions we drew at the end of the last chapter chime well with Aquinas's understanding of temperance as the *via media* between two extremes, and the recognition that there can be no one legalistic way to locate where that *via media* lies. It takes prudence to discern where that point is (II–II.47.7), and that point will vary according to individual circumstance and cultural context. Many of us reading this will resonate with Aquinas's view that 'temperance takes the need of this life, as the rule of the pleasurable objects of which it makes use, and uses them only for as much as the need of this life requires' (II–II.141.6), both in the sense of only using something as one has need, and also in the sense that such a use can be pleasurable.

This account of temperance is helpful, providing a constructive framework for our desire as Christians to resist the societal pressure that gives free rein to one's appetites and encourages a person to overconsume. Focusing on temperance alone, however, will not enable us to resist the pressure to focus on ourselves and our own sense of well-being and self-fulfilment, whether physical or existential: a temptation that, as we have seen, is alive and well for many of us, even for those of us trying to live more simply. We must also remember Aquinas's understanding of how the virtues relate together. There is an ecology within the virtues which means that they work together and cannot be read in isolation. In this way, temperance is not temperance unless it is held together with the other virtues of fortitude, prudence, charity and so on. We do not have the space to look at how temperance relates to all the other virtues, but the purposes of this book lead us to focus on one other virtue in particular, and to see how temperance needs to be fortified with justice.

Fitting Aquinas's views on temperance and justice together is a tricky thing and it can be easy to view them as in some sense opposed to each other. Where temperance seems to be concerned with the good of the individual, justice is concerned with actions directed towards the good of the community and of others.[31]

However, on closer inspection this differentiation is too simplistic. Aquinas develops a hierarchy of three levels of need to explain what he means by 'the needs of this life' that are addressed by temperance (II–II.141). First, there is the physical need – what a body needs to live. Second, there is what is needed in order 'to live fittingly' in relation to money and a person's position in society ('offices'). Third, there is what is needed to live fittingly as regards an honourable life of virtue.[32]

In this hierarchy, Aquinas provides a generous account of 'needs', moving away from too austere a position which would hold that 'whoever was to use any pleasure above the need of nature, which is truly content with very little, would sin against temperance', and instead allowing for the moderate use of things which are not absolutely necessary for the maintenance of life, but which also do no bodily harm. The key point is that these things are to be used 'according to the demands of place and time, and in keeping with those among whom one dwells' (II–II.141.6). In other words, these things are to be used with a consideration of what and who is around us. Through this statement, we can see that the main issues with which Thomist temperance is concerned (food, drink and sex) are relational and social in nature and are not to be thought of as purely individualistic matters. Because of this, ethicist and theologian Nick Austin can conclude, 'The need of human life is intrinsically relational, and so, therefore, is the end of temperance.'[33] So we see that temperance is not exclusively concerned with the good of the individual.

Nonetheless, it takes a coupling of temperance with the virtue of justice to bring out this other-directedness more fully. Aquinas's discussion on justice is extensive and complex. It is multi-layered and we are not going to attempt a full exploration of it, but will focus on how it relates to temperance.

In summary, the virtue of justice is, for Aquinas, concerned with actions directed towards the good of the community and of others. This being the case, rather than being rooted in the appetites (i.e. feelings and desires), it is rooted in the will. The will is the immediate source of those actions. To quote Porter, 'Justice involves a disposition of rationally informed commitments to maintaining certain kinds of relationships with others, rather than a disposition to feel and respond in a particular way.'[34] Central to Aquinas's notion of justice is the claim that 'just as love of God includes love of our neighbour, as stated above (II–II.25.1), so too the service of God includes rendering to each one his due' (II–II.58.1). Such an understanding means that justice requires us to respect the rights of others, regardless of whether we want to or not – which is why justice is an act of the will rather than the emotions. Justice is thus an absolutely necessary virtue, because people's natural orientation is towards their own good.[35]

The key question for our purposes is this: what is the relationship between temperance and justice, between the individual good and the good of others and/or the common good? So far as Aquinas is concerned, there is no conflict. He locates his reasoning for this in his understanding of anthropology (i.e. what it means to be human), which he roots strongly in being made in the image of God (I–II, Prologue). Now it needs to be said that Aquinas's anthropology is distinctly hierarchical, and this raises many problems, not least for those who seek to recover an egalitarian understanding of the relationship between women and men, and for those who are attempting to move away from a domineering view of humanity's relationship with the wider creation. Nonetheless, one positive aspect of his theological anthropology is that when looking at what it means to be made in the image of God, he insists that human beings are social beings – male and female, made in the image of a trinitarian God, as we have already considered in the Introduction. Aquinas believed that 'man is naturally a social being, and so in the state of innocence he would have led a social life' (I–II.96.4). It is within this social framework that a person grows towards perfection.

I love the way Susanne DeCrane from the University of Maryland expresses this:

> The goodness of the human person is not one that can be pursued by the person in isolation. By the very constitution of the person, her good is one that is authentically pursued in the company of others . . . Aquinas valued the material and social dimension of the person as important to her growth in perfection and goodness and did not expect a person to transcend or reject her materiality to choose a gnostic type of good.[36]

Aquinas has no hesitation in asserting that 'the common good transcends the individual good of one person' (II–II.58.12). Yet this does not mean for him that the good of an individual is thereby ignored. Rather, 'he that seeks the good of the many, seeks in consequence his own good . . . because the individual good is impossible without the common good of the family, state, or kingdom' (II–II.58.10). In this way, as Porter says, 'the well-being of individual and community are interrelated in such a way that what promotes one promotes the other, and what harms one harms the other as well'.[37]

When we reflect back on the strands of thought that have been running through this book, it will become apparent how relevant this understanding is. We have been thinking throughout how we might live rightly in our contemporary context (as Aquinas would say, 'according to the demands of place and time'): how might we live well in relation to God; in relation to others both locally and globally; in relation to the wider creation; and in relation to ourselves? Aquinas's thought provides a framework that brings these different elements together and, instead of trying to hold them apart as rivals, draws them together as vital constituents of a life moving towards perfection in God. For Aquinas, therefore, love of self – rightly understood – is secondary only to love for God (II–II.26.4). This is helpful material to bring into our discussions, to help us articulate a robust understanding of *eudaimonia* which sees that self-fulfilment can actually only be found when our lives are other-focused, practising justice. Our own good will be found when the good of other people, our communities and the natural world is also found.

Temperance is thus integrally bound up with justice (and likewise with charity). It is subsumed into the *telos* – the end or goal – of justice, so that justice functions as a motivator to act 'for the good of the other'.[38] In order to understand this more fully, a tight distinction must be made between self-restraint and a Thomist understanding of temperance as a virtue. Akin to our earlier discussion on asceticism, self-restraint is broad-ranging and can cover a number of different aims, some of which Aquinas highlights, such as improving one's health. Not every aim of self-restraint, though, is orientated towards the kinds of goals we have been identifying (goals of relational well-being, on all levels) – and for Aquinas such self-restraint is admirable, but it is not temperance.

Those who lack other virtues, through being subject to the opposite vices, have not the temperance which is a virtue, though they do acts of temperance from a certain natural disposition, in so far as certain imperfect virtues are either natural to man, as stated above (I–II.63.1), or acquired by habituation, which virtues, through lack of prudence, are not perfected by reason, as stated above (II–II.141.1).

For an act truly to be temperate, it must be drawn by the particular ends of justice. In other words, 'temperance, without justice, would not be a virtue' (I–II.68.5).

One of the threads running through this book has been the recognition that those of us living in more economically developed situations must think carefully about, and reduce, our resource use, both for our own sakes and for the sake of our relationships with God and his human and non-human creation. In Part Three we will be exploring what that might look like in practice, but for now, the Thomist understanding of temperance we have been developing provides theological content to these ideas and helps draw out the overriding motivation for our desire to live more simply, with justice at its heart.

This articulation of temperance gives to the practice of simplicity its particularly Christian underpinning. There are many different traditions of simplicity, arising from all faiths and none, but our research has helped us frame a truly Christian simplicity which arises from a desire to promote the welfare of the other, rather than from predominantly self-centred aims, and which sees that embracing such a life is an essential part of moving towards God.

One important thing for us to note here is that, seen in this way, temperance is not the be-all and end-all of Christian practices of justice, but it forms a partial expression. At the end of chapter 1 we saw the criticism coming from Humphery concerning a lack of political and macro-level engagement that can accompany a focus on issues of lifestyle and simple living, and so here too we recognise that temperance in and of itself is not a sufficient expression of justice. There are other practices (e.g. community engagement and campaigning work) that cannot be subsumed under this category, and we will consider these and others in Part Three. Nonetheless, temperance is an important aspect of justice that must not be neglected. Because of this, Austin's statement that 'those concerned for the common good should therefore be committed to temperance as an important social virtue' is an important one that none of us should ignore.[39]

It is important also to highlight at this point that living a life based on these understandings – in the face of a culture that so often pushes in the opposite direction – can be hard, and the bass notes of sacrifice that have appeared at various points throughout this book must not be forgotten. It is here that the flaws of Aristotle's *Nichomachean Ethics* become readily apparent, as it is incapable of equipping the Christian for a life directed towards God and all that entails. Aquinas's finely held balance between the individual, others and the community is an ideal. But we need to recognise that the person who pursues this ideal in a fallen world may end up making choices that lead to a life which is actually detrimental to a thin understanding of well-being. The importance of justice as a matter of the will is crucial here (sometimes decisions have to be made through gritted teeth), as is the foundational nature of grace. To live in such a way requires the virtues to be infused in one's life. In particular, although I have chosen to focus on temperance and justice, neither are complete without *caritas* – 'charity' (to use the old-fashioned term) or 'love'. Our desire for justice is inspired by God's love and thus arises out of love – for God and God's creation – and it is such love that keeps us on the hard path, enabled to live sacrificially.

One aspect of Aquinas's exploration of justice that is relevant for our concerns is his understanding of theft. So far as Aquinas is concerned, theft has two dimensions to it. At its most obvious, theft is to be condemned when one person takes the personal property of another individual (or of the state). Aquinas thus supports the notion of private property, rooting it as he does in natural law (i.e. the idea that we can draw universal moral principles from the world around us): God has, 'according to His providence, directed certain things to the sustenance of man's body. For this reason man has a natural dominion over things, as regards the power to make use of them' (II–II.66.1). The second dimension, however, is that Aquinas does not see ownership of property as an absolute right or good, for the self-same reason that all things are received from God (II–II.66.1). Because of this, there will be times when it is theft to keep from someone what is their due. In particular, where there is extreme need, Aquinas does not see it as theft to take another's goods in order to ameliorate that need. 'It is not theft, properly speaking, to take secretly and use another's property in a case of extreme need: because that which he takes for the support of his life becomes his own property by reason of that need' (II–II.66.7).

There is much in Aquinas's words on these matters that would make for provocative discussion at a governmental level, particularly his views that, if need be, goods can be taken by force in order to meet the needs of the common good if those goods are not willingly given up (II–II.66.8). Our interest, though, is on the implication this has for individuals. We have been concerned throughout this book about the ways in which high levels of consumption and resource use perpetuate injustice. Many of us feel keenly that such consumption and resource use is not only unfair, but actually comes *at the expense* of others who are thereby impoverished as a result. To live in such a way is not only callous but, in Aquinas's terms, actually constitutes theft. Looked at from this perspective, Aquinas's repetition of Ambrose's statement that 'he who spends too much is a robber' (II–II.66.2) is a powerful and painful commentary on the lives that many of us lead. Aquinas's views on theft – as part of his broader understanding of the virtue of justice – thus provide a strong imperative for us to look at our own consumption and resource use and see where we might make some changes.

These views on theft bring us back to the question that occupied us for most of the last chapter – what is a Christian approach to money and possessions? – and it is interesting to see what place Aquinas gives to material goods in the eudaimonist life. His overall view seems to be summarised in his agreement on this point with Aristotle that 'riches we do not desire except in so far as they are useful for a human life'.[40] Two points arise from this. One is that gaining riches does not constitute the overall thing that is to be desired: a happiness derived from such an attainment would, for Aquinas, be 'a mistaken form of happiness'.[41] At the same time, though, there is also no indication in Aquinas's writings of an outright rejection of riches. While very clearly recognising that 'it is impossible for happiness, which is the last end of man, to consist in wealth' (I–II.2.1), material goods are still seen positively as being useful for human life.

What we see is that Aquinas follows Aristotle in giving a positive place to material goods. Coming from a position of natural law, he sees goods as having been given to human beings by God, for our use. (As with his hierarchical understanding of the image of God, there may be aspects of this that we would want to take issue with, but this is not the place for that discussion.) Indeed, a certain level of material goods is needed in order to be able to pursue a virtuous life, if only because the virtues are never practised in theory; they are enacted precisely through how we use such goods in the normal course of life. Porter thus describes the necessities of life as the 'fields of operation for the virtues'.[42] In this sense, Porter is able to maintain that, for Aquinas, 'the virtuous life will normally be an enjoyable life, satisfying through its participation in the kinds of things that most people, in most times and places, do regard as desirable and fulfilling – marriage, children, a secure place in society, and the like'.[43]

At the same time, however, Aquinas insists that *eudaimonia* does not consist in the acquisition of such goods themselves, but, as stated above, in how they are used in order to move a person towards their end. The concept of right use is thus crucial here, just as we saw it to be earlier, particularly when we looked at the early Church's attitude to material things: how might one use one's own goods in a way that is prudent, courageous, temperate and just, that befits the person moving towards God? The overriding answer is that material goods are to be used to help others. Standing on the shoulders of what we have already seen to be a strong Christian tradition in this regard, Aquinas is clear and uncompromising:

> Whatever certain people have in superabundance is due, by natural law, to the purpose of succouring the poor. For this reason Ambrose [loc. cit., 2, Objection 3] says, and his words are embodied in the Decretals (Dist. xlvii, can. Sicut ii): 'It is the hungry man's bread that you withhold, the naked man's cloak that you store away, the money that you bury in the earth is the price of the poor man's ransom and freedom.' (II–II.66.7)

*　　*　　*

As we come to the end of this chapter, I hope it is obvious how much there is in Aquinas's thought that helps to give our own thinking and actions a theological framework. His emphasis on *eudaimonia* gives us a good way forward, highlighting as it does the positive approach to life that emerges from a desire to live more simply, while also bringing in the different debates and tensions that we have noted.

As a part of this, the central role that the virtues play in such a life provides a valuable tool with which to navigate the many quandaries that accompany our efforts to walk well through contemporary life. For individuals marred by sin, living within sinful structures, in a world that is itself a 'world of wounds',[44] the question of how to live well does not offer up easy answers. The path we are identifying through this book – which we will turn to more specifically soon in Part Three – is often marked with conflict and the need to make hard choices. In such circumstances, theologian and ethicist Celia Deane-Drummond is surely right to say that the virtuous person will act 'in pain and regret', and in the knowledge that, whatever action they decide to take, they will be 'marred in some way'.[45]

It is in this context that the doctrine of the golden mean, with which we started this chapter, finds its force. As we seek to hold together the tensions we have discussed in Part Two of this book, we attempt to walk that middle line. The imprecision of where that *via media* lies and the relation it has to each person's individual circumstances is not to be viewed as a problem. Rather, it gives us freedom and allows us to recognise that we will not always be able to determine where that middle line sits exactly. It is something we can hold ahead of us as a state we desire to reach: an ideal for us to wrestle with and debate.

Aquinas's eudaimonist ethic, as we have seen, arises from his understanding of the true end of humanity, found ultimately in the beatific vision, yet also allowing for a present, 'imperfect' happiness. That ultimate end in God has implications for how our present life is to be lived, rooted in a reading of Scripture that sees God's work in Christ as operating on more than an individual level alone, reaching into the whole creation and having radical implications for the value of that creation and for our place within it as human beings. With this understanding, taking our responsibility to our human and non-human neighbour seriously is a key way by which we move closer to God, not something that stands outside that movement.

Within our current global and societal context, that responsibility cannot be taken seriously without a consideration of our own levels of consumption and personal expenditure. Aquinas's discussion on the virtues of temperance and justice brings us a deeper understanding of what is taking place in the decision to live more simply. On the one level we can recognise that over-consumption is bad for us as human beings, causing us physical and psychological harm. To be a more temperate person, there-fore, is to demonstrate a wise consideration for our own well-being (the physical and existential 'needs of this life').

But temperance does not end there. It gets caught up into the virtue of justice, which then widens out the remit for deny-ing ourselves to incorporate the notion of making positive choices that build relationships and protect the wider creation. 'Frugality' can be a helpful contemporary term for this prac-tice. Thinking back to our discussion in chapter 5, it may also be useful to think of the practices of, and motivation for, living more simply as a type of generous or kindly asceticism. We are reminded again of the rhythm of retreat and engagement as, through temperance, our acts of justice involve withdrawing from unhelpful practices of overconsumption, but we then also engage in positive practices that foster restorative relation-ships. Aquinas thus helps us gain a fuller appreciation of how the practices involved in living well in our contemporary culture can change our understanding of what constitutes well-being, and can help individuals embrace the challenges of a life lived sacrificially.

Here it is worth emphasising again that Aquinas is able to take us so much further than Aristotle in this regard. For Aristotle, the good life is a life fulfilled in the present through philosophical contemplation and the practice of the virtues. For the Christian, however, this is more problematic because the good life is not necessarily the wholesome, fulfilled life: it might be a life spent for others that is painful and difficult. Aquinas's discussion on the virtues, and his understanding of the place of riches in the Christian life, gives us resources to cope with this. By focusing on a life moving towards God, we can see that notions of well-being, virtues and the cross can be held together, albeit with the recognition that their relationship will always be fragile and, at times, uncomfortable in this present age.

In conclusion, our deliberations in this chapter have brought us to a truly Christian, justice-focused, eudaimonist ethic – one that is alive to the complexities and tensions that exist as we seek to respond to the challenges of globalisation and consumerism. What we need to do now is think what such a response might actually look like in practice, and it is to this we now turn, in Part Three.

PART THREE

A Life Well Lived –
Putting It All Together

Introduction

Andie and Ian have been working in Tanzania since 1994. They lived there for nine years with their four children, starting up and running a fantastic dental charity called Bridge2Aid that trains indigenous healthcare workers to provide basic dental care, in a country that only has one dentist per 400,000 people. Alongside that, they were involved in a village for people with leprosy and other disabilities, renovating and transforming it. A few years ago they moved back to the UK and set up home in Leeds. Ian works as a dentist in a socially deprived area and Andie is mostly at home, helping the family adjust to life in the UK and giving her time as a governor for the local primary school. She is the second-hand queen and can find anything you need in a charity shop! She has also turned part of her garden into a thriving vegetable patch and has – her friends might say – become somewhat obsessed with chutneys. Together they have worked hard at finding a church life that works for all the family.

Louise is a political activist. Back in 1998 she started SPEAK, a network of students and young adults who pray and campaign on a range of different global issues and also share their faith with other activists. Their aim is both to campaign for change and to demonstrate that God cares for the poor and the oppressed and that people are treated unfairly. She lives in a part of north London where you can still buy a cup of tea for 50p and, as well as working with SPEAK, she runs Music Speaks, which supports poets and musicians and helps them speak out against injustice. She does not have a paid job as such, but is supported financially by people who believe in what she is doing.

Jean and David are retired and now live in south-west England, moving there when Jean's elderly mother needed support. Jean worked in publishing as an editor and David was a management consultant, but now they enjoy being full-time volunteers. They are committed to living as simply as they can, for example deliberately choosing a house that was near to the town centre so they would not have to be car-dependent; cutting down their meat eating; monitoring and reducing their household energy consumption. They are very careful about the things they buy and the amount of waste they generate, and Jean is particularly proud that even her mother-of-the bride outfit for their daughter's wedding was second-hand!

Andy and Jenny live in a flat on a working-class estate in south London, where they moved when they got married. They set up a Tenants and Residents Association and every fortnight have 'Neighbour Night' in their flat, when they invite people from the estate round for food. They both have part-time jobs with a secure income, and then work part time in other ways to give themselves more space to just 'be' around their neighbourhood. Jenny runs a small theatre company and Andy is a musician, writing and singing songs about justice.

They are part of a missional community expression of church called The Well.

Rick and Kirsty have inherited a large family estate of 6,000 acres, made up of woodland, in-hand farms, tenanted land and quarries. Having read theology and environmental ethics at university, they were determined to try to manage the land in ways that reflected the principles they learned there. On their in-hand farm, they are part of the extensive conservation programme called Higher Level Stewardship, which is a ten-year agreement with the UK government. This is principally focused on creating habitats for farmland birds, but also leads to them running their farm in ways that benefit many different species of wildlife (including the landowners, they say!). Many of their tenant farms are three-generational tenancies, which helps the farmers take a long-term view on soil fertility and encourages them to manage their farms sustainably. Alongside the farms, they have given over the management of 160 acres to their local community to run as a conservation project that includes a wide range of educational, research and community activities.

Keren has lived all round the world for work, but currently lives in the UK. For seventeen years she worked at George at Asda, working her way up from trading manager to director of sourcing for Asia and then lastly director of brand development in South Africa. Committed to social and environmental issues, she worked hard to bring those concerns into her job and find ways of integrating ethical considerations into George's clothes sourcing policies. Following some time developing artisans into export-ready, ethical suppliers, she now runs a social enterprise called Made in Africa that is developing clothing factories in Africa to be 'future factories'. Keren's aim is to ensure measurable social and environmental impact and show that you can compete on cost with efficiency and have ethical practices and living wages. She also gives a lot of her time elsewhere, using her business expertise to help the development of positive initiatives.

Peter and Jeanette live in a London suburb. With Peter working as a chartered accountant, they enjoy a high level of income. This has freed Jeanette to be at home full time for their children and to give some of her time to volunteering in the local school. They live well beneath their means and put the money they do not need into a trust fund, which they use to bless others.

There are so many friends of mine I could have included here: people from all sorts of different backgrounds, in all sorts of different situations, but all trying their best to live well in our consumer society.

Having looked at the context within which we are living, and having provided something of a theological basis for some of the key issues we face as we try to live as followers of Jesus in this context, now we come to the most challenging part of the book: how do we actually do it?

Through my doctoral research and what I have learned through speaking and writing on these things and making attempts to live in ways that match what I say, I have identified seven areas I think are foundational to a life lived well in response to our globalised, consumerist world. These seven areas are the focus of this last part of the book. My aim is to make this as practical as possible. I want you to go away with things you can actually do; practices and habits you can form in your life to equip you in your walk with God.

I also hope to start a discussion. I have no doubt there will be other things you will want to add to what I talk about here. Each area could, of course, take up a book in its own right, and I know I will not be able to cover every single thing that could be said or done. I would love to hear other thoughts and ideas from you, so please feel free to be in touch via my website (www.ruthvalerio.net). It will become obvious, too, that the lines between the sections are somewhat blurred, but that's OK.

Finally, I will talk quite a bit in these sections about what I have tried to do myself, and changes we have made as a family. I hope it is obvious that I do not see myself as the epitome of perfection on these matters! I do try to do most of what I talk about here, but it wouldn't take much for you to discover that I am still learning and failing and compromising along with everyone else. Every day is a new challenge to live as well as we possibly can.

A Global Social Concern

At the start of this book, in the Introduction, we laid out the biblical framework that has underpinned all we have been discussing. We saw there that relationships are at the heart of what it means to be human – in fact, they are at the heart of the whole way in which God has created this world – and that a crucial element is our relationships with each other.

We look forward to a time when there will be *shalom*, when there will be no more mourning or sickness, when God will wipe every tear from our eyes. But in the meantime we are painfully aware that we live in a world of immense suffering, inequality and injustice. Part of following a God of justice and compassion, who looks after the stranger and the needy, is that we are to be and do likewise. A fundamental element of a life lived well in contemporary society is therefore, as Isaiah 58:10 tells us, to focus on spending ourselves on behalf of the hungry and satisfying the needs of the oppressed.

How can we ensure that this is a core part of our lives? The first thing I would say is that we need to find ways to learn about, experience and engage with the lives of others around the world who are in situations of need and poverty. One way to do that is actually to go, get stuck in and help. If you are a young person coming up to your gap year, give a year or six months to help a community and gain some life-changing experiences at the same time (Tearfund do great gap year trips). If you are older, why not take a special holiday and go on an overseas trip that will use your skills to help others? If you are retired, could you turn your latter years into an adventure, maybe through going abroad or volunteering in some way?

I am very sensitive to concerns about the carbon emissions from flying and about the cost of these sorts of trips (wouldn't we be better just giving that money to charity?). Flying *is* immensely damaging and we will look further at that in the next section, but I think it is worth doing occasionally and there is something irreplaceably valuable about going abroad at least once in your life to experience the reality of poverty and let it impact you. I still remember the first time I walked around the slums of Addis Ababa in my early twenties: it was a life-changing experience for me as I came into contact with a level of poverty I had not encountered before. As I explained in the Introduction, it changed how I saw the world and developed in me a determination to live in ways that did not forget these people.

The crucial thing about engaging with and experiencing the lives of others is that we open ourselves up to listen to them. We do not go with our own agendas and prescribed solutions. We go to listen and learn.

The key for me is finding ways to open ourselves up to the reality of how so many people live today and not let ourselves become immune to it. So don't let yourself succumb to compassion fatigue. You don't have to go abroad for that. I remember watching Comic Relief one year and finding myself in floods of tears (more than is normally the case!) as I felt God breaking my heart for the different situations and people being shown, both abroad and closer to home. I encourage you to ask God to break your heart and show you how you can respond and act and not grow complacent.

One of those ways is to pray. Through prayer we connect with the people and places we are praying for. I find the different prayer diaries produced by various organisations helpful. Personally I like those created by Christian Aid and Tearfund, but there are many others. My mum has a heart for the persecuted church and she prays each day with the Open Doors prayer diary. At A Rocha UK we produce a quarterly 'Prayer ENews' that helps people pray for situations and communities impacted by environmental breakdown. Or you might just want to take whatever situation is currently in the news and pray for that. Remember, you cannot pray for everything, but God will put particular things on your heart for which you can commit to pray.

And then we can give. This is a really tangible way by which we can connect with others around the world and use our money to help them (something we will pick up again later, when we look at how we can live out a Christian approach to money and possessions). As with prayer, so with giving: we cannot support any and every cause. We will have to make our commitments and decisions and stick with them. But take a few moments now to stop reading and think about how much money you give away. Is there work that you support regularly (charities find it so much more helpful to have regular support than one-off donations, as much as they appreciate those)? If not, think through which areas of need in this world you would most like to help, and then begin supporting a charity working in that area. Some years ago I felt particularly burdened over the HIV/AIDS epidemic in Africa, and so we have been supporting the amazing work of WeSeeHope, set up by Wendy and Phil Wall.[1] When our girls began to be aware of wider issues, we wanted to help them grow in their understanding and decided that child sponsorship would be a helpful way, connecting them directly to two other girls their age. We decided to go through a charity called Grassroots, run by friends of ours, Sharon and Hugo Anson.[2] Through them we give our money and sponsor two Indian girls from the Dalit slums in Chennai.

One other thing I have found helpful is to instil a small discipline in my life that whenever a particular disaster hits the news (often triggering involvement from the Disasters Emergency Committee), I will give a larger amount of money than normal. I hope in this way both to respond compassionately to some awful situations that desperately need our help, and also to make sure I do not become immune to what is happening around me.

As we pray and give and open our hearts to the different needy situations of our world, we will inevitably become aware of some of the root causes of these needs. Sometimes they are unavoidable natural disasters, but more often than not it is injustice that lies at the root – and even with natural disasters, how well people cope is often linked to equality (e.g. you are more likely to lose all your possessions if you cannot afford insurance). To draw on the analogy of the river story that we saw earlier: while we help rescue people who are drowning in the river, we must also work upstream to stop them being pushed into the river in the first place. We will look more at this area later on when we consider activism, but we must bring it in here too. Speaking up on behalf of those who cannot speak for themselves is a critical part of how we engage with issues of global social concern.

Finally, I would really encourage you to find ways of doing these things with other people. If you live in a household, why not decide together to skip one meal a week and give that money to a charity of your choice? Or take one day a week when you eat more frugally than normal (maybe just eat rice and lentils that day) and give the money away. Doing so both releases money to help people who need it more than we do, and helps us stand in solidarity with them. Taking part in a scheme such as 'Live Below the Line' can be a great way to do this kind of action.[3] You could undertake these things as a whole church, too, and use it as an opportunity to focus on issues of poverty, both in your own country and further afield.

One thing we have loved as a family has been Christian Aid's 'Count Your Blessings' Lent scheme. Each day during Lent the scheme has some sort of reflection based around a situation or issue in our world, which encourages us to be aware of how much we have and then give in response. So, for example, one such reflection has been, 'We often run water until it's the right temperature. But 748 million people don't have access to safe water. That's the combined population of Brazil, Russia, the UK, US and Zimbabwe. Give 10p every time you run water today.' We look at it each evening over dinner and write on a piece of paper the amount, then add it up at the end of Lent and give the total to Christian Aid. It has been a great way to help us all learn about these different issues and then, practically, to release some of our money to help.

As you do these things, you may find that God leads you to open your own lives and homes, and your churches, to the victims of social injustice. Praying *about* and giving *to* both carry the danger of being arm's-length activities. Don't be surprised if God calls you into deeper and more direct involvement with specific people and their situations. That has certainly been the case for us in a number of different ways.

One of the things about the relational scheme that provides a foundation for all we are looking at in this book is that it brings everything together in a holistic way, so we don't pit different aspects of the Christian life against each other. This is important to remember when we consider our global social concern, because we should not set it against evangelism. We live in a world where people need both to hear about Jesus and experience the transformation that is brought about by a fully holistic understanding of salvation. For all its failures and weaknesses (and who of us will cast the first stone?), this has always been the understanding of the missionary movement, combining evangelism and social transformation (I think, for example, of my grandfather's life as a missionary in China, where he planted churches and established a hospital, both of which still stand today).

Maybe as you read this, God is calling you not just to pray, campaign and give (and to shop mindfully of others too, but we will come to that later), but to take a bigger step. I think of friends of ours – Mark and Jo – who left their secure jobs as teacher and nurse to join Andie and Ian (whom we met earlier) in Tanzania and help them with the dental charity. I think of

Simon and Julia, who stepped out in faith and set up Dalit Goods, raising awareness of the plight of the Dalit people in India and selling candles and spices to raise funds for the charity. And I think of Liza and David who, once they reached retirement age, moved to Kenya to work with the local churches in their area on issues of reconciliation. Has God put something on your heart, and is it time you did something about it?

Placing the needs of other people around the world at the heart of who we are and what we do is a good place to begin living well in our world today. But there is so much more we can do too.

An Ecological Concern

How often do you spend time outdoors? As I sit down to write this, I have just come back from an hour or so on the allotment, planting and weeding. The flowers and the sun were both shining and the blackbirds were in full voice. When I lifted up some black covering we use for land that isn't currently being grown on, a little frog hopped away and two slow-worms slithered out. I gathered them up and put them near the compost bin. At one point I uncovered an ants' nest and I watched with fascination as the poor things hurried around, picking up the hundreds of eggs that were now in danger, carrying them along the tracks of the nest and down into the myriad of little holes in the ground. I left that area alone and dug somewhere else.

I don't spend enough time outside (in fact my eldest daughter, Mali, said to me earlier today, 'Mum, do you spend *all* your time at your computer?' Oh dear!), but when I do, I know that something happens to me. It is as if a part of me gets switched on that otherwise lies dormant, in darkness.

Having an ecological concern is not a theoretical matter where we are only interested in issues that are thousands of miles away from us: it starts with connection; with learning about, experiencing and engaging with the natural world. Why? Because connection leads to love, which leads to action.

There is a tree on the green on the estate where we live that I find particularly beautiful. I love it and would never want it cut down. A developer would have no problem cutting it down, however, because they do not know it as I do. The first step to take is to reframe our attitude when it comes to the natural world. This is not about 'the environment', an inert and passive platform on which we live our lives. This is about the world that we are a part of, that intertwines with our selves and inter-acts with us in ways we can only begin to fathom. It is a world that has its own characteristics and personalities, that can be wounded and can heal, that mourns and rejoices: a community in which we dwell, and with which we join in singing the praises of our Creator.

Key for us to develop, therefore, is what has been called 'ecological literacy': an understanding of the world around us. Could you name five wild flowers that grow in your area? Do you know what your soil is like and what grows best? Where does your water come from and where does your waste go? Do you know what geological forces led to the formation of your country? What social forces have moulded it – why does the land look like it does? How important are the seas to the health of your place? What other countries share an interest in the well-being of the sea and its inhabitants?[1]

Cultivate an interest in the natural world and learn its work-ings, both by getting outside regularly and meeting the land and the inhabitants with whom you share your local area (and thereby learning about them), and by taking time to read books, articles and watch programmes, involving your children if you have them. Go for a walk in your lunch break rather than sitting at your desk reading emails. Join organisations that will broaden your horizons. A Rocha UK produces a twice-yearly magazine that is a quality mix of information about aspects of the natural world, biblical reflection, discussion on crucial issues and ideas for practical action. It also produces a quarterly 'Conservation ENews' that keeps you up to date with topical conservation issues.[2] Ask God to grow a love in you for what you see and experience and allow him to stir your heart over these things. As you can see, part of living well in our consumer culture is having a soft heart that is easily broken and also inspired and thrilled.

As this happens, we will inevitably want to live in ways that do as little damage as possible to the natural world and even try to live in ways that do some good. There are many things we can do (and some of these things will come into the other sections), but the biggest issue we need to tackle is seriously reducing our resource use. Food is an important area and we will consider that later under 'ethical consumerism'. Waste and water are also significant, but there is not the space to look at everything so we will focus on two crucial areas.[3]

First, let's consider our energy usage, thinking particularly about the energy we use in our homes. For most of us this will primarily be gas and electricity, the majority of which comes from fossil fuels. Heating our homes is where the biggest amount of our energy goes, followed by heating our hot water, then using our appliances, and lastly cooking our food. The biggest step we can take is to *reduce* our energy usage in the first place. Insulate everything you can: your walls, your loft, your hot water tank. Turn the heating down and get used to living in a house that is colder than you might ideally want it to be (recognising health needs, of course). In the winter, try turning the heating on fifteen minutes later than it is currently set for and turn it off fifteen minutes earlier, and see if you survive. If you do, reduce it some more. Try the same for your hot water. Keep your appliances for as long as you can and repair them if they break, only replacing them when all else has failed. When you do replace, go for the highest efficiency you can.

Alongside reducing all you can, switch to a 100 per cent renewable energy supplier, one that invests its money in generating more renewable electricity, such as Good Energy or Ecotricity. That way you are directly supporting the renewable industry while also sending a message to the big fossil fuel energy suppliers that you do not want their dirty energy. You can sign up for a smart meter trial, or install an energy dashboard display so you can see how much energy you are using at any one time. It is amazing how energy conscious this will make you. There are also great control systems (such as Hive) you can install to improve your efficiency.

Take advantage of any incentives that are around which will help you install renewable energy. We were able to put in solar panels some years ago and we now also have a solar iBoost, which diverts our excess electricity to an immersion heater and heats up our hot water. They have both been fantastic and we use half the electricity that we used to, as well as significantly less gas (we haven't yet had the iBoost long enough to know exactly how much our consumption has fallen).

Second, we should examine our travel. Unless cycling or walking, all our travel is powered by fossil fuels and we must be prepared to travel less, particularly by car and aeroplane. Are we willing to bite the bullet when it comes to our flying habits? Will we change our holiday patterns so we only fly abroad, say, every five or ten years, or not at all? Will we refuse to fly domestically and only travel by public transport? It is a sacrifice we must be willing to make. There probably will be times when we decide to fly – on holiday, for business, or to see family – and then I recommend offsetting through Climate Stewards, an A Rocha project that helps you offset unavoidable carbon emissions by supporting community forestry and cookstove projects in Ghana, Kenya and Mexico.

Do you commute to work? If so, think about switching to public transport or cycling if possible. Even just getting out of the car one day a week makes a difference.

We need to think about our driving habits too. This is a constant challenge for me, with children needing to be taken to clubs all over the place. I'll be honest here: I do my best and walk or cycle quite a lot, and my children get themselves to and from school and are pretty good at walking or cycling to places, but still I drive more than I would like to. My challenge is to lengthen the distance I think I can walk or cycle and make sure I leave the time to do that so I don't have to jump in the car at the last minute. Alongside this we should think about our car choice. There are many efficient cars available and even if you are a real car-lover, there is no excuse for not having one that is economical. It is also worth looking into whether there are any car share or leasing schemes available, especially in some of our bigger cities.

So how about it? What changes could you make to your travel so that you are reducing the amount of fossil fuels you use, and what else might need to change in your life to facilitate those alterations?

When we have spent the rest of this book thinking about huge concepts like globalisation and consumerism and the massive challenges they pose, and discussing big theological notions like *eudaimonia* and the virtues, deciding to put panniers on your bike and cycle to the shops rather than drive, or to put on a jumper rather than turn on the heating, can seem too small and inconsequential to be worth writing about, let alone actually bothering to do. The message I want to give you, though, is that there are big steps we can take (installing renewable energy, stopping flying, eating meat only a couple of times a week, for example), and take them we must. But there are also many little steps that on their own hardly seem worth talking about, but together do make a difference. My personal motto is, 'Many little steps in the right direction.' That is what keeps me doing the little things – day in, day out – as well as trying to take the bigger, more demanding actions as well.

Overall, we each need to ask ourselves, what would the world look like if everyone lived the way I do? Would it be a flourishing world, or a world that was being used harmfully in order to make my life more comfortable? I am reminded here of theologian John Carmody's statement, 'If I cannot extrapolate my standard of living for the whole world and still find nature flourishing, my standard of living is immoral.' It can be difficult to know exactly how to measure this, but I have found it helpful to use an online carbon calculator.[4] Of course these things are never entirely accurate, but they can give you some sense of what your level of living is like. From using such a calculator, I know that my standard of living can still be called immoral: there are more steps I need to take.

One final point as we come to the end of this section concerns the role of the Church, which, as we saw in chapter 3, has been recovering an environmental theology. The sleeping giant is beginning to wake up! It is yawning and stretching and pulling back the bedclothes, but it is still woefully slow when it comes to taking wider creation care seriously in its actions.

I have a clear vision. I want it to be as commonplace for the Church to be engaged in acts of environmental care as it is for it to be engaged in acts of community and social involvement. Think about it: you would be hard pressed nowadays to find a church that isn't involved in its community in some way or another through food banks, street pastors, toddler groups, and so on, or that isn't supporting some kind of overseas poverty and/or mission work. If you were to find such a church, you would, I'm sure, feel it to be deficient. The same should be true environmentally: if we are in or leading a church that is not integrating environmental concern and action across its life, then we should feel that the church is not fully living out its Christian faith.

If this is something you know your church needs to take on board, then A Rocha UK's Eco Church scheme may be the best way to go about it. Working across the denominations, and in partnership with Tearfund and Christian Aid, Eco Church is an award scheme that takes your church through a process to help it integrate wider creation care across the whole of church life, from worship and teaching, to buildings and grounds, to the personal lifestyle of members, and to community and global engagement.[5]

A Christian Approach to
Money and Material Goods

We have looked long and hard at this subject in various places throughout the book – considering what the Bible has to say, looking at how the earliest believers attempted to live out a Christian approach, and examining the thoughts of St Benedict, St Francis and Thomas Aquinas. We have encountered different understandings and different emphases, but we were able, at the end of chapter 5, to distil it all down to some basic principles.

In our approach to money and material goods we see clearly demonstrated our double movement. On the one hand, there is much about money and possessions that is to be rejected: they can so easily be what we search after instead of the kingdom of God; they can come at the expense of other people and the natural world, causing immense harm; we can use them to judge and discriminate against others. They must, indeed, be handled with immense care. On the other hand, that does not lead us to reject them entirely, because we recognise that we have been created as material beings in a material world. We do not work out our Christian faith by shutting ourselves away from society, but by engaging with it constructively. Money and material things can have immense power for good, helping to forge relationships and bring about positive change.

What we are talking about here is a reappropriation of material goods, using them in ways that facilitate life and relationship (using them for our 'focal concerns', as we saw in chapter 3, and not letting them use us). Maybe what we could search for is what Humphery describes as a 'new materialism', in which there is 'a valuing of material objects and forms that does not privilege endless consumption'. Humphery draws on the work of Csikszentmihalyi and Rochberg-Halton, who distinguish between 'terminal materialism' (whereby the 'habit of consumption can become an end in itself, feeding on its autonomous necessity to possess more things, to control more status, to use more energy'), and 'instrumental materialism' (which involves 'the cultivation of objects as essential means for discovering and furthering goals', primarily 'the fuller unfolding of human life').[1] Catholic theologian Christine Firer Hinze has encapsulated this wonderfully when she says, 'A new ethic of enough will require not an asceticism that glorifies self-denial or impugns the bodily, but a joyful and life-affirming engagement in and with the material world.'[2]

Trying to work this out in practice brings Aquinas's golden mean into play as we look to walk a very difficult line between having too much and having too little; loving things too much and loving them not enough. There are two things for us to remember in this regard. One is the recommendation from both Aristotle and Aquinas that the mean is not a mathematical middle: to steer that line will often be about veering away from the side that is most likely to be our weakness. While this will not be the case for us all, I would humbly suggest that for many of us our weakness is to have too much rather than too little, and that is the side about which we need to be most wary. The second thing to bear in mind is that the mean in our case is a global mean, not the mean of the top 5 per cent of the world, which probably would include all of us reading this (or even the top 1 per cent). In other words, it is easy to feel that our standard of living places us in the middle of those around us (after all, there are many who consume way more than I do) and forget that this still makes us incredibly privileged and rich on a global level.

So what can we do? First, budget. FBI director Edgar Hoover said, 'A budget tells your money where to go, otherwise you wonder where it went.' For some of us the most simple step is to get our money under control so we know how much we have coming in and how much we have going out. That will enable us to see what sorts of things we spend our money on, whether any of that can be reduced, and how much money we have available to use to bless others. The Money Charity can help you do this.[3]

Second, have one or two trusted friends with whom you can talk about your money. One of the most helpful things I ever did, many years ago, was to get together with two of my best friends and go through our family finances. We took it in turns to work through our budgets: our monthly expenditures and incomes, our savings, mortgages, pensions and so on. Everything was laid out on the table and open for questioning, not out of judgementalism or nosiness, but because we wanted to try to bring our attitudes and practices in line with what we saw in the Bible. That was probably about fifteen years ago, but we still talk openly together and it has been helpful over the years, as we have found ourselves in different life situations, to ask each other's advice and opinion. It has also helped me to remember not to judge other people's lifestyles too quickly when they are different from my own, as I may not know what is going on behind the scenes.

Third, practise generosity and give as much as you can. Actively look for opportunities to give away both your money and your things. Having an open-handed approach is one of the best ways to ensure that we are living out a good approach to our money and possessions. I will be honest here: this is one of the areas I have struggled with the most. I was brought up to be very careful with money and I know, for me, that this developed into stinginess. God has had to prise open my tightly shut fists and teach me to let go of things. And of course he has not done that in an abstract way; he has done that through other people: through my husband Greg, who has a completely different attitude to money, and through some of my closest friends, who have given me such wonderful examples of how to live generous lives that I have not been able to do anything but learn from them and try to follow suit.

We touched on this already in our consideration of how to respond to global social issues, but I would encourage all of us to give regularly to particular work we want to support. Organisations really do need our financial help, so let's give as much as we can. And then let's also look for ways to give spontaneously: be open to hearing about a particular one-off need and giving some money to help. You might find it helpful to put money aside regularly for just that purpose. And always ask yourself, am I really giving away as much I can, or am I giving out of my excess and keeping most of it for myself? Some serious honesty is needed here, and a willingness to allow God to speak.

When it comes to generosity, sharing can be as important as giving. In fact for some of us, sharing can be harder! Are you able to lend things to people and then not get upset if they come back in a worse condition?

Finally, we must remember our investments. A contemporary Christian approach to money is not only about how much we give away, but is also about what we do with the money we keep. If you have a bank account, a pension scheme or investments of any sort, then your money is being used by others to finance projects. What a terrible pity it would be if you scrupulously gave away as much money as you could to support positive things, but then discovered that your savings were being used to finance destruction. Let us instead make sure that our money is being used for good by looking carefully at which bank we use and ensuring that our pensions and savings are invested ethically.[4]

This is something that has been important to me because I have a modest share portfolio as the result of some family inheritance. Early on in my adult life, I met the stockbroker who manages it and went through my conditions of investment (including no mining of any sort and a commitment to look for positive investments where possible), and we have stuck to that resolutely. We have also tried to be creative and take risks by selling shares in the regular stock market and putting money into one or two smaller, more relational and beneficial businesses.

When it comes to a Christian approach to money and possessions, there is no one clear way ahead. Each of us reading this lives in a different situation from the next person and what is right for us might not be right for them. We need grace when it comes to this topic, courage to take bolder steps than our society might expect us to take, and a determination to keep pushing and challenging ourselves so that we do not get complacent.

One of the principles we saw at the end of chapter 5 is that money and possessions should never be gained at the expense of other people or the wider creation. John Wesley's well-used principle is helpful to remember here: 'Earn all you can, save all you can, give all you can, but not at the cost of conscience.' Perhaps it would be right to accompany this with an additional principle that money and things should also never be *kept* at the expense of other people or the wider creation. Theoretically, the Bible teaches that there is nothing intrinsically wrong with money and that it *can* be a sign of God's blessing. In practice, however, in our world today of extreme poverty and inequality, it should become almost impossible for a follower of Jesus to be wealthy. Why? Because whenever we have money and things that are additional to our needs, we should give them away.

(You will notice that I am not talking about tithing here because, as we saw in chapter 5, I do not think it is a principle that Christians are expected to follow, although it can be a helpful pragmatic guideline. The only specific teaching we have on giving – beyond Jesus' words to do so in secret – is in 1 Cor. 16:2, where Paul says that each person should give 'in keeping with your income'.)

Generosity is thus a key word for us. The other key word is contentment. As we saw in chapter 2, we live in a society that thrives on making us discontented so that we always want, and think we need, more. 'Keep your lives free from the love of money and be content with what you have' (Heb. 13:5) is perhaps one of the most important sentences for us in the entire Bible. This is also a critical aspect of living out the ecological concern we saw in the previous section. We simply consume too many resources through all the things we buy and expect to have in our houses and on ourselves. If we are content, then we will live more frugally, buying significantly fewer things, thus reducing our resource use and freeing up more money to use for the benefit of others and the natural world.

Contentment says, 'I have enough.' The secret to being able to say this is learning to be thankful. It does not ignore the struggles and pains that most of us reading this will carry at different points in our lives, but it still says, 'Thank you, God. Thank you for what I have. Thank you for the birds and the trees and the flowers. Thank you for the family you have placed me in. Thank you for the meaning and purpose you have given my life. Thank you that you hold my future in your hands, however much financial security I may or may not have.'

Let us make it a practice, every day, to put aside a few minutes to stop, think and say 'thank you'.

Ethical Consumerism

Do you remember Wham's 'Choose Life!' t-shirts, back in the 1980s? They were designed by leading fashion lady Katharine Hamnett. Some years ago, she designed some t-shirts for something Greg was doing with the words 'How you spend controls what happens on the planet' emblazoned across them.

Nine words will never do justice to the complexities behind the mess our world and its inhabitants are in. Nonetheless, it wasn't a bad attempt.

As we think about ethical consumerism, we pick up our discussions from Part Two around living out a double rhythm of retreat and engagement. Our consuming activities can do a huge amount of damage, both to people and to planet, and where that is the case we choose to withdraw – to retreat – wherever possible from those practices and reject those negative aspects of consumerism. I cannot emphasise strongly enough how essential it is that we consume less. But as we do that, we can also engage positively and, when we do consume, we can use our consumer power for good.

Ethical consumerism in the UK has seen incredible growth over recent years, thanks in large part to the success of the fairtrade concept. It is now possible to buy ethically (i.e. to buy products that have not been produced or grown in a socially or environmentally harmful way, and often are positively beneficial) in nearly all areas of consumer life, even if some areas are harder than others.

The good news is that buying ethically really does make a difference. There are many wonderful and inspiring stories that I could tell, but let me just focus on one – fairtrade gold, which is a product close to my heart given the role that Greg has played in its development.

Gold is a filthy product. Globally, around 100 million people are dependent on small-scale mining, of which gold plays a major part. Small-scale miners account for 90 per cent of the labour for gold extraction and yet they receive only 15 per cent of the money generated by gold. Labourers earn an average of $2 a day, child labour is rife, as is indentured labour, gender exploitation is routine, and health and safety issues are regularly ignored. Environmentally, gold uses cyanide and mercury as part of the extraction process. These can, and often do, leach into the water and soil, polluting the local ecosystem and damaging all who rely on that. Deforestation and (literally) blowing up mountains are the obvious results of extracting gold and gemstones. It is shocking to realise that for every 10 grams of 18-carat gold that comes to the high street, 20 tonnes of toxic waste will have been created. For every kilogram of gold from small-scale miners, 3 kilograms of mercury are needed to amalgamate it from the hard rock.

Thanks to the hard work of Greg and the Fairtrade Foundation, we can now buy gold (and silver) that avoids all these problems. Fairtrade gold is fully traceable right back to the mine and miners it came from. The miners receive a minimum price and a premium, and there are strict standards for working conditions, environmental protection and impact, and child labour. In Peru, as a result of the fairtrade premium, villages have installed electricity for the first time, and they have connected electricity to schools and their medical clinic. They now have a phone mast, enabling much-needed improvements in communication, and they are in the process of installing access to fresh water, which they currently have to bring in by lorry.

With this example of the benefits of ethical consumerism to encourage us, how can we go about becoming ethical consumers ourselves?

The first thing is simply to stop and think. We are conditioned in our society to buy whatever we are presented with, without asking any questions. In chapter 2 we saw how contemporary consumerism relies on detachment, with the result that we do not know where a product has come from, how it was made or who it was made by. One of the biggest steps we can take is to stand against that detachment and do all we can to build up the links and connections between ourselves and the products we buy.

So, before buying anything, stop, think and ask yourself what you know about the product. Do you know where it has come from? Do you know whether it was made by someone in good working conditions? Has it been made from environmentally harmful materials? Has it or any of its components been tested on animals? Has an inordinate amount of energy been needed to make it? Will it make the producer's life better if I buy it? Is this company involved in supporting an oppressive regime, or does it engage in unhelpful political activity such as lobbying? Does it allow trades unions to operate? Are the directors paid disproportionately high salaries in comparison to the wider workforce? Will this purchase foster good relationships between myself and other people and the wider world? One very simple discipline I have instilled is that I do not allow myself to impulse buy. If I happen to be somewhere and see something I like, I have to go home and think about it first before buying it. It is amazing how effective that simple rule can be!

Answering these questions, of course, can often be incredibly difficult and I am in no way underestimating the task ahead of us if we want to be as ethical as possible in our consumer habits. We need to increase our knowledge massively on these issues by reading around the topics and generally taking an interest in them. The *Ethical Consumer* magazine is the best way I have found for doing this.[1]

Overall, we need to develop a sort of 'ethical instinct': an underlying understanding of how our consumer system works and the main issues to look out for (which tend to cluster around the four areas of people, the environment, animals and politics). We may not be able to give the ins and outs of every product, but we will develop a pretty reliable 'nose' that will help us sense whether something is a good thing to buy or not.

We also need to recognise that there can be a tension involved in buying more expensive products, but buying more ethically and buying less. It is sometimes the case that to buy something made well, using sustainable materials and local labour or fairly traded labour from abroad, is more expensive. Balancing budget and ethics can often be tricky and is something I have wrestled with a lot.

In this section we do not have the space to look at every area of consumer activity and think how to approach it ethically, which is why developing an 'ethical instinct' is such a crucial thing for us to do (I am very aware, for example, that clothing is something I am not looking at specifically here). But there is one area we have not considered so far, which is absolutely fundamental to the global systems of our world and the most important when it comes to ethical consumerism. That area, of course, is food.

We live in a crazy world when it comes to food.[2] Despite the very real prevalence of hunger, we actually produce enough food in the world to provide every woman, man and child with 2,700 kilocalories each day, several hundred more than most adults need (an average of 2,300 kilocalories a day). The good news is that 132 million fewer people were hungry between 1990–92 and 2010–12, and the proportion decreased from almost 1 in 5 of us (18.6 per cent) to 1 in 8. In fact, during the last fifty years, world food production has consistently increased faster than population growth. There is more food per capita available than there has ever been.

And yet, the fact that 1 in 8 people in the world is malnourished is still shocking, particularly when you consider that 1 in 3 adults in the world is overweight.

The craziness of our world continues when you realise that just four companies control around 80 per cent of the global grain trade, and only half of the world's grain harvest is eaten directly by people. A third is fed to animals (a shocking 80 per cent of US corn is fed to animals) and a further sixth goes to biofuels. Globally, meat eating is set to double by 2050, by which point the world's entire grain harvest will be needed to feed animals. A third of all the food grown in the world is wasted and, if current trends continue, all the world's fish stocks will be exhausted by 2048.

The environmental impacts of the way we do food around the world are severe. Climate change; high energy and resource use, particularly water, oil and chemicals; soil erosion; nitrogen over-balance; overfishing; ocean acidification and issues around animal welfare are all involved here. On a more specifically human level, rising food prices, the exploitation of workers and producers, and land grabbing are some of the big issues we face. In the UK we have seen the rise of food banks (in 2013 the Trussell Trust gave out over 900,000 food parcels through its network) and a situation whereby 61 per cent of adults and a third of children in the UK are overweight or obese, with most of the nation now living on diets that are low in vegetables and fruit, and high in protein, saturated fat, salt and sugar. This has led to a new understanding of malnutrition and health in the UK (and in other countries too), which is no longer about the quantity of food, but about the affordability and accessibility of healthy options.

With this dizzying array of complicated issues, all tangled up with each other, what can we do to try to eat more ethically? The good news is that there are actually some quite simple steps we can all take which will mean that we are not contributing too much to the global food industry but are taking some power and control back into our own hands. These things are still complex, and I could add caveats to every point. But for the sake of enabling us to take some steps forward, here is what I recommend and try to live by as best I can.

(1) Eat less meat. Along with changing our flying habits, this is the biggest step we can take to make a difference in this world and reduce our resource consumption. Our high meat (and dairy) diets consume vast amounts of resources because of all that is needed to produce the feed the animals are given (water, land, grain, pesticides to grow the grain, oil to power the machinery, etc.), plus the water and land they need to be produced on. They also produce an awful lot of greenhouse gases from their 'backside emissions' and huge amounts of slurry – too much to be dealt with sustainably, thus leading to the poisoning of the land and water around intensive farms as the slurry leaches out.

From a resource perspective, we do not need to go fully vegetarian, although that is better than the diets most of us currently have. But we do need to reduce our intake significantly so that we only eat a small portion of meat two or three times a week (and remember that beef consumes a lot more resources than chicken, with pork and lamb in between).

(2) If/when we do eat meat, consider where it has come from and how it has been reared. The best type of meat comes from animals that have been reared on marginal lands. That means land that could not be used to grow crops. So, down my way, Three Harbours beef is from cattle grazed on the salt marshes as a beneficial part of the management of that area. Issues of animal welfare are crucial for us as Christians: I would go so far as to say it is un-Christian to eat meat from intensive systems. That includes meat that carries the Red Tractor logo, which in reality stands for very little. Instead, go for the RSPCA Freedom Food logo as a minimum, with Free Range and Organic as the best, as your budget allows.

(3) Buy fish and seafood carefully. As with meat, if you are buying farmed fish, make sure it is RSPCA certified or organic. If it is wild, ensure it carries the MSC ecolabel. If in doubt, don't be afraid to ask where it has come from and how it has been caught. Always avoid anything that has been caught using trawler nets.

One of my best recent food experiences has been joining a local fish co-operative called Community Fish Box, which supports a local fisherman from the coast near us at a place called Emsworth. You sign up for a season and pay up front and then collect a regular delivery of fish, which consists of what has been caught that night, so it is wonderfully fresh. You can get all sorts of things (I've had bass, mullet, mackerel, plaice, skate, cuttlefish, dogfish and crabs) and you take them as they come, which means you have to descale and gut them (and deal with the cuttlefish and crab appropriately). I have never been very good with fish and joined up as a bit of a challenge. All I can say is, it has been a lot of fishy fun!

(4) Grow and/or rear your own. This has been one of the things that has been most enjoyable (and educative) in my attempts to live more sustainably. As I read about the horrors of our food system, it became very clear to me that the best way I could have control over what I ate and fed my family, at a price I could afford, was to produce it myself. And so began the adventure of trying to do just that, leading to me having an allotment with friends, keeping chickens in the garden, and starting up a pig co-operative, which I now don't lead any more but do still take part in, with about twelve other families.[3] The wonderful thing is that the pig group was so successful and attractive that it spawned a number of others in my area too.

You don't have to be an expert in any of this – I certainly wasn't. You just have to give it a go, even if it is just some runner beans, tomatoes and potatoes.

(5) Alongside that, eat local and seasonal wherever you can. That will happen naturally, of course, if you are growing your own, but you can also use local farm shops and box schemes, all of which have the added bonus of taking a little bit of money and power away from the supermarkets and putting it into the local economy instead.

(6) Eat as unprocessed as possible. So many of the problems associated with our food system are related to processed foods, so one of the simplest things we can do is cook food and make things from scratch whenever we can. As sales of ready-made and microwaveable foods are soaring, let's buck the trend and make things ourselves. Yes, it takes a bit more time and planning, but it is one of the best ways of making sure we know, and are completely happy with, what is going into the food we eat. And of course, homemade food so often tastes nicer too – at least, that is what my children tell me!

(7) Join with others and be creative. One of the most pleasurable things about my adventures with food is that it has nearly all been done with other people. At one point Greg and I looked into the possibility of living in the countryside and having our own smallholding, but I was too committed to our estate to move so I had to find ways of eating ethically right here, in my urban situation. It has been great fun, chatting while working on the allotment with my girlfriends; learning how to pluck and eviscerate chickens with other friends; looking after the pigs and trying our hand at making sausages with a whole group of people; running a food co-operative (whereby

we buy in bulk from an ethical wholesalers called Infinity Foods) with my church small group, and so on. It has also made everything cheaper and has been less time consuming than if we were doing it all by ourselves. Of course that is not to say there is anything wrong with going the smallholder route, but in our increasingly urbanised world that will be the exception rather than the norm. The days of self-sufficiency are over: we need community and co-dependency instead.

If you have children, involving your family is an important part of all this. Thankfully my kids have always been up for the challenge of experimenting and trying new things. They understand the principles behind why I do what I do food-wise and have taken that into their own lives too (Jemba has not eaten anything with palm-oil in it since she was eight, and has chosen to be vegetarian). I understand that some family members might be less enthusiastic, so I recommend taking things slowly, introducing things bit by bit, explaining your reasons all the time, and finding ways to involve everyone in what you are trying to do.

(8) Finally, think and plan. As with so much of what we have seen already in Part Three, a lot of how we live comes down to stopping, thinking, and not just going along with society's assumptions. Thinking and planning is essential if we are to reduce our food waste. Plan your week's menu (but not so tightly that you can't be spontaneous if someone drops by). Draw up a shopping list and stick to it. Label anything you put in the freezer. Be savvy about sell-by and use-by dates. Move things that need eating to the front of the fridge so you don't forget about them. Learn your portions and only cook what you need. Discover the joys of leftovers. Don't let yourself buy

any reduced items to put in the freezer until you have used up what is there already. And so on – I am sure you have your own ideas too.

Food is a wonderful thing: a good gift, given to us by a good God. So most of all, enjoy it, appreciate what you have, share it with others, and have fun experimenting.

Local Community

Do you know the names of the people living next door to you ... two doors along ... three doors along? How many people do you know well enough to say 'hello' to in your street?

In our thinking on ethical consumerism we remembered what we saw in chapter 2 about consumerism's tendency towards detachment. This chimes well with the theological framework of our Introduction, with its emphasis on relationship and on living in ways that foster those relationships, working against the forces of detachment. A part of how we do that is through consuming ethically and connecting around the world in that way. But sometimes that is the easy bit: the hardest connections to make can be with those who live next door!

It is ever so important to include something on community in our thinking about how to live well in consumer culture. Our highly mobile, time-poor lives can mean this is an area that gets forgotten, and we can end up doing all we can to reduce our energy usage, live frugally and help people in need thousands of miles away, but in a way that is individualistic and forgets the needs of the people and places immediately around us.

This is something I have learned a lot about over the last twenty years, as Greg and I have spent our married life living on a social housing estate in Chichester (which some years ago would have been called a council estate). This was an area in which our church had invested for a number of years through running an annual summer playscheme on the green that sits at the centre of the estate. The church wanted to build on that and have more regular input into the estate, but recognised that no one from the church actually lived there, so a few of us opted to move in (some of us renting, some of us buying). For Greg and me, as we were in the early years of discovering the Bible's clear emphasis on social justice and poverty, it was an opportunity to explore more practically on a local level what we were already trying to outwork abroad.

It was not the worst estate in the UK, but relative to the general area it was pretty bad: run down, dogged by youth gangs and violence (some of it racial), the place where people were put when they were evicted from other estates. I wouldn't have walked around it alone at night, and in fact we had two separate occasions when friends of ours were beaten up as they tried to walk home alone after coming to us for dinner. I was chatting recently to one of my daughter's teachers who said her partner remembered having a pizza delivery job in Chichester years ago, and it had been company policy that you couldn't go onto the estate on your own in the evening.

Even writing that brief description of how the estate used to be surprises me, and I wonder if I'm making it up or over-dramatising it, because it is so different now. As I write this, I can see out of my kitchen window onto the green. I can see people walking their dogs; families playing; students relaxing on the grass; young people playing football on the multi-use games area (surely it is ironic that its acronym MUGA sounds like 'mugger'). The green has paths and flowers and trees, little hilly areas and a wildflower patch. In one corner is a bandstand, surrounded by a community mosaic we helped create some years ago. Sometimes when I look out I'll see the community wardens walking around carrying out their estate check-ups and talking to people as they go.

How has the change occurred? In 1991, a wise-headed city councillor looked at our estate and realised that, unless something was done, it was heading towards becoming a sink estate that would cause increasing amounts of problems for the district. He raised the money to employ a community development worker (John) to work on the estate for a year. The first thing John did was send round a questionnaire, asking people for their thoughts on the estate. It finished with two questions: 'Do you think it would be good to have a community association?' and, 'If so, would you be willing to be a part of it?' And so the Whyke Estate Community Association (WECA) was begun. I took on the role of co-chair from the start and did that job for twelve years. I insisted that the position of chair be a shared role primarily because I didn't feel confident to do it on my own, but it has turned out to be a positive thing, meaning that overall leadership is shared and no one person has the 'power'.

We started ever so slowly: we had no idea how the local councils worked (we have three in our area, all responsible for different things, which is very confusing); there were so many problems to tackle; residents laughed and told us we'd achieve nothing; our meetings were long and frustrating with too many voices and opinions and axes to grind. I remember our first AGM. John stood up and said he wanted to congratulate us because we were a success: the fact that we were still meeting after a year and hadn't fallen apart was an achievement in itself, even if we hadn't achieved anything else (which we hadn't)! That was such an encouragement, and it gave us what we needed to keep going.

Gradually as a committee we wised up, toughened up, learned who to talk to for what issues (generally, go straight to the person at the top) and how to raise money for projects. Most importantly, we've lasted the course. Committee members came and went, but a few of us stayed dedicated throughout. When it first started, I told myself I was going to be 'the last one standing', and that little covenant with myself kept me going through all the times when I would really rather have just given up, closed my front door and spent the evening watching television.

The result over the years is what I see when I look out of my kitchen window. Together (and it really has been together) we turned our estate from a 'bad' estate that people desperately wanted to move away from, to a 'good' estate that people now queue up to move into. Crime rates have dropped and it wouldn't cross my mind now to be nervous of walking across the green at night. We have won a number of awards (including several Britain in Bloom awards), and apparently our story is used as a case study in various places.

It has not all been plain sailing, and getting involved in our local communities will never be so. WECA now sadly does not exist. A couple of years ago a very disruptive person moved into the estate, stirred up gossip and ill feeling and caused such trouble that WECA had to be closed down. I was heart-broken to see it come to an end, but there clearly wasn't any other way. The legacy is still there, though. The community orchard that we planted recently is thriving and we still work on that, and when I walk or cycle anywhere I will always go past people I know and can say 'hello' to. I know this is just a hiatus and that things will be picked up again when the time is right.

My story of an estate in Chichester is very specific to me. I'm as surprised as anyone by what has happened and I can only see that it has been a God-thing. You will have your own story to write, but write it you must. So how can you go about playing your role in the community around you?

To begin with, I would really encourage you to find out what structures already exist. Is there a local residents' association or neighbourhood committee of any sort? If so, join it! It is the best way of being part of what is going on, meeting new people and finding out what issues people really care about. If you're not sure if such a group exists, your local council should be able to tell you.

If there is not such a group, then why not start one up? You could identify which area you want to focus on and put a simple flyer through people's doors (get your friends and family to help), asking if a neighbourhood group is something they would like and, if so, if they would be interested in getting involved. If you get positive responses back (with contact details), then arrange a time to meet and take it from there.

One thing we found invaluable was involving and working with the local authorities right from the start. For us that was the city, district and county councils, the police, the social landlord, and the youth service. They were helpful in a number of ways, but particularly in showing us how to access funds. Not everyone will have such a positive experience of their local authorities, and I know of people for whom it is much more of a battle, but I would really encourage you to draw them in as much as possible.

Outside of residents' groups, there are other groups you can also get involved with. Like my friend Andie, mentioned at the start of Part Three, you might want to consider becoming a school governor. Or you could find out if your area is part of the Transition Towns movement, which can be a great way of getting to know people and doing things that fit right into the themes of this book.[1] Maybe there is a conservation group near you. Or could you get involved in local politics and consider becoming a local councillor?

If you are part of a local church, I am sure there will be a number of community-related activities you can join in with that demonstrate God's love for the people of your area and provide more verbal opportunities to share the gospel as well: food banks, street pastors, groups for parents or elderly people, Alpha courses, and so on. When we considered poverty at the start of Part Three, we focused mostly on global poverty, but of course poverty is right on our own doorsteps as well – sometimes shockingly so – and finding ways of tackling that in our own communities is crucial. The only word of caution I would add about this is that, while I think many local schemes do brilliant things that are much needed, they can often be about *us* helping *them*. I would encourage you also to be involved in things that are about people doing things and solving problems *together*.

If all this feels too much and you know this is beyond your capacity, then don't despair: there are other smaller things you can do that are simply about getting to know the people around you. Food, of course, is so often the key to this. I love Jenny and Andy's fortnightly 'Neighbour Night' when they are deliberate about having people over for some food. They draw in people from their church, too, so there is a mix of people.

My most memorable meal was one I hosted for my co-chair at the time (a tough trades unionist and hardened carnivore) and another of the key members of our committee and his wife (hippy, yoga-teaching vegetarians). I worked hard at producing a delicious vegetarian dinner, and my poor co-chair, who had never eaten a meal in his life that didn't centre around meat, told me later that it had been 'disgusting' and he had left my house and gone straight to the kebab shop to get some 'proper food'!

It can help to find an occasion that gives you a reason to do something (and it can help those invited too if they similarly feel nervous). Christmas can be one of those occasions. We have sometimes held an open house at some point during the Christmas season, inviting our neighbours over for drinks and nibbles. Local anniversaries can provide a good excuse too. When we discovered that it had been seventy years since the first foundations of our estate were laid, we held a picnic on the green, with bunting and games. National events such as a coronation or a significant sporting event are great excuses for a party of some sort. And don't forget the Eden Project's 'Big Lunch' idea: a simple initiative that encourages people to get together with neighbours on the first Sunday in June. Millions take part all round the country.[2]

Involving children and families can also be good. Thinking back to the summer playschemes that the church put on all those years ago, some of the children now live on the estate with children of their own, and still talk about those play-schemes very fondly.

Personally, having my children involved with what we have done on the estate has been important to me, and they have helped me put leaflets through doors, set up for meetings, and many other things. When things were collapsing with WECA, I had to endure a number of painful meetings (at one of them, a woman I had known for years stood up in front of everyone, pointed at me and shouted, 'You can't trust a word she says'). Jemba – then aged ten – sat with me through each of them, sometimes holding my hand, and she helped me get through those tough times.

I am sure you have other ideas and more stories of things you have done as part of your local community. If so, I would love to hear them. Whatever you do, though, even if it is just walking around your area every now and then to pray for those who live there, remember to do it with a smile.

Finally, community can start right in your home: you might open it up to having other people come and live with you, if you have the capacity, or you could explore the idea of a larger 'intentional community'.[3] When Greg and I got married, Greg was fostering an older teenager who needed his help when he reached sixteen and left the care system. He gave us six weeks' space after our wedding, then moved back in. We have had people living with us ever since.

When we moved to the estate, we deliberately bought a four-bedroomed house (three bedrooms with a loft conversion). We knew it gave us a high mortgage to pay, but we did it as an act of faith because we wanted the space to have others living with us in some sort of a community. Over the years, we have had a wonderful variety of people coming through our house, some staying for a few years, others for a few weeks, and some of their stories have been colourful to say the least. For many years most of those people had some sort of connection with our church, but nowadays we have overseas students from a local college who live with us. It is a lovely way of introducing these young people to what a Christian faith looks like, and for our children it has been a great way of helping them grow up with an understanding of hospitality and how you engage and welcome someone who is a stranger.

So community is what goes on around you, and it is also what goes on in your home. Wherever you choose to place your emphasis, there is one thing I can guarantee: you may do this out of a desire to help and see others change, but what you will learn most will be about yourself, and what will change most will be you.

Activism

In chapter 1, in our discussion about Beck and 'sub-politics', we noted the concerns of Mary Grigsby and Kim Humphery that focusing primarily on issues of personal lifestyle will not bring about the changes we long to see. There are major political and economic shifts that must take place, and changing our lifestyles (reducing our levels of consumption; practising generosity, etc.) *will* make a big difference but will not take us the whole way. For that to happen, our governments, economic institutions and businesses need to make major changes too, and experience tells us that the majority don't do this voluntarily: we have to push, encourage, shame, congratulate and cajole them into making those changes.

An essential part of living well as followers of Jesus in our contemporary culture is getting involved in these bigger, structural issues, and fighting to see change in these areas as well as in our own lives. When we think about our rhythm of retreat and engagement, here we are talking full-on engagement! This is about getting stuck into the issues of our world; speaking up for those (human and other-than-human) who cannot speak for themselves; working to see unjust systems challenged and turned around; and having the courage to speak the truth and bring light into situations of darkness.

So how can we go about making sure that this is a part of our lives? There are two models I want to explore that I think can help us.

First, we can work from the inside. Joseph gives us an example of this, although his role was not so much about changing structures as using them to bring about good. His life was used by God to bring about the saving of many lives when the seven years of famine hit Egypt and the surrounding region. He was led by God, through a winding series of events, into a position of power that meant he could act when the need arose. Interestingly, he did not plan for any of it to happen; it just did.

I think of the work that Greg has done, too, to bring about change within the jewellery industry. He realised early on that campaigning against its evils and shouting from the sidelines would not be effective. He needed to be in the industry itself and demonstrate that another way was – is – possible. Like Joseph, Greg could never have predicted where the twists and turns of his earlier life would end up taking him.[1]

Many of you reading this can be – and will already be – inside activists through your paid employment. You will be in institutions where you can work for change. Maybe you work for a company, a local authority, or the government. Maybe you are an economist or an engineer; a scientist or an architect. Whatever it is and wherever you are, there will be things you can do to bring about good.

You may feel you have very little power, and that may indeed be the case. But remember, change can come about through the little as well as the big. Change the culture of your office by being a positive presence, always ready to encourage and say a nice word, noticing what is going on with the people around you. Talk to your boss about thinking through a sustainability policy that takes steps towards reducing your work's resource consumption. How about having a charity lunch once a month where people bring their own food to share and make a small financial contribution to a charity? People can take it in turns to choose their charity, or you could use the lunch to support a child sponsorship scheme between you. Could you be bold enough to have a confidential prayer box, where you let people know that prayer is important to you and that if they have something they would like prayer for they can slip a note into the box (with or without their names on it) and you will commit to praying for whatever is in there? Once you start thinking, you realise there are many things you can do to make a difference. It just takes a bit of creativity and courage.

It may be that you are in a position of greater power and opportunity within your work structures. If that is the case, then that also gives you greater responsibility to use it well, beyond providing an income for yourself. I suggest you take some time, in the light of what you have read so far, to think through and talk with others about where changes need to take place within your sphere, how you might take steps to bring those changes about, and what support you will need from those around you as you do so. I don't say that lightly. It can be incredibly hard to bring about change. Speaking out and doing things differently might make you unpopular. It could cost you your job. You may even come to the conclusion that your work is finally incompatible with Christian principles of justice and ecological care, and choose to leave. The question that is easy to ask and hard to answer is, are we seeking first God's kingdom and his righteousness before anything else?

Do not count yourself out if you are not in paid employment. Whatever the reason for that might be, you will still be in a sphere that you can influence. Think through the different issues we have looked at in this book: issues of social justice and earth care; how we use our money to help other people and places; the need to integrate our evangelism into these other concerns; the importance of living our lives from the basis of the relational framework we have discussed. What could you do to be an activist and bring these things to bear in your primary life situation?

Being an activist is therefore partly about working from the inside, being actively involved in bringing about good in the different areas of our involvement. But of course, the second model is about working from the outside.

Amos is a good example of this. Some of the prophets (such as Jeremiah and probably Isaiah) were priests, already integrated into the Israelite system of power, but Amos was completely different. He was simply an ordinary person, with no particular social standing. He was a shepherd and an agricultural worker: not the sort of person anyone was likely to listen to anytime soon. And yet he was courageous enough to be God's mouthpiece and to speak out about the terrible situation the Israelites were in: a situation where they had walked away from following God and were trampling on the poor, resulting in the land itself responding by trembling and convulsing, almost as if it was rebelling in disgust at how the people were living. Read Amos 8 and see how familiar the description sounds.

Like Amos, we must have confidence to have our say in telling the power systems of our world where we want them to change and how we want them to act. How do we do that?

The good news is that help is at hand from the many organisations already involved in this sort of work. Campaigning work is now such a well-recognised part of the landscape that almost every organisation you might want to support will be involved in it in one way or another. So get on and do your bit: send those emails and sign those postcards and online petitions. It is even better to go a step further by personalising emails you send, and even better than that is to write a letter. Alongside all this, make the effort to attend rallies and marches so that your physical presence counts as well.

It is worthwhile meeting your MP in person, too, as that has more impact than anything else. The same goes for MEPs, councillors and MSPs or Assembly members if you have them. If you want to contact a government minister, or even the prime minister, the best way is through your local MP. If you contact your MP and ask them to pass on your concerns to the minister who is responsible for the issue you are concerned about, the minister will usually reply faster, sign the reply personally, and notice it more. Do also remember to pray for the people you lobby, and take an attitude that is neither too trusting nor too suspicious.

Don't be afraid to get creative. The arts can be an incredibly powerful tool in the fight for justice. They might not take you down the corridors of power, and some people scoff at these more carnivalesque-type actions, but I think they are an important arrow in the campaigning quiver: something that complements other actions that are taking place, reinforcing what is being said through the more conventional routes of postcards and emails, and demonstrating further the strength of public opinion.

And be persistent. I remember years ago, before the fair-trade idea became more mainstream in the supermarkets, noticing that my supermarket only stocked small jars of Cafédirect coffee, but large jars of everything else. I asked them why that was and was told it wasn't possible to get large jars. I knew that wasn't the case, as I could get them at my local Oxfam shop. I told them so. They told me it couldn't be done. I repeated that it could, because I could buy them elsewhere. They told me they were special catering jars and supermarkets couldn't stock them. I asked them to look into changing that. They told me that, actually, they were about to meet with Cafédirect so they would put that on the agenda. Some while later, walking past the coffee section, I saw large jars of Cafédirect, and they have been there ever since. It may have been a complete coincidence, but I like to think I played a part in broadening the fairtrade options in that particular supermarket!

So be encouraged. When we take these actions, they do not fall on deaf ears, even if it might sometimes feel like they do. It can be easy to be overwhelmed with the number of causes and issues to speak up for, but don't let that feeling lead you to do nothing. If it helps, trim things down to two or three organisations whose campaigning efforts you will support. But do take those actions. Our relational framework is about love and connection. Where there is no love there is, literally, apathy (*a-pathe*, 'without feeling'), but love leads to action – and in our globalised, consumerist world, act we must.

Time

A woman came to talk to me after I had spoken at an event recently where I was looking at how we can live more lightly on this earth. She said to me, 'What you're talking about is more than just making a few changes to how we live. If I'm going to do this properly, I'm going to have to reframe my whole life.'

She was absolutely right, and as we approach the end of this book, it is apt that we finish with thinking about our time. If we are to live well in our consumer culture, we may well have to reframe our whole lives, and to do that takes time.

Time is a peculiar thing. It can be a social divider: separating out those who have too much from those who have too little. How often is busyness used as a social marker, to signal that we are important people, in much demand? In my early adult life my church context was full of busy leaders and I remember feeling that I ought to show myself in the same light if I wanted to be accepted as one of them. How often do we say, 'I don't have the time', but then happily sit and watch the television for a couple of hours every day? Our lives are filled with time-saving gadgets, but we seem to have less and less of it and get frustrated if a website takes more than a few seconds to load.

I suggest that the final thing we can do to put into practice the things we have been considering through this book – and particularly in the last six sections – is to take some control over our time and be intentional about how we use it. That does not mean descending into control-freakery. For some of us, 'wasting time' could be the most healthy thing we could do. What it does mean is thinking about our relationships (with God, the rest of creation, other people and ourselves) and working out how we can use our time for the good of each of those areas.

A good place to start would be to keep a record of your time for a month. As you go through your days, jot down what you have done and for how long. Be honest with yourself (funny how hard that can be!). At the end, take a look. Better still, go through it with someone else who is doing the same exercise and talk about it together. What does the way you spend your time say about you and your priorities? Thinking about the different areas of relationships, are you giving time to them all, or are there some that are missing out? What steps could you take to bring balance into your life, if you think that is needed?[1] Does the way you spend your time reflect the rhythm of retreat and engagement that we have been considering?

Much of what we have looked at in Part Three (though not everything, of course) has been related to using our time in ways that engage with what is around us, and so I want to spend the remainder of this section focusing instead on creating time to retreat. As we have been thinking through how we might maintain a healthy rhythm of retreat and engagement in relation to the world around us, so too it is helpful to think about the rhythms of our own lives and ensure that we have good practices built in to take care of and nurture ourselves. I am a firm believer in eating healthily and keeping fit, and I know those things don't just impact my body, they impact every aspect of my being. Of course they do: God has not created us to be separated into different compartments (body, mind, spirit, heart, etc.); we have been created as integrated beings where all these things flow together.

One thing I believe to be crucial when we consider our time is building a rhythm into our lives that includes gaps when we can stop, be still, reflect and simply be. For many, a helpful way for this to happen is through the practices of silence, solitude and contemplation. Writing on the Desert Mothers, Mary Earle has said that a life without silence is like trying to read with no spaces between the words.[2] I would encourage us all to build those spaces into the pages of our own busy lives.

Creating such a rhythm is also a key way by which we build resilience into our lives and find sustenance for the journey. Sometimes the MP doesn't listen. Sometimes the supermarket moves away from its fairtrade ethos. Sometimes the neighbours refuse friendship; the recipe goes wrong; our plans fail and success comes disappointingly slowly, if at all. Sometimes the sheer scale of the problems around us is overwhelming. When that is the case, we remember that we are not the saviour of the world: that honour belongs to God alone. Our job is to be faithful and to keep walking.

So how do we build rhythms of space and silence into our lives? First, let us think about those natural spaces that occur in our daily lives. They may just be a couple of minutes when we are boiling the kettle, or sitting at the station waiting for a train, or waiting to pick our children up from somewhere, or standing by the photocopier. Maybe there are moments you naturally fill by turning on the radio or checking your emails. Why not use those moments instead to be quiet and remind yourself that God is with you and you are with God?

Second, we should find a more regular, set-aside time (each day if we can) when we create the space to sit more intentionally in God's presence. There are different things we can do during this time that are more akin to the traditional 'quiet time': using some sort of daily Bible notes and bringing particular prayer requests to God. Alongside these things, though, let us also discover the prayer that is silence.

Mother Teresa was once asked about her prayer life. The interviewer asked, 'When you pray, what do you say to God?'

Mother Teresa replied, 'I don't talk, I simply listen.'

Thinking he understood what she had said, the interviewer asked, 'And what is it that God says to you when you pray?'

Mother Teresa replied, 'He also doesn't talk. He also simply listens.'

This sounds wonderful, but it can be much harder to put into practice, so I would suggest you start small. When you have your set-aside time, start by practising five minutes of silence. Settle into a comfortable position; set the alarm on your phone so you aren't worrying about the time; close your eyes if you find that helpful, and then just sit. I often start by telling God that I am giving him this time and giving him permission to do what he wants. And then I just do . . . nothing.

You will probably find after a short while that your mind suddenly bursts into life and all sorts of things begin rushing round your head. Don't worry about that; it's fine. Just acknowledge those thoughts and let them pass by. You might find it helpful to focus on your breathing for a while: taking in long, slow breaths, breathing in the good things of God, breathing out your worries and failures. It can be helpful to have a word or short phrase you use to bring you back into focus. For a while, mine was 'Here I am', which sometimes was what I said to God and sometimes was what I felt God was saying to me. Now it is simply 'Thank you, God'. When my mind is wandering and I realise I've been meditating on next week's shopping list, then I say that phrase to bring me gently back. I find that my head rushes around for quite a long time, but at some point it gives up and settles itself down. I have to allow it to go through that process.

After doing this for a little while, your alarm will go too quickly and five minutes will feel too short. When that happens, take it up to ten minutes . . . and then to fifteen . . . and so on. At the moment, twenty minutes is the right length of time for me, although I am beginning to want more. However, the constraints of my day mean I am stopping at twenty, for now anyway.

I have found three images helpful in my understanding of what is taking place in this process of silence, although you may well find God gives you other pictures that are more personal to you. The first is the cross-section of a river. Running along the top is the flow of the river, and that is all my thoughts that course along constantly. When I am aware of particular thoughts coming into my head, I can consciously throw them into that river of my life and into God's care. At the bottom of the river, though, is the riverbed where the rocks lie motionless, and it is there, at that still point, where I meet with God when I am sitting in silence. It can be helpful, if my mind is wandering, to remind myself that my thoughts may be flowing freely across the top, but underneath God is meeting me in the stillness.

The second image is of being at the dentist's or on the operating table for a localised operation. You are awake, but you sit or lie there patiently while the dentist or surgeon does their necessary work. My sitting in silence is my waiting in patience while God does his work. I told this to Ian the dentist, whom we met at the start of Part Three, and he said that he needs his patients to do two things: the first is to trust that he knows what he is doing; the second is to be still and not move.

The third image actually is more of a feeling. Sometimes I almost physically feel a connection from God to my sternum. It is as if there is an umbilical cord from him to me, and the silence allows his nourishment to flow into me and connect me deeper into him.

So setting aside time each day for silence can be crucial for us as we live out our faith in a noisy, busy society. But a third way of creating space is to build in occasional times when we go away for a day or longer. For various reasons (mostly to do with being away too much anyway and not wanting to do something else that takes me away from my children), this is not something I have done, and so I have asked my good friend Margot Hodson[3] to write of her experiences.

As an activist, I always struggle to take time out of modern life. I have found that going on retreat is one way in which I can make myself slow down and listen to God. I always come away feeling rebalanced and back on course. Taking time to go on retreat is not easy or even possible for everyone: work, families and other commitments can make it difficult but it is well worth doing if you can, even if just for a day. Costs vary and some places ask for a donation.

There are several ways to do retreats. Many retreat houses offer day or residential guided retreats. These usually have some input in the form of talks and then time to yourself to reflect and pray on the theme of the day. They provide food and often have places to walk as well as space indoors. A guided retreat is a really good way to start.

Most retreat centres also have room for guests to come on their own. For many years I have taken days at a centre called Stanton House, near Oxford. Here meals are provided and you are given a room to yourself. I take a Bible and sometimes another book to reflect on. I always have a note pad and usually decide beforehand on a section of the Bible to read slowly through the day. I arrive with things to give thanks for, things that are worrying me and things that are upcoming. I look back on the notes I have made on previous days and it is amazing to see how God has been working in my life. I come away feeling refreshed and with a better perspective on the demands of my life.

As a vicar, I am supposed to take one week a year on retreat, which is an amazing gift for me. I go to Hilfield Friary in Dorset, which is an A Rocha UK partner. This is a community of Anglican Franciscans and you join the family of monks, lay community members, other guests and anyone who drops in. You are given a simple room to yourself and the days have a rhythm of worship in the chapel; family style meals together in the refectory; time just to be; walking on the Dorset heath, or in the grounds; and any volunteering in the community that you might like to do. At Hilfield, God speaks to me as much through the life of the community as through shafts of inspired insights. My life is simplified again and I come away feeling that my relationships with God, people and creation have been restored and deepened.

There are other ways to go on retreat. Some people like to fast. There are centres that offer prayer for healing or individual prayer. The most important thing is to find a place where you feel secure enough to pray.

As we take control of our lives in this way – thinking through how we spend our time; asking ourselves how we can use our time to facilitate our relationships; building in rhythm and space – so we will find that we will be naturally trained away from being such exhausted consumers, because our focus and priorities will be elsewhere and the need to consume will die away.

Actively caring for the lives of people around the world caught up in injustice and poverty; actively caring for the world we live in and all its inhabitants; developing a Christian approach to money and material goods; becoming an ethical consumer; involving ourselves in our local communities and opening up our homes; engaging in advocacy and actively working for good in our different contexts; and using our time to balance our activism with retreat – all of these, I believe, are essential components of how we can live faithfully as followers of Jesus in our consumer society.

As we do these things, we hold the tension of the double movement of retreat and engagement: retreating where there are aspects of our culture that we want to resist and not be a part of, but engaging where there are areas we can get involved in to bring in the light and truth of the gospel and the values of the kingdom of God. Each side needs the other, and it is as we hold them together that we develop lives that are just and that live well with God, other people, the wider creation and ourselves.

Final Words

It feels apt that I am writing these final words at the triennial A Rocha Forum. Every three years, the lead people from the various national A Rochas around the world get together for five days. People have come from all around the world (Australia, South Africa, Ghana, USA, Peru, France, Finland, New Zealand, Kenya, the UK, Nigeria, the Czech Republic, Spain, Uganda, Portugal, India, Canada, Brazil, Costa Rica, Switzerland and the Netherlands) to meet each other, talk, cry, pray, inspire, encourage, worship, strategise, laugh and eat together. In case you are wondering, all the flights are offset via Climate Stewards.

This time we are meeting in Portugal, on the north coast, in an Ignatian retreat centre. In the midst of a full-on schedule of plenary sessions, focus groups and workshops, I have also been taking time out in the afternoons to develop my own rhythm of writing and taking breaks to walk along the beach and scramble over the rocks. Conversations over mealtimes and sitting out in the courtyard into the evening have been rich, and they have helped inform some of what has gone into Part Three.

There are amazing things being done by the people I am meeting – conserving precious species and ecosystems; helping improve the lives and livelihoods of local people; trying to engage the Church wherever they are and help them see how this is vital gospel work. Last night I sat and talked with Sir Ghillean and Lady Ann Prance. Ghillean has conducted 39 expeditions up the Amazon, discovered 450 new species, had 51 species and one genus named after him, and has collected 30,919 plants! For a lot of their married life the couple lived very simply in various places around the Amazon, with hammocks for beds.

What comes through from every conversation is the pressure that comes from human development (particularly the problems of our increasing global urbanisation), the greed and corruption of so many people in different positions of power, and the complexities of our global and local situations. I am reminded that, although I have been writing from a primarily UK-based perspective, the issues we have been looking at are relevant for people the world over, and the practices we have outlined in Part Three are not only appropriate for wealthy developed nations.

I am also reminded of the interconnectedness of the whole creation. We simply cannot divorce human needs from the needs of the other-than-human world and try to prioritise one over the other. We are all living parts of this wonderful world that God has made, and we must learn how to live together in it.

Through the course of *Just Living* we have looked at a number of complex and challenging issues, both socially and theologically. I know what I have written won't be the last word, but I hope it will provoke further thought and discussion on these vitally important topics. Most of all, though, I hope it will lead to action. The whole point of the book has been to provide deep foundations on which we can stand, secure in the knowledge that the things we have been looking at in Part Three are not optional extras for a minority of Christians who are interested in these issues, but are central components of what it means to follow Jesus today.

I want to encourage you to do all you can to develop the practices outlined in the last section of this book. None of us will ever be able to do everything, but each of us can do something . . . and a bit more. Don't worry about what you cannot do, but challenge and stretch yourself to do what you can. I worried constantly throughout Part Three that my desire to be practical and realistic meant I wasn't being radical enough, while also being aware that what I was outlining there could appear overwhelming and intimidating to readers just starting out on this path. If you can go above and beyond what I have suggested, then I will be delighted. Likewise, I will be thrilled if all of this is new and it helps you take those first steps forward.

Whatever stage you are at, why not look back over Part Three and choose one thing from each of the seven areas that you could do: one change you can make as a result of what you read there. I would love to know what you decide to do: you are more than welcome to find me on Twitter or Facebook and tell me. And then don't put this book back on the shelf to gather dust. Come back to it in six months' time to see how you are doing and choose another thing in each of the areas to do.

Even better, do this as part of a church group. Although I have tried to weave church suggestions into the practices of Part Three, I am aware that I could be criticised as having forgotten the hugely important area of the Church and its call to be 'an embodied question mark in society'.[1] That is not the case. As believers in Jesus Christ, we are part of his body, both locally and globally, and we are at our best when we work as part of that body. Let us commit ourselves to living out these practices together, as communities of people dedicated to seeing the multi-faceted good news of Jesus impacting all areas of our world and the people, places and other species that share that world with us. So get together with other people – in your church or beyond – to think, discuss and pray about the things we have looked at and then, vitally, to act.

To act in these ways will take courage, determination and commitment. But I can promise you one thing: you will also have a lot of fun along the way.

Acknowledgements

My life is a network of relationships and without them I could not have written this book. Thank you, first, to beautiful Tamsen, who has walked with me every step of the way and encouraged me constantly. A huge thank you, too, to Katherine, my editor, who has done her job brilliantly and been like a midwife, helping me bring this thing to birth. She gently but firmly steered me through the process, never afraid to tell me where something didn't work, always confident that I had more in me than I realised. I owe a big debt of thanks to Luke Bretherton, who was my main doctoral supervisor. He helped me believe in my ability to think, and he helped me articulate the tensions that we explore in Part Two and that have become such a key part of my thinking. Thank you, also, to Rich and Jack Bull, Ben Niblet and Esther Reed, who read through and commented on various chapters, and to Anna Rowlands who so helpfully supervised my final doctoral stages. My Facebook and Twitter friends have played a significant role in *Just Living* too: always on hand to answer and debate the many questions I've fired out over the years, and at one critical moment when I nearly gave up writing this book, they gave me the encouragement and support I needed to take a deep breath and keep going. Finally, Greg, Mali and Jemba: for your wonderful company, for embracing all my strange eco-eccentricities so enthusiastically, and for putting up with the hours of writing this has taken me: thank you.

Notes

Introduction

1. Natural England, 'Childhood and Nature: A Survey on Changing Relationships with Nature across Generations' (Natural England, 2009).
2. National Trust, 'Wildlife Alien to Indoor Children', survey (National Trust, 2008).
3. R. Louv, *Last Child in the Woods*: *Saving Our Children from Nature-Deficit Disorder* (Chapel Hill: Algonquin Books of Chapel Hill, 2005).
4. There is so much written on this that a simple Google search can be quite overwhelming, but a helpful place to start is with Matt Freer's chapter, 'The Power of Nature Connection to Change the World', in B. Stanley and S. Hollinghurst (eds), *Earthed: Christian Perspectives on Nature Connection* (Llangurig: Mystic Christ, 2014), and to see his references there.
5. University of Essex, 'What is the Best Dose of Nature and Green Exercise for Improving Mental Health? A Multi-Study Analysis' (2010), available at http://pubs.acs.org/doi/abs/10.1021/es903183r.

6. S. Bouma-Prediger, *For the Beauty of the Earth* (Michigan: Baker Academic, 2001), p. 105. He is following the work of Beldon Lane (*The Solace of Fierce Landscapes: Exploring Desert and Mountain Spirituality*, New York: Oxford University, 1998) in his thinking here.

7. C. Seaton, *Whose Earth?* (Cambridge: Crossway Books, 1992).

8. J. Odgers, *Simplicity, Love and Justice* (London: Alpha International, 2004).

9. I carried out my research on people from Breathe, which was a network of people committed to the concept of simple living and trying to outwork its practice in various ways.

10. There are many excellent books written on the relationship between faith and science and on issues around creation and evolution. The molecular biologist Denis Alexander is one well-recommended writer in this field.

11. There is a very close relationship between *'adam* and the Hebrew word for earth, *'adamah*: we are literally made from the earth; humans from the humus. Adam is not a proper name until Eve is created in Genesis 2: until that point Adam is more like a description.

12. C.J.H. Wright, *Old Testament Ethics for the People of God* (Leicester: IVP, 2004), p. 119. Other versions have 'let us make humankind in our image, in our likeness, and let them rule over the fish of the sea . . .', and then do not build such a clear link between being made in God's image and ruling over the rest of the created order. Wright is keen to stress that we should not see the image of God in humanity as being exclusively about 'our dominion over nature', since 'human beings are, and do, very much more than [that]'. I see that as being its primary meaning,

though, and the reason why we have been given intellect, the ability to love, and a moral conscience – precisely so that we might carry out this job well.

13. J.D. Zizioulas, *Being as Communion: Studies in Personhood and the Church* (Crestwood: St Vladimir's Seminary Press, 1993).

14. Michael Northcott writes brilliantly about the fate of the cedars of Lebanon during the course of Ancient Near Eastern history and how their destruction mirrors 'the turning of the nomadic and pastoral ethic of the patriarchs and early settlers of Canaan into the more elitist urban social forms of the later Hebrew monarchy' (M. Northcott, *A Moral Climate: The Ethics of Global Warming*, London: Darton, Longman and Todd, 2007, p. 104).

15. Luke 2:14 (translation from N.T. Wright's *The New Testament for Everyone*, London: SPCK, 2011). Strictly speaking, the angels speak the words, but it is so much nicer to imagine a choir of angels singing!

16. C. Gunton, *Christ and Creation* (Carlisle: Paternoster, 1992), p. 64.

Part One: The Air We Breathe – the Context

Chapter 1: The Elephant and the Blind Men

1. P. Spufford, 'The Comparative Mobility and Immobility of Lollard Descendants in Early Modern England', in M. Spufford (ed.), *The World of Rural Dissenters, 1520–1725* (Cambridge: Cambridge University Press, 1995), p. 310.

2. I. Linden, 'Globalization and the Church: An Overview', in C. Reed (ed.), *Development Matters: Christian Perspectives*

on Globalization (London: Church House Publishing, 2001), p. 3.

3. S. Panitchpadki, 'Preface to the Report of the Secretary-General of UNCTAD to UNCTAD XIII' (28 November 2011), available at http://www.policyinnovations.org/ideas/policy_library/data/01619.

4. D. Held and A. McGrew, *Globalization Theory: Approaches and Controversies* (Cambridge: Polity Press, 2007), p. 4.

5. Although I am choosing to concentrate on the economic, political, technological and cultural dimensions of globalisation, Held et al. also highlight military globalisation and the globalisation of labour. See D. Held, A. McGrew, D. Goldblatt and J. Perraton, *Global Transformations: Politics, Economics and Culture* (Stanford: Stanford University Press, 1999), p. 25. It could be argued, however, that these are further subsets of the main categories on which I am focusing.

6. Address given at the University of Chicago (12 June 1999), available at http://www.state.gov/1997-2001-NOPDFS/policy_remarks/1999/990612_clinton_chicago.html.

7. The full text of the address can be read here: http://www.washingtonpost.com/wp-srv/nation/specials/attacked/transcripts/bushaddress_092001.html.

8. A helpful exploration of these issues is found in Gavin Fridell's chapter, 'Free Trade and Fair Trade', in P. Haslam, J. Schafer and P. Beaudet (eds), *Introduction to International Development Studies: Approaches, Actors and Issues* (Canada: Oxford University Press, 2012).

9. See, for example, some of the high-profile economists mentioned in D. Rodrik, 'The Death of the Globalization

Consensus', 25 July 2011, available at http://www.poli-cyinnovations.org/ideas/commentary/data/000072.

10. D. Rucht, 'Social Movements Challenging Neo-Liberal Globalization', in P. Ibarra (ed.), *Social Movements and Democracy* (Basingstoke: Palgrave Macmillan, 2003), p. 214.

11. G. Pleyers, *Alter-Globalization: Becoming Actors in the Global Age* (Cambridge: Polity Press, 2010).

12. Avaaz (www.avaaz.org) and 350.org (www.350.org) are two of the best-known global organisations. Avaaz has 10.5 million members. In the UK, 38 Degrees has become a thorn in the side to whichever government is in power (www.38degrees.org.uk).

13. Theos, Cafod and Tearfund, *Wholly Living: A New Perspective on International Development* (London: Theos, 2010), p. 15. And see R. Kaplinsky, *Globalization, Poverty and Inequality* (Cambridge: Polity Press, 2005), p. 45.

14. See the graphic descriptions throughout B. McKibben, *Eaarth: Making a Life on a Tough New Planet* (New York: Times Books, 2010).

15. See, for example, the current report and future analyses provided in the UNDP's *Human Development Report 2011* (New York: UNDP, 2011).

16. The International Union for Conservation of Nature's 'Red List of Threatened Species' contains vast amounts of information on this topic (see http://www.iucnredlist.org/).

17. Tearfund's 2015 report, *The Restorative Economy: Completing our Unfinished Millennium Jubilee*, is an excellent look at how unsustainable development is impacting

the poor severely (available at http://www.tearfund.
org/~/media/Files/Main%20Site/Campaigning/
OrdinaryHeroes/Restorative%20Economy%20long%20
report%20HR%20singles.pdf). The 2015 report from the
Lancet/University College London Institute for Global
Health Commission similarly concluded that climate
change could derail the previous fifty years' progress in
global health (available at http://www.thelancet.com/
commissions/climate-change).

18. Kaplinsky, *Globalization, Poverty and Inequality*, pp. 7,
233–4.

19. I. Christie, 'Human Flourishing and the Environment',
briefing paper for the 'Wholly Living' project on development and flourishing (London: Theos/Cafod/Tearfund,
2010), p. 3.

20. There has been good work done on developing such a
model. See, for example, Herman Daly and Dan O'Neill's
work on the Steady State Economy, and Ellen MacArthur's
work on the Circular Economy.

21. R. McCloughry, *Living in the Presence of the Future*
(Leicester: IVP, 2001), p. 40.

22. http://unfccc.int/resource/docs/2013/cop19/eng/
inf04.pdf.

23. M. Steger, *Globalization: A Very Short Introduction*
(Oxford: Oxford University Press, 2003), p. 51.

24. G. Monbiot, 'We Need a New Law to Protect our Wildlife
from Critical Decline', *Guardian*, 21 November 2014,
available at http://www.theguardian.com/environment/
georgemonbiot/2014/nov/21/we-need-nature-wellbeing-
act-protect-wildlife-decline?CMP=EMCENVEML1631.

25. Unite, 'Tories in 1.5 Billion Pound NHS Sell-off Scandal', 4 October 2014, available at http://www.unitetheunion. org/news/tories-in-15-billion-nhs-sell-off-scandal/.

26. A. Giddens, 'Globalisation' (Reith Lectures no. 1).

27. See http://www.itu.int/net/pressoffice/press_releases/ 2015/17.aspx#.VZPyHaZgOL0. It needs to be noted that this still leaves 60 per cent of the global population without internet access: again, highlighting the inequality of our world.

28. McCloughry, *Living in the Presence of the Future*, p. 38.

29. A. Giddens, 'Family: Washington DC', in 'Runaway World' (Reith Lecture no. 4).

30. Family studies within sociology is an area far larger than this one short paragraph would suggest. For a helpful overview into the many debates that it involves, see C. Smart, *Personal Life: New Directions in Sociological Thinking* (Cambridge: Polity Press, 2007).

31. This categorisation comes from R. Cox, 'Civil Society at the Turn of the Millennium: Prospects for an Alternative World Order', in L. Amoore (ed.), *The Global Resistance Reader* (Abingdon: Routledge, 2005), pp. 108–9.

32. Z. Bauman, *Globalization: The Human Consequences* (Cambridge: Polity Press, 1998), p. 2.

33. U. Beck, *World Risk Society* (Oxford: Blackwell, 1999), p. 6.

34. W. Berry, *Sex, Economy, Freedom and Community* (New York: Pantheon Books, 1992), p. 8.

35. See http://index.gain.org/.

36. Z. Bauman, *Liquid Times: Living in an Age of Uncertainty* (Cambridge: Polity Press, 2007), p. 33 (italics his).

37. Beck, *World Risk Society*, p. 18.
38. U. Beck, *Risk Society: Towards a New Modernity* (London: Sage Publications, 1992), p. 21.
39. Beck, *World Risk Society*, p. 23.
40. ibid., p. 112, quoting A. Giddens and C. Pierson, *Conversations with Anthony Giddens: Making Sense of Modernity* (Cambridge: Polity Press, 1998), p. 105.
41. ibid., p. 11.
42. A. Giddens, *Sociology* (Cambridge: Polity Press, 2009, 6th edn), p. 102.
43. See, for example, Rucht, 'Social Movements Challenging Neo-Liberal Globalization', in Ibarra, *Social Movements and Democracy*, p. 217.
44. See http://www.ukpolitical.info/Turnout45.htm, and http://www.york.ac.uk/news-and-events/news/2005/uk-elections/.
45. This political reconstitution receives negative and positive appraisals by different commentators. See L. Bretherton, *Christianity and Contemporary Politics* (Chichester: Wiley-Blackwell Publishing Ltd, 2010), pp. 6–10.
46. Beck, *World Risk Society*, p. 91 (italics his).
47. ibid., p. 93; and from the abstract to U. Beck, 'Subpolitics: Ecology and the Disintegration of Institutional Power', *Organization and Environment* 10:1 (1997), p. 52. It might be of interest to some to note that this view reflects the 'double-movement' thesis of Polanyi: that the principle of economic liberalism is accompanied by the reaction of social protection. See K. Polanyi, *The Great Transformation: The Political and Economic Origins of our Time* (New York: Octagon Books, 1975), Part II.

48. M. Micheletti, *Political Virtue and Shopping: Individuals, Consumerism, and Collective Action* (New York: Palgrave Macmillan, 2003), p. 2.

49. K. Humphery, *Excess: Anti-Consumerism in the West* (Cambridge: Polity Press, 2010), pp. 67–71.

50. ibid., p. 71.

51. M. Grigsby, *Buying Time and Getting By: The Voluntary Simplicity Movement* (New York: State University of New York Press, 2004).

52. ibid., ch. 5.

53. ibid., p. 185. These writers are not lone voices and others talk on a similar theme. Alan Durning, for example, states that 'voluntary simplicity, or personal restraint, will do little good, however, if it is not wedded to bold political steps that confront the forces advocating consumption' (A. Durning, 'How Much is Enough?', in M. Schut (ed.), *Simpler Living, Compassionate Life: A Christian Perspective* (Downers Grove: IVP, 1999), p. 98).

Chapter 2: Skinny Jeans and a Broken Nose

1. V. Miller, *Consuming Religion: Christian Faith and Practice in a Consumer Culture* (New York: Continuum, 2003), pp. 46–7.

2. ibid., p. 71.

3. W. Cavanaugh, *Being Consumed: Economics and Christian Desire* (Grand Rapids: William B. Eerdmans, 2008), pp. 36–47.

4. S. Hauerwas, *A Better Hope: Resources for a Church Confronting Capitalism, Democracy, and Postmodernity* (Grand Rapids: Brazos, 2000), p. 148, cited in M. Northcott,

'Being Silent: Time in the Spirit', in S. Hauerwas and S. Wells, *The Blackwell Companion to Christian Ethics* (Oxford: Blackwell Publishing Ltd, 2nd edn, 2011), p. 418.

5. T. Veblen, *The Theory of the Leisure Class: An Economic Study of Institutions* (New York: Penguin Books, 1979, first published 1899).

6. P. Bourdieu, *Distinction: A Social Critique of the Judgement of Taste* (Oxford: Routledge, Kegan and Paul, 1984, 2010).

7. ibid.

8. Z. Bauman, *Consuming Life* (Cambridge: Polity Press, 2007), p. 83.

9. This idea of consumerism as being akin to an arms race has been developed in J. Heath and A. Potter, *The Rebel Sell: How the Counterculture Became Consumer Culture* (Chichester: Capstone Publishing, 2005). In this regard, they use the phrase 'defensive consumption'.

10. ibid., pp. 102–6. Sen's phrase is used by J. Urry in 'Consuming the Planet to Excess', *Theory, Culture and Society*, 27:2-3 (2010), p. 203.

11. A point made by a number of commentators, for example, A. Warde, 'Setting the Scene: Changing Conceptions of Consumption', in A. Anderson, K. Meethan and S. Miles, *The Changing Consumer: Markets and Meanings* (London: Routledge, 2002), pp. 17–19.

12. Bretherton, *Christianity and Contemporary Politics*, p. 181.

13. D. Miller, *The Comfort of Things* (Cambridge: Polity Press, 2008). See also D. Miller, *Stuff* (Cambridge: Polity Press, 2010).

14. This positive dynamic to supermarket shopping has been highlighted by the Italian sociologist Roberta Sassatelli in

Consumer Culture: History, Theory and Politics (London: Sage Publications, 2007), p. 63.

15. Miller, *The Comfort of Things*, p. 1.
16. J. Twitchell, *Lead Us into Temptation: The Triumph of American Materialism* (New York: Columbia University Press, 1999), p. 33.
17. For a fuller explanation of this list and an accompanying bibliography, see Warde, 'Setting the Scene', in Anderson, Meethan and Miles, *The Changing Consumer*, pp. 13–17.
18. C. Lury, *Consumer Culture*, pp. 30–31.
19. Sassatelli, *Consumer Culture*, p. 11. See also J. Baudrillard, *The Consumer Society: Myths and Structures* (London: Thousand Oaks, 1998), p. 81.
20. M.H. Jacobsen and S. Marshman, 'Bauman's Metaphors: The Poetic Imagination in Sociology', *Current Sociology*, 56:5 (2008), p. 805.
21. Z. Bauman, *Liquid Modernity* (Cambridge: Polity Press, 2000), p. 6.
22. M. Davis, *Freedom and Consumerism: A Critique of Zygmunt Bauman's Sociology* (Aldershot: Ashgate Publishing, 2008), p. 52.
23. Bauman, *Liquid Times*, p. 11.
24. ibid., ch. 1.
25. M. Davis, 'Bauman's Compass: Navigating the Current Interregnum', *Acta Sociologica*, 54:2 (2011), p. 186.
26. Bauman, *Liquid Modernity*, p. 7.
27. See their extended discussions in U. Beck, A. Giddens and S. Lash, *Reflexive Modernization: Politics, Tradition and Aesthetics in the Modern Social Order* (Cambridge: Polity Press, 1994).

28. See, inter alia, Bauman, *Consuming Life*, pp. 9, 111; *The Art of Life* (Cambridge: Polity Press, 2008), ch. 2; and *Liquid Modernity*, p. 62.

29. Bauman, *Liquid Modernity*, p. 64.

30. Bauman, *The Art of Life*, p. 53.

31. ibid., p. 109.

32. Z. Bauman, *Liquid Love: On the Frailty of Human Bonds* (Cambridge: Polity Press, 2003), pp. 10, 41, 90; *The Art of Life*, p. 15.

33. Bauman, *Liquid Times*, p. 24.

34. Bauman, *The Art of Life*, p. 5.

35. Bauman, *Liquid Love*, p. 35; Davis, *Freedom and Consumerism*, pp. 69–70. It is surprising that Bauman has not extended this discussion to social networking sites such as Facebook and Twitter and to the updating of mobile phones to smartphones.

36. For 'exclusion' see particularly Z. Bauman, *Work, Consumerism and the New Poor* (Milton Keynes: Open University Press, 1998). For 'human waste' see, for example, *Consuming Life*, ch. 4.

37. Bauman, *Consuming Life*, pp. 29, 36–7.

38. Bauman, *The Art of Life*, pp. 2–3.

39. ibid. p. 9.

40. Smart, *Personal Life*, p. 189.

41. Taken from the Office for National Statistics data, 'Divorces in England and Wales 2012'. See http://www. ons.gov.uk/ons/rel/vsob1/divorces-in-england-and- wales/2012/stb-divorces-2012.html.

42. See http://www.footprintnetwork.org/images/article_ uploads/EarthOvershootDay_2014_PR_General.pdf.

43. See http://www.stockholmresilience.org/21/research/ research-programmes/planetary-boundaries.html.

44. See http://faostat3.fao.org/browse/FB/FBS/E. It is important to remember that inequalities exist within countries too, and it is a shocking fact that there are 48 million 'food insecure' people in America (T. McMillan, 'The New Face of Hunger', *National Geographic*, August 2014, p. 73).

45. See http://www.happyplanetindex.org/

46. A. Druckman, D. Hirsch, K. Perren and J. Beckhelling, 'Sustainable Income Standards: Possibilities for Greener Minimum Consumption', RESOLVE Working Paper Series 14-11 (University of Surrey, 2011).

47. See http://www.jrf.org.uk/topic/mis.

48. See http://www.jrf.org.uk/sites/files/jrf/Minimum-income-standards-2014-FULL.pdf.

49. New Economics Foundation, *The (Un)Happy Planet Index 2*, (New Economics Foundation, 2009) pp. 46–7.

Chapter 3: Of monks and men

1. R. Sider, *Rich Christians in an Age of Hunger* (London: Hodder & Stoughton, 1990), pp. 184, 159.

2. R. Foster, *Freedom of Simplicity* (London: Triangle/ SPCK, 1981), p. 3.

3. ibid., p. 177 (italics his).

4. ibid., p. 4.

5. You can find out more about that at http://ww.lausanne. org/gatherings/issue-gathering/ international-consultation-on-simple-lifestyle-2.

6. S. Claiborne, *The Irresistible Revolution: Living as an Ordinary Radical* (Grand Rapids: Zondervan, 2006), p. 113.

7. ibid., p. 163.

8. See http://www.businessinsider.com/bottled-water-costs-2 000x-more-than-tap-2013; http://caraobrien.tumblr.com/ post/605286421/americans-spend-20-billion-on-ice-cream-a-year-it.

9. See http://e360.yale.edu/feature/consumption_dwarfs_ population_as_main_environmental_threat/2140/.

10. J. Stott, *The Radical Disciple* (Leicester: IVP, 2010).

11. ibid., p. 79 (he is quoting from the Lausanne Evangelical Commitment to Simple Lifestyle).

12. See arocha.org.uk/livinglightly.

13. L. White, 'The Historical Roots of Our Ecologic Crisis', *Science*, 155:3767 (1967), pp. 1203–7.

14. John of Damascus (675–749), *Treatise*, cited in 'Teaching on Creation through the Ages', in M. Maudlin and M. Baer, *The Green Bible* (London: HarperCollins, 2008), p. 101.

15. Quoted in 2006 at www.cofe.anglican.org/about/church-commissioners/news/environment/resources.html/ quanda.doc.

16. See www.cofe.anglican.org/info/ethical/policystatements/ environment.pdf.

17. Mission and Public Affairs Council, *Sharing God's Planet: A Christian Vision for a Sustainable Future* (London: Church House Publishing, 2005); and see www.shrinking-thefootprint.cofe.anglican.org.

18. See the work of Bright Now (http://brightnow.org.uk/).

19. Evangelical Alliance and Christian Research, *21st Century Evangelicals: A Snapshot of the Beliefs and Habits of Evangelical Christians in the UK* (London: Evangelical Alliance, 2011), p. 5.

20. See http://www.theguardian.com/world/2015/jun/13/pope-francis-intervention-transforms-climate-change-debate?CMP=share_btn_tw.

21. See http://www.archbishopofcanterbury.org/articles.php/5404/archbishop-invites-young-christians-to-spend-year-praying-at-lambeth-palace.

22. See Rutba House (ed.), *School(s) for Conversion: 12 Marks of a New Monasticism* (Eugene: Cascade Books, 2005).

23. ibid., p. ix.

24. Society of St John the Evangelist, *Living in Hope*, p. xvi.

25. ibid., p. viii.

26. Bauman, *Liquid Times*, p. 49.

27. B. McLaren, *Finding Our Way Again: The Return of the Ancient Practices*, (Nashville: Thomas Nelson, 2008) pp. 5–6.

28. B. Reay, *The Quakers and the English Revolution* (New York: St Martin's Press, 1985), p. 9.

29. ibid., ch. 6, provides a fascinating account of this period.

30. T. Gorringe, 'Liberation Ethics', in R. Gill, *The Cambridge Companion to Christian Ethics* (Cambridge: Cambridge University Press, 2001), p. 129. Clearly liberation theology is not a singular phenomenon (we could more precisely refer to liberation theologies), even when restricted to the Latin American version, but for the sake of these brief paragraphs its differentiations are not being explored.

31. R. Goizueta, 'Gustavo Gutiérrez', in W. Cavanaugh and P. Scott (eds), *The Blackwell Companion to Political Theology* (Oxford: Blackwell Publishing, 2004), p. 290.

32. G. Gutiérrez, *A Theology of Liberation* (London: SCM Press, 1974), ch. 13, but especially pp. 171–3.

33. Goizueta, 'Gustavo Gutiérrez', in Cavanaugh and Scott (eds), *The Blackwell Companion to Political Theology*, p. 292.

34. Miller, *Consuming Religion*, ch. 3.

35. ibid., p. 73.

36. ibid., p. 195.

37. These things are explored more by the American theologian Marve Dawn, in her book *Unfettered Hope: A Call to Faithful Living in an Affluent Society* (Louiseville: Westminster John Knox Press, 2003), pp. 52–6.

38. M. Budde, *The (Magic) Kingdom of God: Christianity and Global Culture Industries* (Boulder: Westview Press, 1997).

39. M. Budde, 'Collecting Praise: Global Culture Industries', in Hauerwas and Wells, *The Blackwell Companion to Christian Ethics*, p. 124; Budde, *The (Magic) Kingdom of God*, p. 82.

40. This point is also strongly made by James Smith in *Desiring the Kingdom: Worship, Worldview and Cultural Formation* (Grand Rapids: Baker Academic, 2009).

Part Two: **Breathing In, Breathing Out – the Theology**

Chapter 4: **Get Thee to a Nunnery?**

1. J. Lacarriere, trans. R. Monkcom, *The God-Possessed* (London: George Allen & Unwin Ltd, 1963), pp. 15–16.

2. S. Ramos, trans. N. Russell, *Like a Pelican in the Wilderness: Reflections on the Sayings of the Desert Fathers* (Brookline: Holy Cross Orthodox Press, 2000), p. 12.

3. H. Waddell, *The Desert Fathers: Translations from the Latin* (London: Constable and Company Ltd, 1994), p. 9.

4. ibid., p. 10. Care should be taken not to give the impression that the desert dwellers were only interested in

solitary living. For an approach that emphasises the communal dimension of the Desert Fathers, see G. Gould, *The Desert Fathers on Monastic Community* (Oxford: Clarendon Press, 1993). Nonetheless, whether alone or with others, the point remains that they retreated from 'the world'.

5. L. Regnault, *The Day-to-Day Life of the Desert Fathers in Fourth-Century Egypt* (Petersham MA: St Bede's Publications, trans. 1999), pp. 7–8.

6. T. Martin, 'Augustine and the Politics of Monasticism', in J. Doody, K. Hughes and K. Paffenroth (eds), *Augustine and Politics* (Lanham: Lexington Books, 2005), pp. 167–9.

7. J.D. Hunter, *To Change the World: The Irony, Tragedy, and Possibility of Christianity in the Late Modern World* (Oxford: Oxford University Press, 2010).

8. ibid., p. 151.

9. N. Biggar, 'Seek the Welfare of the City: A Response to *Christianity and Contemporary Politics*', *Political Theology*, 12.3 (2011), p. 454.

10. Bretherton, *Christianity and Contemporary Politics*, p. 191.

11. R. Markus, *Christianity and the Secular* (Notre Dame: University of Notre Dame Press, 2006).

12. ibid., p. 5.

13. ibid., p. 39.

14. ibid., p. 13.

15. L. Bretherton, '"How Shall We Sing the Lord's Song in a Strange Land?": A Response to the Symposium', *Political Theology*, 12:3 (2011), p. 466; Markus, *Christianity and the Secular*, p. 5.

16. Markus, *Christianity and the Secular*, pp. 5–6.

17. Something that Bretherton highlights in '"How Shall We Sing the Lord's Song in a Strange Land?": A Response to the Symposium', p. 469.

18. Some people have trouble with the doctrine of the atonement that Townend puts forward in his lyrics. That is not the point I am making here.

19. M. Percy, *Words, Wonders and Power: Understanding Contemporary Christian Fundamentalism and Revivalism* (London: SPCK, 1996).

20. ibid., ch. 4.

21. ibid., pp. 64–5.

22. ibid., p. 75.

23. Chris Voke has written a very helpful book on how we can ensure our worship gives a proper place and value to the wider creation: C.J. Voke, *Creation at Worship: Ecology, Creation and Christian Worship* (Milton Keynes: Paternoster, 2009).

24. See http://www.jesus4u.co.uk/study-sheets/victorian_hymns.

25. See http://www.billboard.com/charts/christian-songs. Those songs were: 'Something in the Water' (Carrie Underwood); 'Oceans (Where Feet May Fail)' (Hillsong UNITED); 'He Knows My Name' (Francesca Batestelli); 'Greater' (Mercy Me); and 'He Knows' (Jeremy Camp). The billboard chart measures radio airplay plus sales and streamlining data for the US. There is not an equivalent UK chart for UK Christian songs, only an album chart.

26. A. Anderson, *An Introduction to Pentecostalism* (Cambridge: Cambridge University Press, 2004), p. 229.

27. P. Ward, *Selling Worship: How What We Sing Has Changed the Church* (Milton Keynes: Paternoster Press, 2005), pp. 1, 198.

28. ibid., pp. 206–7.

29. Anderson, *An Introduction to Pentecostalism*, pp. 25–7.

30. ibid., p. 28.

31. C. Campbell, *The Romantic Ethic and the Spirit of Modern Consumerism* (Oxford: Blackwell Publishers, 1987).

32. P. Sedgwick, *The Market Economy and Christian Ethics* (Cambridge: Cambridge University Press, 1999), p. 3; Campbell, *The Romantic Ethic*, p. 31.

33. See particularly his discussion in ch. 5.

34. Campbell, *The Romantic Ethic*, chs 4 and 5.

35. See, for example, p. 140.

36. He has refined his thesis in the years since his work was first published. See, for example, his introduction to P. Falk and C. Campbell (eds), *The Shopping Experience* (London: Sage Publications, 1997).

37. D. Bebbington, *Evangelicalism in Modern Britain: A History from the 1730s to the 1980s* (London: Unwin Hyman Ltd, 1989), pp. 50–55, 80–81.

38. Campbell, *The Romantic Ethic*, pp. 138. For Polanyi, see Polanyi, *The Great Transformation*.

39. E. Gregory, *Politics and the Order of Love: An Augustinian Ethic of Democratic Citizenship* (Chicago: Chicago Press, 2008), p. 369.

Chapter 5: In Plenty or in Want

1. You can read more about this in his fantastic autobiography, G. Valerio, *Making Trouble: Fighting for Fairtrade Jewellery* (London: Lion Hudson, 2013).

2. D.L. Okholm, 'Asceticism', in D. Atkinson and D. Field (eds), *New Dictionary of Christian Ethics and Pastoral Theology* (Leicester: IVP, 1995), p. 173.

3. World Council of Churches, *A Spirituality for Our Times: Report of a Consultation on Monastic Spirituality* (Geneva: World Council of Churches, 1986), p. 9.

4. J. Ziesler, *Christian Asceticism* (London: SPCK, 1973), pp. 4–5.

5. M.A. Tolbert, 'Asceticism and Mark's Gospel', in L. Vaage and V. Wimbush (eds), *Asceticism and the New Testament* (New York: Routledge, 1999), p. 45.

6. Ziesler, *Christian Asceticism*, pp. 5–7.

7. Kallistos Ware, 'The Way of the Ascetics: Negative or Affirmative?', in V. Wimbush and R. Valantasis (eds), *Asceticism* (New York: Oxford University Press, 1995), p. 3, cited in A. Saldarini, 'Asceticism and the Gospel of Matthew', in Vaage and Wimbush (eds), *Asceticism and the New Testament*, pp. 14–15.

8. V. Wimbush (ed), *Ascetic Behavior in Greco-Roman Antiquity: A Sourcebook* (Minneapolis: Fortress Press, 1990), p. 2, cited in M. MacDonald, 'Asceticism in Colossians and Ephesians', in Vaage and Wimbush (eds), ibid., p. 270.

9. R. Valantasis, 'Constructions of Power in Asceticism', *Journal of the American Academy of Religion*, 63 (1995), p. 797, cited in MacDonald, ibid., p. 270.

10. Tolbert, 'Asceticism and Mark's Gospel', in Vaage and Wimbush (eds), ibid., p. 31.

11. Wright, *Old Testament Ethics for the People of God*, p. 149.

12. An interpretive warning sounded in A. Perriman (ed.), *Faith, Health and Prosperity: A Report on 'Word of Faith' and 'Positive Confession' Theologies* (London: Paternoster Press, 2003), p. 101.

13. The different views are helpfully set out in the various chapters in D. Fiensy and R. Hawkins, *The Galilean Economy in the Time of Jesus* (Atlanta: Society of Biblical Literature, 2013).

14. Some of the following paragraphs are based on the writing I did in 'M is for Money', in my *L is for Lifestyle: Christian Living that Doesn't Cost the Earth* (Leicester: IVP, 2nd edn, 2008).

15. D. Kraybill, *The Upside-down Kingdom* (Basingstoke: Marshalls, 1978), pp. 114–29, cited in Valerio, ibid., p. 88.

16. And, it has to be said, Mrs Zacchaeus as well. For a lovely and amusing take on what this incident must have been like for Zacchaeus's wife, see A. Guinness and M. Guinness, *The Word of the Wives* (Milton Keynes: Authentic Media, 2010).

17. Perriman (ed.), *Faith, Health and Prosperity*, pp. 164–7.

18. M. Hengel, *Earliest Christianity: Containing 'Acts and the History of Earliest Christianity' and 'Property and Riches in the Early Church'* (London: SCM, 1986), pp. 179–82.

19. D. Batson, *The Treasure Chest of the Early Christians: Faith, Care and Community from the Apostolic Age to Constantine the Great* (Leominster: Gracewing, 2001), pp. 90, 62.

20. Tertullian, *Adv. Marc.* 4, 15, 8, cited in Hengel, *Earliest Christianity*, p. 210.

21. J. Gonzalez, *Faith and Wealth: A History of Early Christian Ideas on the Origin, Significance, and Use of Money* (San Francisco: Harper & Row, 1990), p. 205. See also M. Mitchell, 'Silver Chamber Pots and Other Gods Which Are Not Good: John Chrysostom's Discourse Against Wealth and Possessions', in W. Schweiker and C. Mathewes (eds), *Having: Property and Possession in Religious and Social Life* (Grand Rapids: William B. Eerdmans, 2004).

22. Clement, *Quis dives salvetur? – Who Is the Rich to Be Saved?*, p. 11, cited in Gonzalez, *Faith and Wealth*, p. 112.

23. *Quis dives salvetur*, p. 14, cited in Gonzalez, ibid., p. 113.

24. Gonzalez, ibid., p. 228.

25. Hengel, *Earliest Christianity*, p. 217.

26. Although Gonzalez sees it continuing at least well into the second century and in some forms throughout most of the third (Gonzalez, *Faith and Wealth*, p. 226).

27. P. Barry (trans.), *St Benedict's Rule: A New Translation for Today* (York: Ampleforth Abbey Press, 1997), p. 4.

28. C. Butler, *Benedictine Monachism: Studies in Benedictine Life and Rule* (Cambridge: Speculum Historiale, 1924), p. 32.

29. ibid., p. 152.

30. Barry (trans.), *St Benedict's Rule*, p. 40.

31. ibid., p. 41.

32. Butler, *Benedictine Monachism*, pp. 149–50.

33. W. Short, *Poverty and Joy: The Franciscan Tradition* (London: Darton, Longman and Todd, 1999), pp. 60–61; M. Robson, *St Francis of Assisi: The Legend and the Life* (London: Geoffrey Chapman, 1997), p. 94; K. Johnson,

The Fear of Beggars: Stewardship and Poverty in Christian Ethics (Grand Rapids: William B. Eerdmans, 2007), p. 31.

34. Short, *Poverty and Joy*, p. 67; Robson, *St Francis of Assisi*, pp. 109, 112.

35. Johnson, *Fear of Beggars*, pp. 28–31.

36. Of course there are many other examples we could have looked at, throughout church history, but I decided to focus on Benedict and Francis because of the renewed interest in monasticism that we saw in chapter 3.

37. If you are interested in looking more at this topic, then the best book to read is C. Blomberg, *Neither Poverty Nor Riches: A Biblical Theology of Possessions* (Leicester: Apollos, 1999).

38. Perriman (ed.), *Faith, Health and Prosperity*, pp. 207–11.

39. ibid., p. 207.

40. ibid., p. 208.

41. ibid.

42. ibid.

Chapter 6: Temperance, Justice and Human Flourishing

1. The translation being used is that provided by C. Rowe in S. Broadie and C. Rowe, *Aristotle: Nicomachean Ethics. Translation, Introduction, and Commentary* (Oxford: Oxford University Press, 2002).

2. A full understanding of Aristotle's ethics can only really come from a full understanding of his view of the human soul, but to discuss that takes us outside the remit of what we are considering here.

3. S. Broadie, *Ethics with Aristotle* (Oxford: Oxford University Press, 1991), p. 3.

4. See Broadie's commentary on 1106b7 in Broadie and Rowe, *Aristotle: Nicomachean Ethics*, p. 304.

5. A. Tessitore, *Reading Aristotle's Ethics: Virtue, Rhetoric and Political Philosophy* (New York: State University of New York Press, 1996), p. 27.

6. c.f. the discussions in Tessitore, ibid., pp. 62–72, 110–11; Broadie, *Ethics with Aristotle*; and D. Hutchinson, 'Ethics', in J. Barnes (ed.), *The Cambridge Companion to Aristotle* (Cambridge: Cambridge University Press, 1995), pp. 210–12.

7. There is disagreement over whether this tension can be resolved and, if so, how. Broadie's analysis seems most helpful here as she sees Aristotle building his conclusion from the beginning, but saving it till the end ('a slow climb brings us to the previously hidden view of a greater mountain beyond our mountain'). According to Broadie, Aristotle's final position is that he wishes to convince his audience (already of a philosophic inclination) that the best sort of life is, indeed, a life of reflection, but one that is rooted in practical and ethical qualities (Broadie and Rowe, *Aristotle: Nichomachean Ethics*, p. 439).

8. For an overview of the differences between them, see J. Owens, 'Aristotle and Aquinas', in N. Kretzmann and E. Stump (eds), *The Cambridge Companion to Aquinas* (Cambridge: Cambridge University Press, 1993), pp. 38–59.

9. The citations in this and the following paragraph are taken from Aquinas, *Commentary on the Ethics*, Book 1, *lectiones* 9–10, sections 103–11, from C. Martin (ed.), *The Philosophy of Thomas Aquinas: Introductory Readings* (London: Routledge, 1988), pp. 170–73.

10. Aquinas uses *felicitas* when translating Aristotle's *eudaimonia*, and *beatitudo* when undertaking his own treatment of happiness. He seems to treat the two synonymously. See A. Kenny, 'Aquinas on Aristotelian Happiness', in S. McDonald and E. Stump (eds), *Aquinas' Moral Theory: Essays in Honour of Norman Kretzmann* (New York: Cornell University Press, 1998), p. 20. *Eudaimonia* is here translated 'well-being', while other translators use 'happiness'. As previously, I prefer to use the original unless citing another's translation.

11. See, for example, his discussion in 'Article 1: Whether it belongs to man to act for an end' (*Summa Theologiae*, I–II.1.8). See also Aquinas, 'On the Virtues in General', in R. Goodwin (trans.), *Selected Writings of St Thomas Aquinas: The Principles of Nature; On Being and Essence; On the Virtues in General; On Free Choice* (Pearson, 1965), p. 82; and Aquinas, *Commentary on the Ethics*, section 128, from Martin (ed.), *The Philosophy of Thomas Aquinas*, pp. 170–73. Translations of Aquinas use exclusive language and I make no attempt to change them. All citations from the *Summa Theologiae* are taken from the online text found at http://www.newadvent.org/summa.

12. Aquinas, 'On the Virtues in General', in Goodwin (trans.), *Selected Writings*, p. 101.

13. S. DeCrane, *Aquinas, Feminism, and the Common Good* (Washington, DC: Georgetown University Press, 2004), p. 44; J. Wippell, 'Metaphysics', in Kretzmann and Stump, *The Ethics of Aquinas*, pp. 89–93.

14. F. Kerr, *After Aquinas: Versions of Thomism* (Oxford: Blackwell Publishing, 2002), p. 114.

15. J. Porter, *Nature as Reason: A Thomistic Theory of the Natural Law* (Grand Rapids: William B. Eerdmans, 2005), pp. 142–3.

16. ibid. pp. 142–3.

17. ibid., pp. 154–5.

18. ibid., p. 157.

19. ibid., pp. 159–62, 169.

20. Kerr, *After Aquinas*, p. 118.

21. Porter, *Nature as Reason*, p. 162.

22. ibid., p. 174.

23. S. Pope, 'Overview of the Ethics of Thomas Aquinas', in S. Pope (ed.), *The Ethics of Aquinas* (Washington, DC: Georgetown University Press, 2002), p. 34.

24. N. Healy, *Thomas Aquinas: Theologian of the Christian Life* (Aldershot: Ashgate: 2003), p. 119.

25. D. Cates, 'The Virtue of Temperance (IIa IIae, qq. 141–170)', in Pope, *Ethics of Aquinas*, p. 321, drawing on II–II.141.5 and 2.

26. J. Porter, 'The Virtue of Justice (IIa IIae, qq. 58–122)', in Pope, ibid., p. 274.

27. Cates, 'The Virtue of Temperance', in Pope, ibid., p. 323.

28. N. Austin, *Thomas Aquinas on the Four Causes of Temperance* (Boston: Boston University, 2010), pp. 69–76.

29. ibid., p. 226.

30. ibid., p. 220.

31. J. Porter, *The Recovery of Virtue: The Relevance of Aquinas for Christian Ethics* (London: SPCK, 1994), p. 124; Porter, 'The Virtue of Justice', in Pope, *Ethics of Aquinas*, p. 274.

32. Austin, *Thomas Aquinas on the Four Causes of Temperance*, pp. 207–34.

33. ibid., p. 234.

34. Porter, *Nature as Reason*, p. 205.

35. ibid., pp. 217, 207.

36. DeCrane, *Aquinas, Feminism, and the Common Good*, p. 57.

37. Porter, *The Recovery of Virtue*, p. 127.

38. Austin, *Thomas Aquinas on the Four Causes of Temperance*, p. 321.

39. ibid.

40. Aquinas, *Commentary on the Ethics*, section 128, from Martin (ed.), *The Philosophy of Thomas Aquinas*, section 110, p. 171.

41. Porter, *Nature as Reason*, p. 167.

42. ibid., p. 167. Bradley, likewise, describes external goods as 'the necessary conditions of virtuous activity' (Bradley, *Human Good*, p. 400).

43. Porter, *Nature as Reason*, p. 172.

44. A. Leopold, *Sand County Almanac*, p. 197, cited in Bouma-Prediger, *For the Beauty of the Earth*, p. 16. The full citation is, 'One of the penalties of an ecological education is that one lives alone in a world of wounds.'

45. C. Deane-Drummond, *The Ethics of Nature* (Oxford: Blackwell, 2004), p. 7.

Part Three: A Life Well Lived – Putting It All Together

A Global Social Concern

1. www.weseehope.org.uk.

2. http://www.grassroots.org.uk/.

3. See https://www.livebelowtheline.com/uk.

An Ecological Concern

1. I was first introduced to the concept of ecological literacy by Steven Bouma-Prediger in *For the Beauty of the Earth*, pp. 20–23.
2. For more information on any of this, email uk@arocha.org.
3. To look at all of this and more in much more detail, see my *L is for Lifestyle*, and also the many ideas at arocha.org.uk/ livinglightly. I also run a Green Living section on my website (www.ruthvalerio.net) which will be helpful.
4. I have used both http://calculator.bioregional.com and http://footprint.wwf.org.uk and found them both helpful.
5. See www.ecochurch.arocha.org.uk.

A Christian Approach to Money and Material Goods

1. M. Csikszentmihalyi and E. Rochberg-Halton, *The Meaning of Things: Domestic Symbols and the Self* (Cambridge: Cambridge University Press, 1981), pp. 230–31, in Humphery, *Excess: Anti-Consumerism in the West*, p. 175.
2. C. Firer Hinze, 'What is Enough? Catholic Social Thought, Consumption, and Material Sufficiency', in Schweiker and Mathewes, *Having*, p. 188 (fn. 67).
3. See http://themoneycharity.org.uk/advice-information/ create-budget.
4. For more on this, see 'I is for Investments', in my *L is for Lifestyle*.

Ethical Consumerism

1. I would also recommend *The Good Shopping Guide: Certifying the UK's Most Ethical Companies and Brands*, and my *L is for Lifestyle*, as well as the Green Living section on my website (www.ruthvalerio.net).

2. Thank you to Jo Khinmaung, Food Policy Advisor at Tearfund, for the following statistics.

3. The pig co-operative (Sussex Saddlebacks) is a story in itself, but it is situated on land that belongs to a lovely place called Aldingbourne Country Centre, about six miles from Chichester. They had an unused scrubby field and – through contacts – were open to us rearing pigs on it. We run it together, with work days and a rota for feeding. We pay in a certain amount and get the meat when pigs go to slaughter.

Local Community

1. www.transitionnetwork.org.

2. http://www.thebiglunch.com.

3. A helpful book to read if you would like to look at this further is David Janzen, *The Intentional Christian Community Handbook: For Idealists, Hypocrites, and Wannabe Disciples of Jesus* (Brewster: Paraclete Press, 2013).

Activism

1. To read his story, see his *Making Trouble: Fighting for Fairtrade Jewellery*.

Time

1. Two books I have found helpful have been Ian Adam, *Running Over Rocks: Spiritual Practices to Transform Tough Times* (Norwich: Canterbury Press, 2013); and Brian Draper's *Less is More: Spirituality for Busy Times* (London: Lion Publishing, 2012).

2. M. Earle, *The Desert Mothers: Practical Spiritual Wisdom for Every Day* (London: SPCK, 2007).

3. Margot is vicar of the Haddenham Benefice in Oxfordshire and the author of many books, including (with her husband Martin), *A Christian Guide to Environmental Issues* (Oxford: Bible Reading Fellowship, 2015).

Final Words

1. P. Kenneson and J. Street, *Selling Out the Church: The Dangers of Church Marketing* (Nashville: Abingdon, 2003), p. 157.

Bibliography

Adam, B., U. Beck and J. Van Loon, *The Risk Society and Beyond: Critical Issues for Social Theory* (London: Sage Publications, 2000)

Adam, I., *Running Over Rocks: Spiritual Practices to Transform Tough Times* (Norwich: Canterbury Press, 2013)

Adorno, T. and M. Horkheimer, *Dialectic of Enlightenment* (New York: Herder & Herder, 1944; English trans. 1972)

Aldridge, A., *Consumption* (Cambridge: Polity Press, 2003)

Amoore, L. (ed.), *The Global Resistance Reader* (Abingdon: Routledge, 2005)

Anderson, A., *An Introduction to Pentecostalism* (Cambridge: Cambridge University Press, 2004)

Anderson, A., K. Meethan and S. Miles, *The Changing Consumer: Markets and Meanings* (London: Routledge, 2002)

Atkinson, D. and D. Field (eds), *New Dictionary of Christian Ethics and Pastoral Theology* (Leicester: IVP, 1995)

Austin, N., *Thomas Aquinas on the Four Causes of Temperance* (Boston: Boston University, 2010)

Barnes, J. (ed.), *The Cambridge Companion to Aristotle* (Cambridge: Cambridge University Press, 1995)

Barry, P. (trans.), *St Benedict's Rule: A New Translation for Today* (York: Ampleforth Abbey Press, 1997)

Batson, D., *The Treasure Chest of the Early Christians: Faith, Care and Community from the Apostolic Age to Constantine the Great* (Leominster: Gracewing, 2001)

Bauckham, R., *Bible and Ecology: Rediscovering the Community of Creation* (London: Darton, Longman and Todd, 2010)

Baudrillard, J., *The Consumer Society: Myths and Structures* (London: Thousand Oaks, 1998)

Bauman, Z., *The Art of Life* (Cambridge: Polity Press, 2008)

Bauman, Z., *Consuming Life* (Cambridge: Polity Press, 2007)

Bauman, Z., *Globalization: The Human Consequences* (Cambridge: Polity Press, 1998)

Bauman, Z., *Liquid Love: On the Frailty of Human Bonds* (Cambridge: Polity Press, 2003)

Bauman, Z., *Liquid Modernity* (Cambridge: Polity Press, 2000)

Bauman, Z., *Liquid Times: Living in an Age of Uncertainty* (Cambridge: Polity Press, 2007)

Bauman, Z., *Work, Consumerism and the New Poor* (Milton Keynes: Open University Press, 1998)

Bebbington, D., *Evangelicals in Modern Britain: A History from the 1730s to the 1980s* (London: Unwin Hyman Ltd, 1989)

Beck, U., 'Sub-politics: Ecology and the Disintegration of Institutional Power', *Organization and Environment*, 10:1 (1997), pp. 52–65

Beck, U., *The Reinvention of Politics: Rethinking Modernity in the Global Social Order* (Cambridge: Polity Press, 1997)

Beck, U., *Risk Society: Towards a New Modernity* (London: Sage Publications, 1992)

Beck, U., 'Climate for Change, or How to Create a Green Modernity', *Theory, Culture and Society*, 27:2–3 (2010), pp. 254–66

Beck, U., *World Risk Society* (Oxford: Blackwell, 1999)

Beck, U. and N. Sznaider, 'Unpacking Cosmopolitanism for the Social Sciences: A Research Agenda', *The British Journal of Sociology*, 57:1 (2006)

Beck, U., A. Giddens and S. Lash, *Reflexive Modernization: Politics, Tradition and Aesthetics in the Modern Social Order* (Cambridge: Polity Press, 1994)

Berry, W., *Sex, Economy, Freedom and Community* (New York: Pantheon Books, 1992)

Berry, W., *The Art of the Commonplace: The Agrarian Essays of Wendell Berry* (Washington: Counterpoint, 2002)

Biggar, N., 'Seek the Welfare of the City: A Response to *Christianity and Contemporary Politics*', *Political Theology*, 12:3 (2011), pp. 453–7

Blomberg, C., *Neither Poverty Nor Riches: A Biblical Theology of Possessions* (Leicester: Apollos, 1999)

Bouma-Prediger, S, *For the Beauty of the Earth: A Christian Vision for Creation Care* (Michigan: Baker Academic, 2001)

Bourdieu, P., *Distinction: A Social Critique of the Judgement of Taste* (Oxford: Routledge, Kegan and Paul, 1984, 2010)

Bradley, D., *Aquinas on the Twofold Human Good: Reason and Human Happiness in Aquinas' Moral Science* (Washington, DC: The Catholic University of America Press, 1997)

Bretherton, L., *Christianity and Contemporary Politics* (Chichester: Wiley-Blackwell Publishing Ltd, 2010)

Bretherton, L., '"How Shall We Sing the Lord's Song in a Strange Land?": A Response to the Symposium', *Political Theology*, 12:3 (2011), pp. 465–75

Broadie, S., *Ethics with Aristotle* (Oxford: Oxford University Press, 1991)

Broadie, S. and C. Rowe, *Aristotle: Nicomachean Ethics. Translation, Introduction, and Commentary* (Oxford: Oxford University Press, 2002)

Bruges, J., *The Little Earth Book* (Bristol: Alastair Sawday Publishing, 2000)

Budde, M., *The (Magic) Kingdom of God: Christianity and Global Culture Industries* (Boulder: Westview Press, 1997)

Butler, C., *Benedictine Monachism: Studies in Benedictine Life and Rule* (Cambridge: Speculum Historiale, 1924)

Campbell, C., *The Romantic Ethic and the Spirit of Modern Consumerism* (Oxford: Blackwell Publishers, 1987)

Cavanaugh, W., *Being Consumed: Economics and Christian Desire* (Grand Rapids: William B. Eerdmans, 2008)

Cavanaugh, W., *Theopolitical Imagination: Discovering the Liturgy as a Political Act in an Age of Global Consumerism* (London: T&T Clark, 2002)

Cavanaugh, W. and P. Scott (eds), *The Blackwell Companion to Political Theology* (Oxford: Blackwell Publishing, 2004)

Christie, I., 'Human Flourishing and the Environment', briefing paper for the 'Wholly Living' project on development and flourishing (London: Theos/Cafod/Tearfund, 2010)

Claibourne, S., *The Irresistible Revolution: Living as an Ordinary Radical* (Grand Rapids: Zondervan, 2006)

Cray, G., I. Mobsby and A. Kennedy (eds), *Ancient Faith, Future Mission: New Monasticism as Fresh Expression of Church* (Canterbury: Canterbury Press, 2010)

Dandelion, P., *A Sociological Analysis of the Theology of Quakers: The Silent Revolution* (New York: E. Mellen Press, 1996)

Davis, M., 'Bauman's Compass: Navigating the Current Interregnum', *Acta Sociologica*, 54:2 (2011), pp. 183–94

Davis, M., *Freedom and Consumerism: A Critique of Zygmunt Bauman's Sociology* (Aldershot: Ashgate Publishing, 2008)

Dawn, M., *Unfettered Hope: A Call to Faithful Living in an Affluent Society* (Louisville: Westminster John Knox Press, 2003)

Deane-Drummond, C., *Eco-Theology* (London: Darton, Longman and Todd, 2008)

Deane-Drummond, C., *The Ethics of Nature* (Oxford: Blackwell, 2004)

DeCrane, S., *Aquinas, Feminism, and the Common Good* (Washington, DC: Georgetown University Press, 2004)

Department for International Development White Paper, 'Eliminating World Poverty: Making Globalisation Work for the Poor' (DID, 2000)

De Waal, E., *Seeking God: The Way of St Benedict* (London: Fount Paperbacks, 1984)

Doody, J., K. Hughes and K. Paffenroth (eds), *Augustine and Politics* (Lanham: Lexington Books, 2005)

Drake, M., *Political Sociology for a Globalizing World* (Cambridge: Polity Press, 2010)

Draper, B., *Less is More: Spirituality for Busy Lives* (London: Lion Publishing, 2012)

Druckman, A., D. Hirsch, K. Perren and J. Beckhelling, 'Sustainable Income Standards: Possibilities for Greener

Minimum Consumption', RESOLVE Working Paper Series 14–11 (University of Surrey, 2011)

Earle, M., *The Desert Mothers: Practical Spiritual Wisdom for Every Day* (London: SPCK, 2007)

Ekberg, M., 'The Parameters of the Risk Society: A Review and Exploration', *Current Sociology*, 55:3 (2007), pp. 343–66

Evangelical Alliance and Christian Research, *21st Century Evangelicals: A Snapshot of the Beliefs and Habits of Evangelical Christians in the UK* (London: Evangelical Alliance, 2011)

Falk, P. and C. Campbell (eds), *The Shopping Experience* (London: Sage Publications, 1997)

Featherstone, M., *Consumer Culture and Postmodernism* (London: Sage Publications, 1991)

Fiensy, D. and R. Hawkins, *The Galilean Economy in the Time of Jesus* (Atlanta: Society of Biblical Literature, 2013)

Finnis, J., *Aquinas: Moral, Political, and Legal Theory* (Oxford: Oxford University Press, 1998)

Foster, R., *Freedom of Simplicity* (London: Triangle/SPCK, 1981)

Giddens, A., 'Runaway World', Reith Lectures (1991), available at http://www.bbc.co.uk/programmes/p00ghvgj

Giddens, A., *Sociology* (Cambridge: Polity Press, 2009, 6th edn)

Gill, R., *The Cambridge Companion to Christian Ethics* (Cambridge: Cambridge University Press, 2001)

Gonzalez, J., *Faith and Wealth: A History of Early Christian Ideas on the Origin, Significance, and Use of Money* (San Francisco: Harper & Row, 1990)

Good Shopping Guides, *Good Shopping Guide: Certifying the UK's Most Ethical Companies and Brands* (London: Ethical Marketing Group, 2012)

Goodwin, R. (trans.), *Aquinas: Selected Writings of St Thomas Aquinas: The Principles of Nature; On Being and Essence; On the Virtues in General; On Free Choice* (Pearson, 1965)

Gould, G., *The Desert Fathers on Monastic Community* (Oxford: Clarendon Press, 1993)

Gregory, E., *Politics and the Order of Love: An Augustinian Ethic of Democratic Citizenship* (Chicago: Chicago Press, 2008)

Greig, P., *The Vision and the Vow* (Eastbourne: Relevant Books, 2004)

Grigsby, M., *Buying Time and Getting By: The Voluntary Simplicity Movement* (New York: State University of New York Press, 2004)

Gunton, C., *Christ and Creation* (Carlisle: Paternoster, 1992)

Gunton, C., *The Promise of Trinitarian Theology* (London: T&T Clark, 2nd edn, 1997)

Gutiérrez, G., *A Theology of Liberation* (London: SCM Press, 1974)

Haslam, P., J. Schafer and P. Beaudet (eds), *Introduction to International Development Studies: Approaches, Actors and Issues* (Canada: Oxford University Press, 2012)

Hauerwas, S. and S. Wells, *The Blackwell Companion to Christian Ethics* (Oxford: Blackwell Publishing Ltd, 2nd edn, 2011)

Healy, N., *Thomas Aquinas: Theologian of the Christian Life* (Aldershot: Ashgate, 2003)

Heath, J. and A. Potter, *The Rebel Sell: How the Counterculture Became Consumer Culture* (Chichester: Capstone Publishing, 2005)

Held, D. and A. McGrew, *Globalization Theory: Approaches and Controversies* (Cambridge: Polity Press, 2007)

Held, D., A. McGrew, D. Goldblatt and J. Perraton, *Global Transformations: Politics, Economics and Culture* (Stanford: Stanford University Press, 1999)

Hengel, M., *Earliest Christianity: Containing 'Acts and the History of Earliest Christianity' and 'Property and Riches in the Early Church'* (London: SCM, 1986)

Humphery, K., *Excess: Anti-Consumerism in the West* (Cambridge: Polity Press, 2010)

Hunter, J.D., *To Change the World: The Irony, Tragedy, and Possibility of Christianity in the Late Modern World* (Oxford: Oxford University Press, 2010)

Ibarra, P. (ed.), *Social Movements and Democracy* (Basingstoke: Palgrave Macmillan, 2003)

Ilmonen, K. (author), with P. Sulkunen, J. Gronow, A. Noro, K. Rahkonen and A. Warde (eds), *A Social and Economic Theory of Consumption* (Basingstoke: Palgrave Macmillan, 2011)

Jacobsen, M.H. and S. Marshman, 'Bauman's Metaphors: The Poetic Imagination in Sociology', *Current Sociology*, 56:5 (2008), pp. 798–818

Jamison, C., *Finding Sanctuary: Monastic Steps for Everyday Life* (London: Weidenfeld & Nicolson, 2006)

Johnson, K., *The Fear of Beggars: Stewardship and Poverty in Christian Ethics* (Grand Rapids: William B. Eerdmans, 2007)

Kaplinsky, R., *Globalization, Poverty and Inequality* (Cambridge: Polity Press, 2005)

Kenneson, P. and J. Street, *Selling Out the Church: The Dangers of Church Marketing* (Nashville: Abingdon, 2003)

Kerr, F., *After Aquinas: Versions of Thomism* (Oxford: Blackwell Publishing, 2002)

Keys, M., *Aquinas, Aristotle, and the Promise of the Common Good* (Cambridge: Cambridge University Press, 2006)

Klein, N., *No Logo: Taking Aim at the Brand Bullies* (New York: Picador, 2000)

Knowles, D., *Christian Monasticism* (London: Weidenfeld & Nicolson, 1969)

Kretzmann, N. and E. Stump (eds), *The Cambridge Companion to Aquinas* (Cambridge: Cambridge University Press, 1993)

Lacarriere, J., trans. R. Monkcom, *The God-Possessed* (London: George Allen & Unwin Ltd, 1963)

Louv, R., *Last Child in the Woods: Saving Our Children from Nature-Deficit Disorder* (Chapel Hill: Algonquin Books of Chapel Hill, 2005)

Lury, C., *Consumer Culture* (Cambridge: Polity Press, 2011, 2nd edn)

Markus, R., *Christianity and the Secular* (Notre Dame: University of Notre Dame Press, 2006)

Martin, C. (ed.), *The Philosophy of Thomas Aquinas: Introductory Readings* (London: Routledge, 1988)

Maudlin, M. and M. Baer, *The Green Bible* (London: HarperCollins, 2008)

McClaren, B., *Finding Our Way Again: The Return of the Ancient Practices* (Nashville: Thomas Nelson, 2008)

McCloughry, R., *Living in the Presence of the Future* (Leicester: IVP, 2001)

McDonald, S. and E. Stump (eds), *Aquinas' Moral Theory: Essays in Honour of Norman Kretzmann* (New York: Cornell University Press, 1998)

McKibben, B., *Eaarth: Making a Life on a Tough New Planet* (New York: Times Books, 2010)

McMillan, T., 'The New Face of Hunger', *National Geographic* (August 2014)

Micheletti, M., *Political Virtue and Shopping: Individuals, Consumerism, and Collective Action* (New York: Palgrave Macmillan, 2003)

Miller, D., *The Comfort of Things* (Cambridge: Polity Press, 2008)

Miller, D., *Stuff* (Cambridge: Polity Press, 2010)

Miller, V., *Consuming Religion: Christian Faith and Practice in a Consumer Culture* (New York: Continuum, 2003)

Mission and Public Affairs Council, *Sharing God's Planet: A Christian Vision for a Sustainable Future* (London: Church House Publishing, 2005)

Moorman, J., *Richest of Poor Men: The Spirituality of St Francis of Assisi* (London: Darton, Longman and Todd, 1982)

Mythen, G., 'Reappraising the Risk Society Thesis: Telescopic Sight or Myopic Vision?', *Current Sociology*, 55:6 (2007), pp. 793–813

National Trust, 'Wildlife Alien to Indoor Children', survey (National Trust, 2008)

Natural England, 'Childhood and Nature: A Survey on Changing Relationships with Nature across Generations' (Natural England, 2009)

Northcott, M., *A Moral Climate: The Ethics of Global Warming* (London: Darton, Longman and Todd, 2007)

Odgers, J., *Simplicity, Love and Justice* (London: Alpha International, 2004)

Panitchpadki, S., 'Preface to the Report of the Secretary-General of UNCTAD to UNCTAD XIII' (28 November 2011), available at http://www.policyinnovations.org/ideas/policy_library/data/01619

Percy, M., *Engaging with Contemporary Culture: Christianity, Theology and the Concrete Church* (Aldershot: Ashgate, 2005)

Percy, M., *Words, Wonders and Power: Understanding Contemporary Christian Fundamentalism and Revivalism* (London: SPCK, 1996)

Percy, M. and I. Jones (eds), *Fundamentalism: Church and Society* (London: SPCK, 2002)

Perriman, A. (ed.), *Faith, Health and Prosperity: A Report on 'Word of Faith' and 'Positive Confession' Theologies* (London: Paternoster Press, 2003)

Pleyers, G., *Alter-Globalization: Becoming Actors in the Global Age* (Cambridge: Polity Press, 2010)

Polanyi, K., *The Great Transformation: The Political and Economic Origins of our Time* (New York: Octagon Books, 1975)

Pontifical Council for Justice and Peace, *Compendium of the Social Doctrine of the Church* (London and New York: Continuum, 2004)

Pope Benedict XVI, *Caritas in Veritate* (Dublin: Veritas Publications, 2009)

Pope, S. (ed.), *The Ethics of Aquinas* (Washington, DC: Georgetown University Press, 2002)

Porter, J., *Nature as Reason: A Thomistic Theory of the Natural Law* (Grand Rapids: William B. Eerdmans, 2005)

Porter, J., *The Recovery of Virtue: The Relevance of Aquinas for Christian Ethics* (London: SPCK, 1994)

Powley, M., *Consumer Detox: Less Stuff, More Life* (Grand Rapids: Zondervan, 2010)

Ramos, S., trans. N. Russell, *Like a Pelican in the Wilderness: Reflections on the Sayings of the Desert Fathers* (Brookline: Holy Cross Orthodox Press, 2000)

Reay, B., *The Quakers and the English Revolution* (New York: St Martin's Press, 1985)

Reed, C. (ed.), *Development Matters: Christian Perspectives on Globalization* (London: Church House Publishing, 2001)

Regnault, L., *The Day-to-Day Life of the Desert Fathers in Fourth-Century Egypt* (Petersham: St Bede's Publications, trans. 1999)

Robson, M., *St Francis of Assisi: The Legend and the Life* (London: Geoffrey Chapman, 1997)

Russell, N. and B. Ward, *The Lives of the Desert Fathers* (Collegeville: Cistercian Publications, 1981)

Rutba House (ed.), *School(s) for Conversion: 12 Marks of a New Monasticism* (Eugene: Cascade Books, 2005)

Sassatelli, R., *Consumer Culture: History, Theory and Politics* (London: Sage Publications, 2007)

Schut, M. (ed.), *Simpler Living, Compassionate Life: A Christian Perspective* (Downers Grove: IVP, 1999)

Schweiker, W. and C. Mathewes (eds), *Having: Property and Possession in Religious and Social Life* (Grand Rapids: William B. Eerdmans, 2004)

Seaton, C., *Whose Earth?* (Cambridge: Crossway Books, 1992)

Sedgwick, P., *The Market Economy and Christian Ethics* (Cambridge: Cambridge University Press, 1999)

Short, W., *Poverty and Joy: The Franciscan Tradition* (London: Darton, Longman and Todd, 1999)

Sider, R., *Living More Simply: Biblical Principles and Practical Models* (London: Hodder & Stoughton, 1980)

Sider, R., *Rich Christians in an Age of Hunger* (London: Hodder & Stoughton, 1990)

Smart, C., *Personal Life: New Directions in Sociological Thinking* (Cambridge: Polity Press, 2007)

Smith, J., *Desiring the Kingdom: Worship, Worldview and Cultural Formation* (Grand Rapids: Baker Academic, 2009)

Society of St John the Evangelist, *Living in Hope: A Rule of Life for Today* (Canterbury: Canterbury Press, 1997)

Spufford, M. (ed.), *The World of Rural Dissenters, 1520–1725* (Cambridge: Cambridge University Press, 1995)

Stanley, B. and S. Hollinghurst (eds), *Earthed: Christian Perspectives on Nature Connection* (Llangurig: Mystic Christ, 2014)

Steger, M., *Globalization: A Very Short Introduction* (Oxford: Oxford University Press, 2003)

Stewart, C., *Prayer and Community: The Benedictine Tradition* (London: Darton, Longman and Todd, 1998)

Stott, J., *The Radical Disciple* (Leicester: IVP, 2010)

Swan, L., *The Forgotten Desert Mothers: Sayings, Lives, and Stories of Early Christian Women* (New York: Paulist Press, 2001)

Tearfund, *The Restorative Economy: Completing our Unfinished Millennium Jubilee* (Tearfund, 2015), available at http://www.tearfund.org/~/media/Files/Main%20Site/Campaigning/OrdinaryHeroes/Restorative%20Economy%20long%20report%20HR%20singles.pdf

Tessitore, A., *Reading Aristotle's Ethics: Virtue, Rhetoric, and Political Philosophy* (New York: State University of New York, 1996)

Theos, Cafod and Tearfund, *Wholly Living: A New Perspective on International Development* (London: Theos, 2010)

Thorn, H., 'Social Movements, the Media and the Emergence of a Global Public Sphere: From Anti-Apartheid to Global Justice', *Current Sociology*, 55:6 (2007), pp. 816–918

Twitchell, J., *Branded Nation: The Marketing of Megachurch, College Inc. and Museumworld* (New York: Simon & Schuster, 2004)

Twitchell, J., *Lead Us into Temptation: The Triumph of American Materialism* (New York: Columbia University Press, 1999)

United Nations, *Millennium Goals Report 2011* (UN, 2011)

United Nations Development Programme, *Human Development Report 2011* (New York: UNDP, 2011)

University of Essex, 'What is the Best Dose of Nature and Green Exercise for Improving Mental Health? A Multi-Study Analysis' (2010), available at http://pubs.acs.org/doi/abs/10.1021/es903183r

Urry, J., 'Consuming the Planet to Excess', *Theory, Culture and Society*, 27:2-3 (2010), pp. 191–212

Vaage, L. and V. Wimbush (eds), *Asceticism and the New Testament* (New York: Routledge, 1999)

Valerio, G., *Making Trouble: Fighting for Fairtrade Jewellery* (London: Lion Hudson, 2013)

Valerio, R., *Environment* (Waverley Abbey: CWR, 2008)

Valerio, R., *L is for Lifestyle: Christian Living that Doesn't Cost the Earth* (Leicester: IVP, 2nd edn, 2008)

Valerio, R., *Rivers of Justice: Responding to God's Call to Righteousness Today* (Waverley Abbey: CWR, 2005)

Veblen, T., *The Theory of the Leisure Class: An Economic Study of Institutions* (New York: Penguin Books, 1979, first published 1899)

Voke, C.J., *Creation at Worship: Ecology, Creation and Christian Worship* (Milton Keynes: Paternoster, 2009)

Waddell, H., *The Desert Fathers: Translations from the Latin* (London: Constable and Company Ltd, 1994)

Walker, A., *Restoring the Kingdom: The Radical Christianity of the House Church Movement* (London: Hodder & Stoughton, 1985)

Walker, A. and L. Bretherton (eds), *Remembering Our Future: Explorations in Deep Church* (Milton Keynes: Paternoster, 2007)

Wannenwetsch, B., '"For in its welfare you will find your welfare": Political Realism and the Limits of the Augustinian Framework', *Political Theology*, 12:3 (2011), pp. 457–65

Ward, B., *The Lives of the Desert Fathers* (London: Mowbray, 1981)

Ward, B., *The Sayings of the Desert Fathers: The Alphabetical Collection* (London: Mowbray, rev. edn, 1981)

Ward, G., *Cultural Transformation and Religious Practice* (Cambridge: Cambridge University Press, 2005)

Ward, P., *Selling Worship: How What We Sing Has Changed the Church* (Milton Keynes: Paternoster Press, 2005)

Warrington, K., *Pentecostal Theology: A Theology of Encounter* (London: T&T Clark, 2008)

Weber, M., trans. T. Parsons, *The Protestant Ethic and the Spirit of Capitalism* (London: Allen & Unwin, 1976)

White, L., 'The Historical Roots of our Ecologic Crisis', *Science*, 155:3767 (1967), pp. 1203–7

Whitmire, K., *Plain Living: A Quaker Path to Simplicity* (Notre Dame: Sorin Books, 2001)

Williams, R., *Silence and Honey Cakes: The Wisdom of the Desert* (Oxford: Lion Hudson, 2004)

World Council of Churches, *A Spirituality for Our Times: Report of a Consultation on Monastic Spirituality* (Geneva: World Council of Churches, 1986)

Wright, C.J.H., *Old Testament Ethics for the People of God* (Leicester: IVP, 2004)
Wright, N.T., *The New Testament for Everyone* (London: SPCK, 2011)
Ziesler, J., *Christian Asceticism* (London: SPCK, 1973)
Zizioulas, J.D., *Being as Communion: Studies in Personhood and the Church* (Crestwood: St Vladimir's Seminary Press, 1993)

Online resources

www.archbishopofcanterbury.org/articles.php/5404/archbishop-invites-young-christians-to-spend-year-praying-at-lambeth-palace
arocha.org.uk
arocha.org.uk/livinglightly
www.avaaz.org
www.billboard.com/charts/christian-songs
breathenetwork.org
http://brightnow.org.uk/
http://calculator.bioregional.com
cofe.anglican.org/about/churchcommissioners/news/environment/resources.html/quanda.doc
cofe.anglican.org/info/ethical/policystatements/environment.pdf
www.ecochurch.arocha.org.uk
faostat3.fao.org/browse/FB/FBS/E
http://footprint.wwf.org.uk
www.footprintnetwork.org/images/article_uploads/EarthOvershootDay_2014_PR_General.pdf

http://www.grassroots.org.uk/

www.happyplanetindex.org/

http://index.gain.org/

www.itu.int/net/pressoffice/press_releases/2015/17.aspx#.
VZPyHaZgOL0

www.jesus4u.co.uk/study-sheets/victorian_hymns

www.jrf.org.uk/sites/files/jrf/Minimum-income-standards-
2014-FULL.pdf

www.jrf.org.uk/topic/mis

www.lausanne.org/gatherings/issue-gathering/international-
consultation-on-simple-lifestyle-2

https://www.livebelowtheline.com/uk

www.monbiot.com/2014/11/18/the-insatiable-god/

www.newadvent.org/summa

www.policyinnovations.org/ideas/commentary/data/000072

www.ruthvalerio.net

www.state.gov/1997-2001-NOPDFS/policy_remarks/1999/
990612_clinton_chicago.html

www.stockholmresilience.org/21/research/research-
programmes/planetary-boundaries.html

www.thebiglunch.com

www.theguardian.com/environment/georgemonbiot/2014/
nov/21/we-need-nature-wellbeing-act-protect-wildlife-
decline?CMP=EMCENVEML1631

http://www.thelancet.com/commissions/climate-change

http://themoneycharity.org.uk/advice-information/
create-budget

www.transitionnetwork.org

www.ukpolitical.info/Turnout45.htm

http://unfccc.int/resource/docs/2013/cop19/eng/inf04.pdf

www.unitetheunion.org/news/tories-in-15-billion-nhs-sell-off-
  scandal/
www.washingtonpost.com/wp-srv/nation/specials/
  attacked/transcripts/bushaddress_092001.html
www.weseehope.org.uk
www.york.ac.uk/news-and-events/news/2005/uk-elections/
www.38degrees.org.uk
www.350.org